Contemporary American Foreign Policy

The Official Voice

Merrill Political Science Series

Under the Editorship of

John C. Wahlke

Department of Political Science
The University of Iowa

Contemporary American Foreign Policy
The Official Voice

Edited by

Gene E. Rainey

The Ohio State University

Charles E. Merrill Publishing Company
Columbus, Ohio
A Bell & Howell Company

Standard Book Number 675-09523-9

Library of Congress Catalog Number: 69-14629

1   2   3   4   5   6   7   8   9   10—73   72   71   70   69

40-5032

Printed in the United States of America

To Dorma

Preface

The purpose of this book is to make available to students a one-volume source of official statements on contemporary American foreign policy. All too often, we who study American foreign policy only evaluate other analysts' evaluations of United States diplomacy, rather than analyzing the decision-makers' statements themselves. There are several reasons for this approach to studying (and teaching) American foreign policy. First, a single volume of contemporary statements of United States policy has been lacking. Several sources of policy declarations exist, but they are published on a year-by-year basis and contain minor and insignificant, as well as major and significant, statements. They are better suited for research than teaching American foreign policy to undergraduates. Second, there is a tendency to neglect policy outcomes in a course on American diplomacy and to concentrate on process questions (*i.e.,* how is foreign policy made?). This is unfortunate, because the issue-outcome questions (*i.e.,* what is American policy on disarmament and in the Middle East?) are usually more interesting to study than the process questions. And finally, the tendency is to approach issue-outcomes from an historical point-of-view. The student, therefore, is led through all the past policy decisions, but is left to shift for himself in the contemporary era.

Foreign policy is dynamic: American diplomacy is no exception to this axiom. American foreign policy is responsive to changes in the international system as well as domestic transformations. The central thought in my mind as I write this Preface is the election of Richard M. Nixon as President of the United States. Will he bring about wholesale changes in American foreign policy? The answer is negative, although he will, no doubt, attempt fresh approaches in selective areas. In general, American diplomacy will remain within the major policy channels dug during the previous administrations. Whatever changes are introduced by the new Nixon Administration, a student should be prepared to evaluate them out of the background knowledge gained from this volume.

Preface

This volume is divided into three parts. In the first section, the Introduction builds a case for analyzing contemporary policy statements made by the Official Voice. A macro-content analysis of the 1966 *Department of State Bulletin* illustrates the composition of one year's output of policy statements. In the second and third parts, I have selected statements on contemporary American foreign policy for nine topics and seven geographical regions. A brief introduction begins each chapter to supply background information for the reader. Whenever possible, statistical data are used to furnish this informational backdrop. These introductions are written, hopefully, without the author's prejudices showing through too often.

I wish to thank *Vital Speeches of the Day* for permission to reprint two addresses that appeared in that journal; also Frederick A. Praeger, Inc., for permission to quote from *The Politics of Disarmament: A Study of Soviet-American Gamesmanship* by John W. Spanier and Joseph L. Nogee; and the Brookings Institution for permission to quote from *The United States and the Unity of Europe* by Max Beloff.

Professors Burton Sapin and James Rosenau made valuable comments on earlier drafts and saved me from many errors of judgment and fact. Also, I should like to acknowledge the research assistance of Douglas Dearth and Michael Buck, the typing assistance of Miss Elizabeth Coy and Mrs. Karen Huffer, and the invaluable editorial aid of my wife, to whom this book is affectionately dedicated.

Finally, I wish to acknowledge the influence on this volume of Mr. Loy W. Henderson, former ambassador and Deputy Under Secretary of State for Administration, and presently Director of the Center for Diplomacy and Foreign Policy at the American University, Washington, D.C. Professor Henderson, who spent almost forty years as a practitioner of American foreign policy, introduced me—as he did all of his students—to the wealth of information contained in contemporary public statements.

G.E.R.
Columbus, Ohio

Contents

Contemporary American Foreign Policy
The Official Voice

Introduction

The Official Voice In American Foreign Policy

Who says what to whom in American foreign policy?

The purpose of this introduction is to answer this question by selecting one year's output of official policy statements printed in the *Department of State Bulletin*.[1] Before examining the specific issue-areas, it would be useful to gain an overview of the many subjects discussed by the American Official Voice.

---

[1] The research technique employed is a macro-content analysis. Each statement was read by two coders with better than 90 percent agreement on 1293 coding decisions contained in the five tables presented in this Introduction. Since the technique is a macro-content analysis, coding decisions were made on the basis of the title of the policy statement. If the title was ambiguous, the major subheadings were used. The position of the speaker and the type of audience were always indicated in the *Department of State Bulletin*.

During 1966, The *Bulletin* carried 234 policy statements; hence, all but two of the statistical tables contained in this Introduction total 234 items. Double counting was a problem only in Table 3. Since the two coders were instructed to indicate themes from the title, and some titles contain two or more themes, the total items were much larger than those contained in Tables 1, 2, 4, and 5. Table 5 involved 235 items and a footnote in the table explains why.

The *Department of State Bulletin* is the official publication of American foreign policy statements. The *Bulletin* reprints statements made by executive spokesmen outside the Department of State, but as a statistical table will show later in this Introduction, non-State officials are decidedly in the minority. The assumption is that the most important foreign policy statements appear in the *Bulletin;* however, there are other official publications, such as the *Department of State Newsletter* and *International Commerce,* as well as unofficial sources (*e.g., Vital Speeches*) which reproduce foreign policy statements from non-State decision-makers. The *Bulletin* publishes most of the news releases written by the White House Offices and the Department of State; those not printed concern topics of little importance, such as announcements of ambassadorial appointments.

The year 1966 was chosen only because it is contemporary and not because it is typical of U.S. foreign policy activity. It may be somewhat skewed by the unusual

Who?

This question focuses on the components of a governmental machine that speaks *officially* for a state in the international system. A nation may have several—indeed, many—voices representing all aspects of governmental and public opinion. But the official voice of a government in international society is the head of state.

In the American political system, the federal Constitution explicitly invests the head of state functions in the executive branch. Article II enumerates the monopolistic powers of the President as Head of State, such as commanding the armed forces and receiving representatives of foreign heads of state. While Article II also lists powers that the executive shares with the legislative branch (*e.g.*, treaty-making and ambassador-appointing functions), and while senators and representatives are outspoken on foreign policy issues, Congress is not the Official Voice of American foreign policy.

The American Official Voice is the President and those executive officials appointed to assist him. This arrangement does not insure an unambiguous Voice, for at times different executive members generate conflicting pronouncements. In moments of crisis when fast-moving events change the complexion of the international system, a single individual (*e.g.*, the Secretary of State) may issue contradictory statements within a short space of time. Yet the President, supported by the massive machinery of the executive branch, is recognized by constitutional and international law as the Official Voice for American foreign policy.

Table 1 indicates the variety of spokesmen that issue foreign policy statements. The President and Secretary of State are the two individuals whose policy pronouncements are most often published. The two largest groups of spokesmen are the Assistant Secretaries of State and the representatives of the U.S. Mission to the United Nations in New York. An Assistant Secretary heads one of the functional or regional bureaus of the Department of State and often delivers addresses on problems that fall within his purview. There are thirteen

---

trip of President Johnson to East Asia and the Manila Conference. However, there is no reason to believe that 1966 data will differ substantially from 1965 or 1967. During 1966, 234 policy statements appeared in the *Bulletin*, which includes addresses, articles, reports, and statements. Also, there were 28 press conferences or interviews published *in toto* or in part; all of these were omitted from the frequency counts. Miscellaneous statements, such as toasts at dinners and greetings at the beginning of state visits also were omitted.

2

TABLE 1

Position of Policy Spokesman

Position	Frequency of statement in 1966	
	Number	Percent
White House Offices		
President	33	14.1
Vice President	5	2.1
Presidential advisers	7	3.0
Department of State		
Secretary	22	9.4
Under Secretary	10	4.3
Deputy Under Secretaries	5	2.1
Assistant Secretaries	31	13.2
Deputy Assistant Secretaries	7	3.0
Other personnel	22	9.4
AID, USIA, Peace Corps, ACDA[a]		
Director or Administrator	9	3.8
Other personnel	3	1.3
Other Executive Personnel		
Secretary of Defense	1	0.4
Secretary of Treasury	2	0.9
Secretary of Agriculture	1	0.4
Secretary of Commerce	3	1.3
Other Commerce personnel	1	0.4
Independent agency	2	0.9
U.S. Diplomatic Representatives		
Ambassadors to UN	50	21.4
Deputy Representatives to UN	5	2.1
Ambassadors to International Organizations other than UN	3	1.3
Ambassadors abroad	10	4.3
Foreign Officials	1	0.4
Totals	234	99.9

[a] AID is the Agency for International Development; USIA is the United States Information Agency; and ACDA is the Arms Control and Disarmament Agency.

assistant secretaries (including the Chairman of the Policy Planning Council whose rank is equivalent to that of an assistant secretary). The role of the U.S. Mission to the United Nations in articulating major policy positions is somewhat unexpected. The Head of Mission has the rank of an ambassador, and two other individuals on the Mission staff are assigned ambassadorial titles as well. In addition, there are three deputy representatives. All together, these six persons generate more published policy statements than any other group of officials. Not only is the Mission staff noted for its verbiage, but individual statements have been singled out as major pronouncements of policy equal in importance to those issued by the Secretary of State.[2]

Individuals with ambassadorial rank other than UN personnel appear to be a frequent source of policy pronouncements. Ambassadors abroad often are called upon to speak to audiences of foreign nationals. Also, diplomatic personnel assigned to international and regional organizations (e.g., Organization of American States and the North Atlantic Treaty Organization) contribute to the record of the Official Voice.

Decision-makers in other executive departments were the authors of four percent of the pronouncements. Statements by non-State Department personnel, such as the secretaries of Commerce and Treasury, were stimulated by the Kennedy Round of tariff negotiations and U.S. balance of payments problems. For an unexplained reason, the Defense Secretary's speeches on national security policy were almost nil in 1966, although Table 1 does not record his three press conferences. Table 1 indicates the diversity of policy statements in the post-war era, for U.S. foreign policy has become more and more complex in the Cold War period as executive voices other than the State Department's are heard and foreign policy issues can no longer be classified as "purely" political.

In this volume, the student might be disappointed that most of the policy statements are not authored by the President or Secretary of

---

[2] Ambassador to the UN, Arthur Goldberg, has functioned often as President Johnson's spokesman on major foreign policy issues. Goldberg's Howard University address, contained in this volume, remains the most comprehensive and well-reasoned examination of American policy on Vietnam. Drew Middleton characterized the Ambassador's address before the General Assembly on September 22, 1966, as "the basic American document on the Johnson Administration's approach to peace in Vietnam, the problem posed in The United Nations by Chinese representation and the need for the rule of law in space." (*New York Times*, July 26, 1967, p. 15).

State. A careful reading of the *Bulletin* reveals that upper echelon decision-makers (such as the President) quite often articulate a new policy, usually to nationwide audience and in language that offers only a general outline. Later, statements made by personnel in the lower echelons of the governmental decision-making pyramid, after a few weeks' or months' time lapse, will analyze and explain the new policy in more specific, concrete terms. They will examine the new policy in detail and perhaps discuss problems encountered in its application. Or the reverse order may occur: a speaker may articulate a "trial balloon" statement which hints that a major pronouncement is to follow given by the President or Secretary of State. For example, Secretary Marshall's famous June 1947 address at the Harvard University commencement was preceded by a little-known speech by Under Secretary Dean Acheson who "tried out" the ideas on European recovery contained in the Marshall Plan.

To summarize: The Official Voice is the voice of the President of the United States. While he himself speaks often, he also speaks through a handful of responsible subordinates in and out of the Department of State.

What?

Two general classifications are employed to analyze the content of the Official Voice: First, what region of the world does the statement pertain to? And secondly, what kind of issue is the primary focus of the statement?

Table 2 offers insight into the regional interest of decision-makers whose statements were reprinted by the 1966 *Department of State Bulletin*. It comes as no surprise that Southeast Asia garners the most attention while East Asia is a distant second. Latin America and Western Europe are respectively third and fourth. Traditionally, United States diplomacy has emphasized Western Europe and Latin America as the two priority areas of the world. Table 2 suggests that a reshuffling has occurred.

Table 3 offers another viewpoint on the "What?" of Official Voice pronouncements during 1966. The most common theme was the Vietnamese conflict, which was mentioned in 19 percent of the statements. But American foreign policy also is oriented toward economics, for the twin topics of foreign trade and aid were referred to in 22 percent of the pronouncements. The large number of references to

5

TABLE 2

Regional Classification for U.S. Foreign Policy Statements

Region	Frequency of statements in 1966	
	Number	Percent
Western Europe	18	6.8
Eastern Europe	11	4.2
East Asia	24	9.1
Southeast Asia	61	23.2
South Asia	2	0.8
Middle East	11	4.2
North Africa	2	0.8
Sub-Sahara Africa	13	4.9
Latin America	16	6.1
North America	3	1.1
Oceania	5	1.9
Multi-regional	16	6.1
Non-regional	80	30.4
Totals	262	99.6

international organization indicates a continuing U.S. interest in the UN and related agencies; however, most of these frequencies occur in statements issued by the U.S. Mission to the UN. Twelve percent of the pronouncements are in-depth analyses of U.S. policy *vis-a-vis* a particular nation, usually delivered by Assistant Secretaries of State responsible for the region in which the country is located. This fact illustrates the point that U.S. foreign policy statements are usually not generalized platitudes with frequent mentions of "peace" and "justice"; rather, they tend to focus on specific problems and issues. The sixth motif is national security policy, which includes references to military strategy and alliances. Since Table 1 reveals that only one of the Defense Secretary's statements in 1966 was published in the *Bulletin,* national security policy is therefore a frequent theme of non-Defense Department spokesmen.

A host of minor topics appear in U.S. foreign policy statements: educational and cultural exchanges, arms control and disarmament, immigration, maritime policy, refugee problems, science and technology, aviation, space, overseas territories, human rights, fisheries, colonial issues, international law, and population. These topics are often

TABLE 3

Themes of U.S. Foreign Policy Statements

Theme	Frequency of statements in 1966	
	Number	Percent
Economics		
Foreign trade	29	8.8
Economic development	44	13.4
Education and cultural	7	2.1
International organization	46	14.0
National security policy	26	7.9
Policy toward individual nations	39	11.9
Vietnamese war	61	18.6
Arms control and disarmament	18	5.5
U.S. Foreign Service	1	0.3
Immigration	1	0.3
Maritime policy	2	0.6
Refugee problems	7	2.1
Science and technology	7	2.1
Aviation	3	0.9
Space exploration	8	2.4
U.S. overseas territories	3	0.9
Human rights	8	2.4
Fisheries	1	0.3
Colonial issues	2	0.6
International law	2	0.6
Population	3	0.9
Foreign Policy formulation	4	1.2
General category	6	1.8
Totals	328	99.8

overlooked in the study of American diplomacy and illustrate the broad range of U.S. interests. While political issues are the most frequent focus, non-political and technical problems also concern the American Official Voice.

Any student of American foreign policy is well aware of the fact that the Official Voice has two channels in diplomacy, one private and secret, and the other public and open. The American public, of course, has access only to the latter; years later the historian may have access to the former. A question then arises: is the "What?" of the public Official Voice substantively the same message as the private Official Voice? An argument can be made that the two channels do not—and indeed should not—carry the same message because goals and strategy must be kept secret. Since secrecy is necessary, foreign policy formulation must be controlled by, and many times limited to, the decision-making elite of government. This position can be labeled the "elitist critique."

The elitist critique may be summarized as follows: the American public possesses neither the interest, the expertise, nor the information to make decisions on foreign policy issues. Therefore, any public discussion of world affairs by executive leaders must be worded in broad generalities. Furthermore, goals must be described in utopian language, such as "justice," that is inappropriate for diplomatic negotiations which demand precision. No national leader—unless he is irrational—will tip his hand and publicize his real objectives to a domestic audience. Foreign policy must be made quietly in times of change on the basis of intelligence reports that cannot be revealed to the public because the enemy would then know the substance of the reports as well as the covert sources which produced them. Covert sources must be protected from enemy counter-intelligence measures. In general, the elitist critique ascribes a minor role to the public in the foreign policy-making process. The public is held to be either incapable of making realistic decisions, or because of the pressure of time, the public must be neglected by the decision-makers. Consequently, the words of the Public Official Voice are meaningless as indicators of policy.

This argument deprecates the public statements of foreign policy and emphasizes private contacts between governments. Senator Fulbright in a February 16, 1967, hearing held by the Foreign Relations Committee exemplified this attitude toward the Public Official Voice. He told Secretary Rusk: "To say we like peace, we are peace-loving people, does not seem to me to mean much. It is what you say privately to the people concerned . . ."[3] The elitist critique would admit that part of the private voice eventually would be made public. Joint communiques, for example, are released after negotiations for public examination. But the decisions on goals and policy implementation, as well as the give-and-take of negotiations should be carried out behind closed doors. Two issues are posed: one is whether or not

---

3 *Washington Post*, February 17, 1966, p. A 10.

public policy statements bear any resemblance to a nation's diplomatic desiderata, and the other is whether or not a national leader's selection and interpretation of facts are in accord with the elusive concept of truth.

It would be foolish to suggest that the Public Official Voice is the only record, or to prove that it is essentially the same record as the Private Official Voice. However, the critique outlined above is too narrow and misses several important considerations by basing its position on four assumptions that must be seriously questioned.

(1) The first assumption is that the crisis situation is the only—or the most important—policy-making context. During crises the context of decision-making does change rapidly and the public is shut off from the foreign policy process for extended periods of time. The news may be "managed" during a crisis; information may be withheld in the interests of national security; and national leaders may verbalize goals in utopian and ideological terms to muster intense public support for the government's policy.

But not all policy statements are within the crisis context. Most are uttered in times of stability and are contained in well-thought-out texts for public perusal. An open society assumes a public kept informed of government policy. All this suggests that the elitist critique overemphasizes the crisis situation as the normal and most common environment in which policy statements are born. Periods of stability exist in which policy statements are made containing amounts of information that are a compromise between the needs of national security and the need for an informed public.

(2) A second assumption is that a monolithic "public" exists as the audience of the Official Voice. This does not distinguish among the different levels of "public" that have become common practice since the writings of Almond[4] and Rosenau.[5] It may be true that a "mass public" or the "man-in-the-street" will pay little or no attention to the Official Voice except in times of crises, and only then when the President himself is speaking. But the Official Voice has more varied sources and is not limited to the President; indeed, the responsible executive officials that attempt to keep the American public informed come from much lower levels on departmental organiza-

---

[4] Gabriel A. Almond, *The American People and Foreign Policy* (New York: Praeger, 1950).

[5] James Rosenau, *Public Opinion and Foreign Policy* (New York: Random House, 1961).

tional charts as Table 1 shows. These officials address groups that represent the "elite" or "attentive" sections of the American public. While a minority, the elite public is informed and interested in issues in world affairs.

(3) The elitist critique further assumes that the Official Voice discusses foreign policy goals in broad generalities because opponents cannot be told precisely about the national desiderata. However, the Official Voice does more than look forward: it glances backward and around as well. A policy spokesman will analyze the past (as many do in this volume) and take note of prior commitments and statements which influence present behavior. A decision-maker's freedom of action is circumscribed by the past Official Voice; at least, it is circumscribed by past commitments that he chooses to honor. A glance backward is highly subjective—indeed, everything that the Official Voice says is subjective—and may differ from interpretations by social scientists who by reason of their research tools or by professional training consider themselves more objective. Nevertheless, justifications for past actions or inactivity are contained in policy statements.

In addition, the spokesman will glance around: he will explain to the attentive public the rationale for present government action within the bounds of intelligence and crisis which were discussed under the first and second assumptions.

Finally, the Official Voice looks to the future and here the assumption that meaningful goals are usually lacking in foreign policy statements should be examined. Unfortunately, "goals" have been neglected in the study of world politics and no data exist that confirms—or invalidates—this assumption. An opposing "hunch" or assumption would be that goals—whether short-range or long-range—are openly discussed in most nations' Official Voice, *but what remains secret is the strategy and tactics for attaining them.* National leaders—Lenin, Stalin, Hitler, de Gaulle, as well as American presidents—have openly publicized objectives of their foreign policy. Goals have been promulgated, usually in banner headlines, in an open society. Robert J. Manning, in a statement before a House committee, outlined several working principles for sharing information on foreign policy with the public. He declared that U.S. foreign policy "must be evolved by open public discussion of proposed policies, of the objectives of these policies, *and in most cases,* of the means to be used to attain those policies." Thus, secrecy primarily shrouds the means of carrying out policy, not the ends. He further argued that secrecy was often necessary during the negotiation stage, after goals and strategy have been debated and decided in public. He said:

> Once a policy has been publicly enunciated to the full, those responsible for carrying out that policy may require certain interludes of privacy in which to get the job done. . . . Without such interludes of privacy—interludes employed to carry out, not to alter, enunciated politices—this government would find it impossible to coordinate with its many allies or seek honorable arrangements with other nations.[6]

(4) The last assumption, and the most difficult to evaluate, is that public statements are mere verbiage which gives little indication of the way that policy actually will be made when a crisis arises. One of the more common comments is that public statements cannot be "trusted," that a decision-maker will purposely say one thing and then do another.

Two issues are involved here. The first is whether the words of the Official Voice encode[7] "reality" as it exists in the speaker's mind, or whether the speaker is consciously or unconsciously attempting to mislead his audience. Secondly, assuming that the Official Voice does encode a reality, what effect does the statement have at the actual moment of decision-making?

An answer to the first issue is quite difficult to frame, but a number of points can be made. If official policy statements are to be questioned constantly on their veracity, then a similar attitude must be shown toward communications in other aspects of life. Because of human nature, because of our political heritage, or because of any number of factors, the American citizen seldom extends to the political spokesman the same level of confidence afforded economic, social, and religious speakers. We normally do not assume that everyone is one hundred percent truthful, but we do assume that most people exhibit a rational pattern of behavior, and will perform consistently with their stated goals (whether their personal objective is to eat dinner or become a doctor). Personal relationships—even the most superficial variety—are built on an acceptance of a communicative

---

[6] Robert J. Manning, "Foreign Policy in the Open Society," *Department of State Bulletin,* Vol. 48 (April 15, 1963) , 577. Emphasis added. This statement was made before the Foreign Operations and Government Information Subcommittee of the House Committee on Government Operations, March 25, 1963.

[7] In communication theory, "encode" means to translate a mental image or concept into a verbal symbol; "decode" means to translate a verbal symbol into a mental image or concept.

interchange over a period of time. In the words of psycholinguistics, verbal expressions *are* nevertheless aspects of human behavior.

On the problem of official lying, reference should be made again to Mr. Manning's comments. He foresaw only two alternatives in public pronouncements on foreign policy: to tell the truth or shut up. "The obligations of the government official is to tell the truth or, if security dictates, to button his lip."[8] The question is not one of morality, he added, for falsehood is simply unnecessary. The frequency of official lying has been exaggerated. There is no doubt that the Official Voice has lied in the past, as seen in President Eisenhower's statement that Francis Gary Power's U-2 airplane was engaged in collecting weather information. However, these instances involve a "cover" story for highly secretive intelligence activities, and not situations in which the decision-maker evaluates past, present, and future policy. Official lies in the U-2 incident involved an event that had happened, and not a declaration of policy intention.

The second issue concerns the influence of the Official Voice at the moment of decision. If the decision-maker is honest in his encoding of policy purposes, is his statement shunted when the time arrives to make a decision? A body of literature exists that evaluates the effect of a speaker's words on his behavior. Bauer summarizes one conclusion of this research: "A communication once completed has an existence external to the originator. It is a sample of his behavior which he must often reconcile—as a result of social or of internal pressure—with other behavior."[9] In other words, the speaker's statement tends to become a commitment. He may have uttered the pronouncement from a variety of motivations, but now it has an existence all its own, and the speaker feels compelled to behave in a way consistent with what he has said.

The Official Voice, furthermore, is an institutional voice. It could be argued that an individual decision-maker might not experience a psychological commitment to his statements uttered in behalf of a faceless organization. Or, if he did, other administrative forces within the institution could frustrate his attempt to honor his words. On the other hand, the fact that the Official Voice is an institutional voice means that it has been coordinated with the major decisional units within the organization. Thus, junior administrators in need of

---

8 Manning, *op. cit.*, pp. 577-578.
9 Raymond A. Bauer, "The Communicator and the Audience," *Journal of Conflict Resolution*, 2:68, March, 1958.

guidance on policy matters will turn to the Official Voice's past commitment rather than ignore it.

Policy will change as the international environment or institutional goals are transformed in the midst of crisis. However, policy changes are limited by previous goals and strategy enunciated publicly and already in effect. Weapons systems, budgetary expenditures, and trained personnel in existence constitute rigidities that cannot be changed overnight: new goals and strategy must "work around" them. The Official Voice sets the initial American response to any crisis. Since international relations is a dynamic subject, policy changes will come, and the changes themselves will be announced by the Official Voice. Hence, public pronouncements on foreign policy "lag" behind the event, *viz.*, the policy change will come and then the public will be told about it. But some public statements "lead" actual changes in policy by preparing the public for new directions, new emphasis, new programs, or in rare cases, complete reversals of policy positions.

The elitist critique, with its four assumptions, gives to the Official Voice private and public channels. It assumes that the private channel is more important and that the Official Voice will send substantially different messages through non-public means. This assumption would be difficult, if not impossible, to confirm. Figure I illustrates the private and public channels of the Official Voice. The primary difference between these public and private channels is that the domestic audience is aware of the former but not the latter. But the question remains: is the policy statement issued through the private channel substantially different than that flowing through the overt channel? In a democratic society, it is doubtful that the two policy statements are *substantially* different, although there may be differences in details. In an autocratic society, however, it is quite possible that the covert channel messages are different both in substance and detail from the overt communications.

In conclusion, the content of the Public Official Voice exhibits a variety of themes that are economic and technical as well as political. There is sufficient reason to accept the Public Voice as a vehicle for conveying policy positions to an attentive public in an open society.

To Whom?

The last question to be answered is to whom are American foreign policy statements addressed? Obviously, the fact that the statement

13

PRIVATE CHANNEL

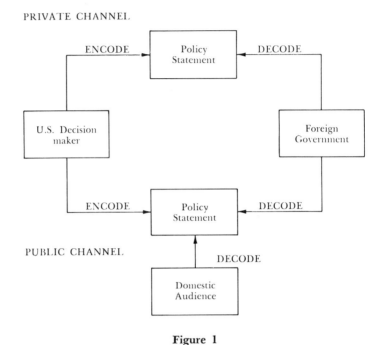

Figure 1

Overt and Covert Channels of the Official Voice

appears in the *Bulletin* indicates that it has a wider audience than the initial group of listeners. Table 4 shows that approximately half of the 234 statements in the 1966 *Bulletin* were presented before domestic audiences in the United States. This fact, of course, is no surprise, except that the total might be expected to be higher.

One-third of the statements were addressed to representatives of foreign governments who were meeting in an international conference. Hence, a sizeable percentage of policy pronouncements was enunciated by accredited U.S. representatives in a formal gathering. To return once more to the public versus private discussion, it is doubtful that the U.S. government would say one thing in public to a foreign representative and another to his government. These statements delivered in a conference setting are policy positions which serve as a basis for compromises and agreements. This audience is hardly the place for abstract and meaningless language.

14

TABLE 4

Classification of Audiences for U.S. Policy Statements

Classification	Frequencies of statements in 1966	
	Number	Percent
American audience in the United States	120	51.3
American audience in a foreign country	3	1.3
Foreign audience in the United States	1	.04
Foreign audience in a foreign country	10	4.3
American and foreign audience in U.S.	4	1.7
American and foreign audience abroad	6	2.6
International organization and conferences	77	32.9
Not applicable[a]	13	5.6
Totals	234	100:1

[a] These statements are articles in the *Bulletin,* or written reports for the President of the United States.

Of 130 statements delivered before domestic audiences, Table 5 shows that the largest percentage was directed to Congress, which again, is not an audience to tolerate the abstract and nondescript statements envisioned by the elitist critique. The second largest domestic audience—academic groups—also tend to be critical of platitudes and utopian goals. The same can be said for other groups, such as mass media (associations of newspaper editors, for example) and foreign policy elites (foreign policy councils, local United Nations Associations, etc.). Largely neglected in 1966 are political parties, labor, and cultural audiences, although this picture might change in other years. For instance, the impression is that Secretary of State Dulles spoke quite often to religious groups. Political organizations, no doubt, are purposely shunned in an attempt at bipartianship in American foreign policy.

TABLE 5

Domestic Audience Groups for Foreign Policy Statements

Group	Frequency of statements in 1966	
	Number	Percent
Nation	4	1.7
Local public	9	3.8
Executive branch		
President	3	1.3
Government group	6	2.6
Congress	33	14.0
Political party	1	0.4
Civic	6	2.6
Religious	2	0.8
Veterans	5	2.1
Labor	0	0.0
Business	11	4.7
Academic	24	10.2
Foreign policy elite groups	10	4.3
Mass media	11	4.7
Cultural	0	0.0
Professional society	5	2.1
Non-domestic group	105	44.7
Totals	235[a]	100.0

[a] One statement was delivered to a group as well as telecast nationwide; thus, it was coded in two categories and this accounts for a higher total for 1966.

Conclusion

The foregoing discussion should furnish an overview of the types of speakers, subjects, and audiences of U.S. foreign policy statements. Additional research on years during other periods of American diplomacy would yield data for comparison. Our concern is contemporary American foreign policy; therefore, the policy statements which follow have been selected to offer in each case the current position of the U.S. government.

A glance at the Contents will indicate that the best-known "news-making" speeches by the President and Secretary of State are omitted. Most of the addresses are delivered by decision-makers hidden deep in the organizational charts of the Department of State. For the most part, the lower-echelon officials in their addresses tend to focus on specific problems and supply facts and figures as well as policy positions. In contrast, a presidential address delivered on radio and television before a nation-wide audience most often is general in tone. While the President will furnish the broad guidelines of policy, it remains for the policy-mechanics to apply the executive decisions to individual cases and make the policy "work." It is important to note that the major policy pronouncements on issues have not all been made recently. For example, no major policy statements on Cuba have been made since Under Secretary George Ball's address in Roanoke, Virginia, on April 23, 1964. This pronouncement illustrates the long-term staying power of some foreign policy positions issued by the Official Voice.

The Official Voice is a multifaceted voice that speaks of many things to many people. A democratic society can disagree with it, but should never ignore it as meaningless.

PART 1

Issues in American Foreign Policy

1

Military Strategy and Doctrine

"National security policy" may be defined as the political, economic, and military strategy developed to insure the survival of a nation against perceived enemies. The political and economic aspects will be discussed in following sections of this volume; this section will focus attention on military strategy. Military strategy is the pattern of decisions made to develop and use national force in the international system. At times the term, military doctrine, will be employed, but there appears to be no conceptual difference between strategy and doctrine. Hence, they will be used interchangeably.

Military strategy has been openly discussed by American policy-makers since the end of World War II for two reasons. In the first place, the U.S. had used two nuclear devices against Japan in a decision which was criticized after the war. Thus, American decision-makers believed that the conditions under which nuclear weapons would be employed should be spelled out clearly for both the American public and a possible adversary. Secondly, the U.S. government was unaccustomed to planning strategy before the fighting started. In the past, American military leaders analyzed foreign wars while protected by two oceans and then updated their strategy and weapons systems on the basis of their observations of the belligerents' strengths and weaknesses. But following World War II, the U.S. was placed in the unfamiliar position of having to devise strategy in a vacuum. Consequently, except for the possible and probable uses of weapons of biological and chemical warfare, military strategy has evolved under the full glare of public opinion. Incidentally, the American government can take solace from the fact that Russian leaders are essentially in the same position. The Soviet Union is relatively new at preparing military strategy *before* the fighting begins. In the past, the

Russians traded territory for time, permitting an invader to occupy vast areas while Russian leaders formulated strategy and built military strength.

Importance of military strategy

The need for pre-conflict planning has been underscored by the nature of contemporary warfare. If the generally accepted estimates are correct, that World War III will be over in a matter of hours or perhaps days, then the military planner will have no opportunity to return to his drawing board and devise new weapons to defeat his enemy. Furthermore, contemporary warfare—at least, the total, unlimited, and nuclear variety—requires highly complex and expensive weapons which may take as many as seven years to design, build prototypes, test, and manufacture in sufficient quantities for the battlefield.

There are historical instances when the military strategist "guessed wrong" and prepared for a type of war that never happened. Based on 19th century experiences, military planners thought that wars would last from six weeks to six months. However, World War I turned out to be a war of attrition when the machinegun, trench, and barbed wire proved that the defense had caught up with the offense. As a result, the French built the most glamorous trench of all—the Maginot line—and trained their troops in the fine art of bayonet charges only to discover that World War II was quite different. The chosen military strategy rigidly molds the initial response of a nation to armed conflict.

Evolution of American military strategy

American military stragegy has evolved through three stages which can be identified with postwar presidential administrations.

Truman Administration

Rapid demobilization after World War II left approximately 400,000 American troops in Western Europe in 1946, and most of these were assigned occupation duties in Germany, Austria, and Italy. A strategy of deterrence began to develop while the Truman administration built a stockpile of atomic warheads and perfected a hydrogen device. According to this strategy, there existed a single source of aggression, the U.S.S.R., and one target, Western Europe. In the event of a Soviet conventional attack on Western Europe, the U.S. would respond with a nuclear attack on the Soviet heartland. Otherwise, instances involving less than total war would be met with the application of increments of power below the nuclear level. The Berlin blockade was an example of a U.S. non-nuclear response to a Soviet policy.

Eisenhower Administration

The Eisenhower administration faced new problems with different strategy needs in the view of American decision-makers. The Soviet Union was no longer the only revolutionary state in the international system. The Peoples Republic of China also presented a source of aggressive intentions. A new military strategy was devised, dubbed "massive retaliation," and announced by Secretary of State Dulles in an address to the Council on Foreign Relations in New York on January 12, 1954. He declared that the United States reserved the option to "retaliate instantly, by means and at places of our own choosing." It was not possible that local defenses could "contain the mighty land power of the Communist world." Thus, the local defenses "must be reinforced by the further deterrent of massive retaliatory power."

Hence, the strategy developed during the Truman Administration was modified substantially. More than one nation could be the target since the Peoples Republic of China now joined the Soviet Union. Nuclear weapons would be employed at any level of conflict—not only in the case of general, unlimited war. The United States reserved the right to retaliate at Soviet and Chinese heartlands in the event that they, singly or united, began a conflict, even though the fighting was limited and only conventional weapons were used. Finally, Secretary Dulles enlarged the region covered by the nuclear umbrella. The U.S. would employ its nuclear arsenal in areas of the world other than Europe.

Kennedy-Johnson Administration

President Kennedy and his advisers questioned the wisdom of responding to every level of conflict with a nuclear attack. In the first

23

place, by 1961, Soviet retaliatory prowess was an established fact, and consequently, exchanges of nuclear weapons in the event of conflict would bring unthinkable devastation to both the United States and the U.S.S.R. Secondly, Soviet or Chinese aggression using conventional or guerrilla tactics with limited objectives presented the dilemma of responding with a nuclear attack or not responding at all. More options were needed by the United States. A new American strategy evolved: The U.S. would meet aggression at the level chosen by the enemy. This decision meant that the United States had to develop military capabilities for guerrilla and conventional types of conflict, as well as nuclear war. The approach of the Kennedy Administration (and that of President Johnson as well) has been labeled "flexible response" or the "McNamara Doctrine."

The present state of American military strategy

An overview of contemporary American military strategy can be gained by examining the five levels at which conflict can and does occur: guerrilla warfare, limited and unlimited conventional warfare, and limited and unlimited nuclear warfare. U.S. decision-makers give uneven attention to these levels, developing detailed strategic plans for some and largely neglecting others.

Guerrilla warfare as a 20th century strategy is new to the American military establishment. The Kennedy Administration attempted to build a counter-insurgency force, led by the elite troops known as the Green Berets, that would meet and, hopefully, defeat enemy guerrillas on their own level. In a true sense, this attempt was a relearning process, for the American revolutionary war (at least in its early stages) was a guerrilla conflict against the British armies. The Americans acted "ungentlemanly" by refusing to stand in ranks and fire volleys. They chose the safety of concealment and were content to fire individually at the bright red coats that made inviting targets. Has the U.S. developed a 20th century capability to fight guerrilla wars? Vietnam is the first true test, but it does not present a clear-cut basis for judgment. Guerrilla fighting has been carried on against the Vietcong; against North Vietnamese regulars, the conflict has been fought on the conventional level. While the final judgment of the Vietnamese conflict is yet to be written, it would appear that the U.S. forces have had more success with conventional battles and a general lack of success at the guerrilla level.

Limited conventional wars have become common fixtures in the post-1945 era. Limited conflicts in Korea, between India and China, India and Pakistan, India and Portugal, and Israel and the Arabs are only a few of the wars fought on the limited conventional level. In an era when the Cold War between two superstates (the U.S. and U.S.S.R.) does not permit unlimited conflict to occur, military engagements of a lower intensity have abounded. What makes a "limited" conflict? Three characteristics must be present: the conflict is limited in geography, weapons systems, and objectives. From a geographical point of view, both sides possess a sanctuary, as in Korea when the Manchurian area was not attacked by the United States and U.S. bases in Okinawa were left alone. Regarding weapon systems, nuclear devices are not employed even though one or both sides possess them. Both sides are willing to settle for less than total victory or the complete annihilation of the enemy.

The strategies worked out within the North Atlantic Treaty Organization are aimed at meeting the threat of a limited conventional thrust by the U.S.S.R. in Western Europe. The emphasis in military preparations has been placed on a strong force of conventional armies under joint NATO command. These NATO forces would serve as a "shield" against a conventional threat from Soviet ground forces attempting to move into Western Europe. According to "forward strategy," the Russian armies would be met as far to the east as possible and checkmated. After the Soviet forces had been stopped, a "pause" would ensue in which the Russian leaders would contemplate the costs and risks of escalating the conflict to nuclear weapons. If the decision is made to escalate, then the NATO "sword," the nuclear air power of the U.S. and United Kingdom, would respond and the conflict then moves to a higher level. While the "sword-shield-forward-pause" strategies have been worked out on paper, the weaknesses of NATO's conventional armies have meant that they could not be implemented. The Gaullist argument is that the four strategies for conventional warfare are unrealistic anyway: if the U.S.S.R. wanted to conquer the world, it would start with a nuclear attack on the U.S. rather than a conventional thrust into Western Europe.

Unlimited conventional wars—the type fought in 1914–1919 and 1939–1945—do not enter into American strategic planning today. Most strategists doubt that the world will ever see an unlimited conventional war again. No nation, losing an unlimited conflict and possessing nuclear weapons, would hesitate to use its entire arsenal to stave off defeat. The only conceivable circumstances under which unlimited conventional war might occur is after a disarmament agreement in which all nations destroyed their nuclear devices and thus were left with only conventional weapons.

Limited nuclear war is a possibility but it is not considered a probability by military strategists. The arbitrary distinction between a tactical nuclear weapon—the only type that would be used in a limited nuclear war—and a strategic nuclear weapon is 20 kilotons, or 20 thousand tons of TNT. Tactical weapons may be fired from artillery pieces and intermediate range ballistic missiles (IRBM) or dropped by airplanes, and they are designed for battlefield targets rather than population-industrial complexes in the enemy's heartland. The problem involved in using tactical nuclear weapons is that of maintaining the limit of the conflict especially if the losing side possesses higher yield weapons.

The last level of warfare, unlimited nuclear conflict, is the subject of the following speech by Mr. McNamara. He argues that American strategy is based on deterrence of Soviet attack by building a "second strike capability." In other words, the U.S. has the capability to absorb a Soviet nuclear missile attack and respond with sufficient nuclear force to destroy the U.S.S.R. The Soviet Union also possesses a similar "second strike capability." Neither nation possesses the means to destroy sufficient numbers of incoming missiles to assure its survival. But the Soviet Union has undertaken an anti-ballistic missile (ABM) system, which Mr. McNamara thinks is spending an enormous sum of money with very little military payoff. He justifies the modest American investment in an ABM on the basis of the Chinese, and not the Russian, threat. Russian intercontinental ballistic missiles (ICBM) are too sophisticated by decoy devices to be hurt by an American ABM system.

Will it ever be possible to employ strategic nuclear weapons in future wars without setting off an atomic or hydrogen holocaust? An attempt to reconcile nuclear weapons to the classical military doctrine (which taught that force should destroy the enemy's will to resist rather than his total resources) was made in 1962 by Mr. McNamara in an address at Ann Arbor, Michigan. He suggested a "counterforce" strategy to replace the "countercity" strategy. He stated that the "principal military objectives, in the event of a nuclear war stemming from a major attack on the alliance, should be the destruction of the enemy's military forces, not of his civilian forces." Instead of targeting cities, the U.S. bombers and missiles would strike military targets and leave the cities intact. The Ann Arbor speech was an indication that U.S. nuclear weaponry development was sufficiently sophisticated and existed in large enough quantities that smaller military targets could be pinpointed and destroyed. Civilian areas could be spared both the blast and the fallout of nuclear weapons. Whether the "counterforce" strategy is now in effect is only a guess, as is any estimate that the Russian military strategist has reciprocated and targeted only American military targets rather than U.S. population areas.

Conclusion

National security policy—the "what" and "how" to use national power—has been debated in a fish bowl since 1946. American decision-makers have been quite unbeguiling about the nature and use of its military might. In the address reprinted below, Secretary of Defense McNamara compares American and Russian strengths, discusses the Chinese missile threat, and points out that national security policy has a psychological dimension.

The Dynamics of Nuclear Strategy

by Robert S. McNamara

Secretary of Defense[1]

I want to discuss with you this afternoon the gravest problem that an American Secretary of Defense must face: the planning, preparation, and policy governing the possibility of thermonuclear war.

It is a prospect most of mankind would prefer not to contemplate. That is understandable. For technology has now circumscribed us all with a conceivable horizon of horror that could dwarf any catastrophe that has befallen man in his more than a million years on earth.

Man has lived now for more than 20 years in what we have come to call the atomic age. What we sometimes overlook is that every future age of man will be an atomic age.

If, then, man is to have a future at all, it will have to be a future overshadowed with the permanent possibility of thermonuclear holocaust.

About that fact, we are no longer free. Our freedom in this question consists rather in facing the matter rationally and realistically and discussing actions to minimize the danger.

No sane citizen, no sane political leader, no sane nation, wants thermonuclear war. But merely not wanting it is not enough. We must understand the difference between actions which increase its risk, those which reduce it, and those which, while costly, have little influence one way or another.

Now this whole subject matter tends to be psychologically unpleasant. But there is an even greater difficulty standing in the way of constructive and profitable debate over the issues. And that is that

---

1 Address made before the annual convention of United Press International editors and publishers at San Francisco, Calif., on September 18, 1967. Printed in *The Department of State Bulletin,* October 9, 1967, pp. 443-51.

28

nuclear strategy is exceptionally complex in its technical aspects. Unless these complexities are well understood, rational discussion and decisionmaking are simply not possible.

What I want to do this afternoon is deal with these complexities and clarify them with as much precision and detail as time and security permit.

"Assured Destruction Capability"

One must begin with precise definitions. The cornerstone of our strategic policy continues to be to deter deliberate nuclear attack upon the United States, or its allies, by maintaining a highly reliable ability to inflict an unacceptable degree of damage upon any single aggressor, or combination of aggressors, at any time during the course of a strategic nuclear exchange—even after our absorbing a surprise first strike. This can be defined as our "assured destruction capability."

Now, it is imperative to understand that assured destruction is the very essence of the whole deterrence concept.

We must possess an actual assured destruction capability. And that actual assured destruction capability must also be credible. Conceivably, our assured destruction capability could be actual without being credible—in which case it might fail to deter an aggressor. The point is that a potential aggressor must himself believe that our assured destruction capability is in fact actual and that our will to use it in retaliation to an attack is in fact unwavering.

The conclusion, then, is clear: If the United States is to deter a nuclear attack on itself or on its allies, it must possess an actual and a credible assured destruction capability.

When calculating the force we require, we must be "conservative" in all our estimates of both a potential aggressor's capabilities and his intentions. Security depends upon taking a "worst plausible case"— and having the ability to cope with that eventuality.

In that eventuality we must be able to absorb the total weight of nuclear attack on our country—on our strike-back forces; on our command and control apparatus; on our industrial capacity; on our cities; and on our population—and still be fully capable of destroying the aggressor to the point that his society is simply no longer viable in any meaningful 20th-century sense.

29

That is what deterrence to nuclear aggression means. It means the certainty of suicide to the aggressor—not merely to his military forces but to his society as a whole.

"First-Strike Capability"

Now let us consider another term: "first-strike capability." This, in itself, is an ambiguous term, since it could mean simply the ability of one nation to attack another nation with nuclear forces first. But as it is normally used, it connotes much more: the substantial elimination of the attacked nation's retaliatory second-strike forces. This is the sense in which "first-strike capability" should be understood.

Now, clearly, such a first-strike capability is an important strategic concept. The United States cannot—and will not—ever permit itself to get into the position in which another nation or combination of nations would possess such a first-strike capability, which could be effectively used against it.

To get into such a position vis-a-vis any other nation or nations would not only constitute an intolerable threat to our security, but it would obviously remove our ability to deter nuclear aggression—both against ourselves and against our allies.

Now, we are not in that position today—and there is no foreseeable danger of our ever getting into that position.

Our strategic offensive forces are immense: 1,000 Minuteman missile launchers, carefully protected below ground; 41 Polaris submarines, carrying 656 missile launchers—with the majority of these hidden beneath the seas at all times; and about 600 long-range bombers, approximately 40 percent of which are kept always in a high state of alert.

Our alert forces alone carry more than 2,200 weapons, averaging more than 1 megaton each. A mere 400 1-megaton weapons, if delivered on the Soviet Union, would be sufficient to destroy over one-third of her population and one-half of her industry.

And all of these flexible and highly reliable forces are equipped with devices that insure their penetration of Soviet defenses.

Now, what about the Soviet Union? Does it today possess a powerful nuclear arsenal?

The answer is that it does.

Does it possess a first-strike capability against the United States?

30

The answer is that it does not.

Can the Soviet Union, in the foreseeable future, acquire such a first-strike capability against the United States?

The answer is that it cannot. It cannot because we are determined to remain fully alert and we will never permit our own assured destruction capability to be at a point where a Soviet first-strike capability is even remotely feasible.

Is the Soviet Union seriously attempting to acquire a first-strike capability against the United States?

Although this is a question we cannot answer with absolute certainty, we believe the answer is "No." In any event, the question itself is, in a sense, irrelevant. It is irrelevant since the United States will so continue to maintain—and where necessary strengthen—our retaliatory forces that, whatever the Soviet Union's intentions or actions, we will continue to have an assured destruction capability vis-a-vis their society in which we are completely confident.

But there is another question that is most relevant. And that is: Do we—the United States—possess a first-strike capability against the Soviet Union?

The answer is that we do not.

And we do not, not because we have neglected our nuclear strength. On the contrary, we have increased it to the point that we possess a clear superiority over the Soviet Union.

We do not possess first-strike capability against the Soviet Union for precisely the same reason that they do not possess it against us. And that is that we have both built up our "second-strike capability"[2] to the point that a first-strike capability on either side has become unattainable.

There is, of course, no way in which the United States could have prevented the Soviet Union from acquiring its present second-strike capability—short of a massive preemptive first strike on the Soviet Union in the 1950's.

The blunt fact is, then, that neither the Soviet Union nor the United States can attack the other without being destroyed in retaliation; nor can either of us attain a first-strike capability in the foreseeable future.

---

2 A "second-strike capability" is the capability to absorb a surprise nuclear attack and survive with sufficient power to inflict unacceptbale damage on the aggressor. [Footnote in original.]

The further fact is that both the Soviet Union and the United States presently possess an actual and credible second-strike capability against one another—and it is precisely this mutual capability that provides us both with the strongest possible motive to avoid a nuclear war.

U.S. Nuclear Superiority

The more frequent question that arises in this connection is whether or not the United States possesses nuclear superiority over the Soviet Union.

The answer is that we do.

But the answer is—like everything else in this matter—technically complex. The complexity arises in part out of what measurement of superiority is most meaningful and realistic.

Many commentators on the matter tend to define nuclear superiority in terms of gross megatonnage or in terms of the number of missile launchers available.

Now, by both these two standards of measurement, the United States does have a substantial superiority over the Soviet Union in the weapons targeted against each other.

But it is precisely these two standards of measurement that are themselves misleading. For the most meaningful and realistic measurement of nuclear capability is neither gross megatonnage nor the number of available missile launchers, but rather the number of separate warheads that are capable of being *delivered* with accuracy on individual high-priority targets with sufficient power to destroy them.

Gross megatonnage in itself is an inadequate indicator of assured destruction capability, since it is unrelated to survivability, accuracy, or penetrability and poorly related to effective elimination of multiple high-priority targets. There is manifestly no advantage in over-destroying one target at the expense of leaving undamaged other targets of equal importance.

Further, the number of missile launchers available is also an inadequate indicator of assured destruction capability, since the fact is that many of our launchers will carry multiple warheads.

But by using the realistic measurement of the number of warheads available, capable of being reliably delivered with accuracy and effectiveness on the appropriate targets in the United States or Soviet Union, I can tell you that the United States currently possesses a superiority over the Soviet Union of at least three or four to one.

Furthermore, we will maintain a superiority—by these same realistic criteria—over the Soviet Union for as far ahead in the future as we can realistically plan.

I want, however, to make one point patently clear: Our current numerical superiority over the Soviet Union in reliable, accurate, and effective warheads is both greater than we had originally planned and in fact more than we require.

Moreover, in the larger equation of security, our "superiority" is of limited significance; since even with our current superiority, or indeed with any numerical superiority realistically attainable, the blunt, inescapable fact remains that the Soviet Union could still—with its present forces—effectively destroy the United States, even after absorbing the full weight of an American first strike.

I have noted that our present superiority is greater than we had planned. Let me explain to you how this came about; for I think it is a significant illustration of the intrinsic dynamics of the nuclear arms race.

In 1961, when I became Secretary of Defense, the Soviet Union possessed a very small operational arsenal of intercontinental missiles. However, they did possess the technological and industrial capacity to enlarge that arsenal very substantially over the succeeding several years.

Now, we had no evidence that the Soviets did in fact plan to fully use that capability. But as I have pointed out, a strategic planner must be "conservative" in his calculations; that is, he must prepare for the worst plausible case and not be content to hope and prepare merely for the most probable.

Since we could not be certain of Soviet intentions—since we could not be sure that they would not undertake a massive buildup—we had to insure against such an eventuality by undertaking ourselves a major buildup of the Minuteman and Polaris forces.

Thus, in the course of hedging against what was then only a theoretically possible Soviet buildup, we took decisions which have resulted in our current superiority in numbers of warheads and deliverable megatons.

But the blunt fact remains that if we had had more accurate information about planned Soviet strategic forces we simply would not have needed to build as large a nuclear arsenal as we have today.

Now let me be absolutely clear. I am not saying that our decision in 1961 was unjustified. I am simply saying that it was necessitated by a lack of accurate information. Furthermore, that decision in itself—as justified as it was—in the end could not possibly have left unaffected the Soviet Union's future nuclear plans.

What is essential to understand here is that the Soviet Union and the United States mutually influence one another's strategic plans. Whatever be their intentions, whatever be our intentions, actions—or even realistically potential actions—on either side relating to the buildup of nuclear forces, be they either offensive or defensive weapons, necessarily trigger reactions on the other side. It is precisely this action-reaction phenomenon that fuels an arms race.

Nonnuclear Forces Required

Now, in strategic nuclear weaponry the arms race involves a particular irony. Unlike any other era in military history, today a substantial numerical superiority of weapons does not effectively translate into political control or diplomatic leverage.

While thermonuclear power is almost inconceivably awesome, and represents virtually unlimited potential destructiveness, it has proven to be a limited diplomatic instrument. Its uniqueness lies in the fact that it is at one and the same time an all-powerful weapon and a very inadequate weapon.

The fact that the Soviet Union and the United States can mutually destroy one another—regardless of who strikes first—narrows the range of Soviet aggression which our nuclear forces can effectively deter.

Even with our nuclear monopoly in the early postwar period, we were unable to deter the Soviet pressures against Berlin or their support of aggression in Korea. Today, our nuclear superiority does not deter all forms of Soviet support of Communist insurgency in Southeast Asia.

What all of this has meant is that we, and our allies as well, require substantial nonnuclear forces in order to cope with levels of aggression that massive strategic forces do not in fact deter.

This has been a difficult lesson both for us and for our allies to accept, since there is a strong psychological tendency to regard superior nuclear forces as a simple and unfailing solution to security and an assurance of victory under any set of circumstances.

What is important to understand is that our nuclear strategic forces play a vital and absolutely necessary role in our security and that of our allies but it is an intrinsically limited role.

Thus, we and our allies must maintain substantial conventional forces fully capable of dealing with a wide spectrum of lesser forms of political and military aggression—a level of aggression against which the use of strategic nuclear forces would not be to our advantage and thus a level of aggression which these strategic nuclear forces by themselves cannot effectively deter. One cannot fashion a credible deterrent out of an incredible action. Therefore, security for the United States and its allies can only arise from the possession of a whole range of graduated deterrents, each of them fully credible in its own context.

Now, I have pointed out that in strategic nuclear matters the Soviet Union and the United States mutually influence one another's plans. In recent years the Soviets have substantially increased their offensive forces. We have, of course, been watching and evaluating this very carefully.

Clearly, the Soviet buildup is in part a reaction to our own buildup since the beginning of this decade. Soviet strategic planners undoubtedly reasoned that if our buildup were to continue at its accelerated pace, we might conceivably reach, in time, a credible first-strike capability against the Soviet Union.

That was not in fact our intention. Our intention was to assure that they—with their theoretical capacity to reach such a first-strike capability—would not in fact outdistance us.

But they could not read our intentions with any greater accuracy than we could read theirs. And thus the result has been that we have both built up our forces to a point that far exceeds a credible second-strike capability against the forces we each started with.

In doing so, neither of us has reached a first-strike capability. And the realities of the situation being what they are—whatever we believe their intentions to be and whatever they believe our intentions to be—each of us can deny the other a first-strike capability in the foreseeable future.

Now, how can we be so confident that this is the case? How can we be so certain that the Soviets cannot gradually outdistance us—either by some dramatic technological breakthrough or simply through our

35

imperceptively lagging behind, for whatever reason: reluctance to spend the requisite funds, distraction with military problems elsewhere, faulty intelligence, or simple negligence and naivete?

All of these reasons—and others—have been suggested by some commentators in this country, who fear that we are in fact falling behind to a dangerous degree.

The answer to all of this is simple and straightforward. We are not going to permit the Soviets to outdistance us, because to do so would be to jeopardize our very viability as a nation. No President, no Secretary of Defense, no Congress of the United States—of whatever political party and of whatever political persuasion—is going to permit this nation to take that risk.

Hope for Arms Limitation Agreement

We do not want a nuclear arms race with the Soviet Union—primarily because the action-reaction phenomenon makes it foolish and futile. But if the only way to prevent the Soviet Union from obtaining first-strike capability over us is to engage in such a race, the United States possesses in ample abundance the resources, the technology, and the will to run faster in that race for whatever distance is required.

But what we would much prefer to do is to come to a realistic and reasonably riskless agreement with the Soviet Union which would effectively prevent such an arms race. We both have strategic nuclear arsenals greatly in excess of a credible assured destruction capability. These arsenals have reached that point of excess in each case for precisely the same reason: We each have reacted to the other's buildup with very conservative calculations. We have, that is, each built a greater arsenal than either of us needed for a second-strike capability, simply because we each wanted to be able to cope with the "worst plausible case."

But since we now each possess a deterrent in excess of our individual needs, both of our nations would benefit from a properly safeguarded agreement first to limit, and later to reduce, both our offensive and defensive strategic nuclear forces.

We may, or we may not, be able to achieve such an agreement. We hope we can. And we believe such an agreement is fully feasible, since it is clearly in both our nations' interests. But reach the formal

36

agreement or not, we can be sure that neither the Soviets nor we are going to risk the other obtaining a first-strike capability. On the contrary, we can be sure that we are both going to maintain a maximum effort to preserve an assured destruction capability.

It would not be sensible for either side to launch a maximum effort to achieve a first-strike capability. It would not be sensible because, the intelligence-gathering capability of each side being what it is and the realities of leadtime from technological breakthrough to operational readiness being what they are, neither of us would be able to acquire a first-strike capability in secret.

Now, let me take a specific case in point.

The Soviets are now deploying an anti-ballistic-missile system. If we react to this deployment intelligently, we have no reason for alarm.

The system does not impose any threat to our ability to penetrate and inflict massive and unacceptable damage on the Soviet Union. In other words, it does not presently affect in any significant manner our assured destruction capability.

It does not impose such a threat because we have already taken the steps necessary to assure that our land-based Minuteman missiles, our nuclear submarine-launched new Poseidon missiles, and our strategic bomber forces have the requisite pentration aids and, in the sum, constitute a force of such magnitude that they guarantee us a force strong enough to survive a Soviet attack and penetrate the Soviet ABM deployment.

Deployment of an ABM System

Now, let me come to the issue that has received so much attention recently: the question of whether or not we should deploy an ABM system against the Soviet nuclear threat.

To begin with, this is not in any sense a new issue. We have had both the technical possibility and the strategic desirability of an American ABM deployment under constant review since the late 1950's.

While we have substantially improved our technology in the field, it is important to understand that none of the systems at the present or foreseeable state of the art would provide an impenetrable shield over the United States. Were such a shield possible, we would certainly want it—and we would certainly build it.

And at this point, let me dispose of an objection that is totally irrelevant to this issue. It has been alleged that we are opposed to deploying a large-scale ABM system because it would carry the heavy price tag of $40 billion.

Let me make it very clear that the $40 billion is not the issue. If we could build and deploy a genuinely impenetrable shield over the United States, we would be willing to spend not $40 billion but any reasonable multiple of that amount that was necessary. The money in itself is not the problem: The penetrability of the proposed shield is the problem.

There is clearly no point, however, in spending $40 billion if it is not going to buy us a significant improvement in our security. If it is not, then we should use the substantial resources it represents on something that will.

Every ABM system that is now feasible involves firing defensive missiles at incoming offensive warheads in an effort to destroy them. But what many commentators on this issue overlook is that any such system can rather obviously be defeated by an enemy simply sending more offensive warheads, or dummy warheads, than there are defensive missiles capable of disposing of them.

And this is the whole crux of the nuclear action-reaction phenomenon.

Were we to deploy a heavy ABM system throughout the United States, the Soviets would clearly be strongly motivated to so increase their offensive capability as to cancel out our defensive advantage.

It is futile for each of us to spend $4 billion, $40 billion, or $400 billion—and at the end of all the spending, and at the end of all the deployment, and at the end of all the effort, to be relatively at the same point of balance on the security scale that we are now.

In point of fact, we have already initiated offensive weapons programs costing several billions in order to offset the small present Soviet ABM deployment and the possibly more extensive future Soviet ABM deployments. That is money well spent; and it is necessary. But we should bear in mind that it is money spent because of the action-reaction phenomenon.

If we in turn opt for heavy ABM deployment—at whatever price— we can be certain that the Soviets will react to offset the advantage we would hope to gain.

It is precisely because of this certainty of a corresponding Soviet reaction that the four prominent scientists—men who have served with distinction as the Science Advisers to Presidents Eisenhower, Kennedy, and Johnson—and the three outstanding men who have served as Directors of Research and Engineering to three Secretaries of Defense have unanimously recommended against the deployment of an ABM system designed to protect our population against a Soviet attack.

These men are Doctors [James R.] Killian, [George B.] Kistiakowsky, [Jerome B.] Wiesner, [Donald F.] Hornig, [Herbert F.] York, [Harold] Brown, and [John S.] Foster.

Offensive and Defensive Capabilities

The plain fact of the matter is that we are now facing a situation analogous to the one we faced in 1961: We are uncertain of the Soviets' intentions.

At that time we were concerned about their potential offensive capabilities; now we are concerned about their potential defensive capabilities. But the dynamics of the concern are the same.

We must continue to be cautious and conservative in our estimates, leaving no room in our calculations for unnecessary risk. And at the same time, we must measure our own response in such a manner that it does not trigger a senseless spiral upward of nuclear arms.

Now, as I have emphasized, we have already taken the necessary steps to guarantee that our offensive strategic weapons will be able to penetrate future, more advanced, Soviet defenses.

Keeping in mind the careful clockwork of leadtime, we will be forced to continue that effort over the next few years if the evidence is that the Soviets intend to turn what is now a light and modest ABM deployment into a massive one.

Should they elect to do so, we have both the leadtime and the technology available to so increase both the quality and quantity of our offensive strategic forces—with particular attention to highly reliable penetration aids—that their expensive defensive efforts will give them no edge in the nuclear balance whatever.

But we would prefer not to have to do that. For it is a profitless waste of resources, provided we and the Soviets can come to a realistic strategic arms limitation agreement.

As you know, we have proposed U.S.-Soviet talks on this matter. Should these talks fail, we are fully prepared to take the appropriate measures that such a failure would make necessary.

The point for us to keep in mind is that should the talks fail—and the Soviets decide to expand their present modest ABM deployment into a massive one—our response must be realistic. There is no point whatever in our responding by going to a massive ABM deployment to protect our population, when such a system would be ineffective against a sophisticated Soviet offense.

Instead, realism dictates that if the Soviets elect to deploy a heavy ABM system, we must further expand our sophisticated offensive forces and thus preserve our overwhelming assured destruction capability.

But the intractable fact is that should the talks fail, both the Soviets and ourselves would be forced to continue on a foolish and feckless course. It would be foolish and feckless because, in the end, it would provide neither the Soviets nor us with any greater relative nuclear capability. The time has come for us both to realize that and to act reasonably. It is clearly in our own mutual interest to do so.

Having said that, it is important to distinguish between an ABM system designed to protect against a Soviet attack on our cities and ABM systems which have other objectives.

Communist China's Nuclear Threat

One of the other uses of an ABM system which we should seriously consider is the greater protection of our strategic offensive forces. Another is in relation to the emerging nuclear capability of Communist China.

There is evidence that the Chinese are devoting very substantial resources to the development of both nuclear warheads and missile delivery systems. As I stated last January, indications are that they will have medium-range ballistic missiles within a year or so, an initial intercontinental ballistic missile capability in the early 1970's, and a modest force in the midseventies.

Up to now, the leadtime factor has allowed us to postpone a decision on whether or not a light ABM deployment might be advantageous as a countermeasure to Communist China's nuclear development. But the time will shortly be right for us to initiate production if we desire such a system.

China at the moment is caught up in internal strife, but it seems likely that her basic motivation in developing a strategic nuclear capability is an attempt to provide a basis for threatening her neighbors and to clothe herself with the dubious prestige that the world pays to nuclear weaponry. We deplore her development of these weapons, just as we deplore it in other countries. We oppose nuclear proliferation because we believe that in the end it only increases the risk of a common and cataclysmic holocaust.

President Johnson has made it clear that the United States will oppose any efforts of China to employ nuclear blackmail against her neighbors.

We possess now, and will continue to possess for as far ahead as we can foresee, an over-whelming first-strike capability with respect to China. And despite the shrill and raucous propaganda directed at her own people that "the atomic bomb is a paper tiger," there is ample evidence that China well appreciates the destructive power of nuclear weapons.

China has been cautious to avoid any action that might end in a nuclear clash with the United States—however wild her words—and understandably so. We have the power not only to destroy completely her entire nuclear offensive forces but to devastate her society as well.

Is there any possibility, then, that by the mid-1970's China might become so incautious as to attempt a nuclear attack on the United States or our allies? It would be insane and suicidal for her to do so, but one can conceive conditions under which China might miscalculate. We wish to reduce such possibilities to a minimum.

Advantages of Light Deployment of U.S. ABM's

And since, as I have noted, our strategic planning must always be conservative and take into consideration even the possible irrational behavior of potential adversaries, there are marginal grounds for concluding that a light deployment of U.S. ABM's against this possibility is prudent.

The system would be relatively inexpensive—preliminary estimates place the cost at about $5 billion—and would have a much higher degree of reliability against a Chinese attack than the much more massive and complicated system that some have recommended against a possible Soviet attack.

Moreover, such an ABM deployment designed against a possible Chinese attack would have a number of other advantages. It would

41

provide an additional indication to Asians that we intend to deter China from nuclear blackmail and thus would contribute toward our goal of discouraging nuclear weapon proliferation among the present nonnuclear countries.

Further, the Chinese-oriented ABM deployment would enable us to add—as a concurrent benefit—a further defense of our Minuteman sites against Soviet attack, which means that at modest cost we would in fact be adding even greater effectiveness to our offensive missile force and avoiding a much more costly expansion of that force.

Finally, such a reasonably reliable ABM system would add protection of our population against the improbable but possible accidental launch of an intercontinental missile by any one of the nuclear powers.

After a detailed review of all these considerations, we have decided to go forward with this Chinese-oriented ABM deployment; and we will begin actual production of such a system at the end of this year.

Psychological Dangers

In reaching this decision, I want to emphasize that it contains two possible dangers, and we should guard carefully against each.

The first danger is that we may psychologically lapse into the old oversimplification about the adequacy of nuclear power. The simple truth is that nuclear weapons can serve to deter only a narrow range of threats. This ABM deployment will strengthen our defensive posture and will enhance the effectiveness of our land-based ICBM offensive forces. But the independent nations of Asia must realize that these benefits are no substitute for their maintaining, and where necessary strengthening, their own conventional forces in order to deal with the more likely threats to the security of the region.

The second danger is also psychological. There is a kind of mad momentum intrinsic to the development of all new nuclear weaponry. If a weapon system works—and works well—there is strong pressure from many directions to procure and deploy the weapon out of all proportion to the prudent level required.

The danger in deploying this relatively light and reliable Chinese-oriented ABM system is going to be that pressures will develop to expand it into a heavy Soviet-oriented ABM system.

We must resist that temptation firmly, not because we can for a moment afford to relax our vigilance against a possible Soviet first strike but precisely because our greatest deterrent against such a strike is not a massive, costly, but highly penetrable ABM shield but rather a fully credible offensive assured destruction capability.

The so-called heavy ABM shield—at the present state of technology—would in effect be no adequate shield at all against a Soviet attack but rather a strong inducement for the Soviets to vastly increase their own offensive forces. That, as I have pointed out, would make it necessary for us to respond in turn; and so the arms race would rush hopelessly on to no sensible purpose on either side.

Let me emphasize—and I cannot do so too strongly—that our decision to go ahead with a *limited* ABM deployment in no way indicates that we feel an agreement with the Soviet Union on the limitation of strategic nuclear offensive and defensive forces is any the less urgent or desirable.

The road leading from the stone ax to the ICBM, though it may have been more than a million years in the building, seems to have run in a single direction. If one is inclined to be cynical, one might conclude that man's history seems to be characterized not so much by consistent periods of peace, occasionally punctuated by warfare, but rather by persistent outbreaks of warfare, wearily put aside from time to time by periods of exhaustion and recovery that parade under the name of peace.

I do not view man's history with that degree of cynicism, but I do believe that man's wisdom in avoiding war is often surpassed by his folly in promoting it.

However foolish unlimited war may have been in the past, it is now no longer merely foolish, but suicidal as well.

It is said that nothing can prevent a man from suicide if he is sufficiently determined to commit it. The question is what is our determination in an era when unlimited war will mean the death of hundreds of millions—and the possible genetic impairment of a million generations to follow?

Man is clearly a compound of folly and wisdom, and history is clearly a consequence of the admixture of those two contradictory traits. History has placed our particular lives in an era when the consequences of human folly are waxing more and more catastrophic in the matters of war and peace.

In the end, the root of man's security does not lie in his weaponry. In the end, the root of man's security lies in his mind.

What the world requires in its 22d year of the atomic age is not a new race toward armament. What the world requires in its 22d year of the atomic age is a new race toward reasonableness.

We had better all run that race—not merely we the administrators but we the people.

2

Foreign Trade, Tariffs, and Investments

The story of United States' trade activities in the post-World War II period is one of affluence followed by a chronic imbalance of payments. The rapid increase in imports, the drain of American gold reserves, and the weakening of the dollar as an international currency have made U.S. foreign economic policy a major concern. One indication of the problem is the decrease in American gold reserves from $24.5 billion in 1949 to $11.4 billion at the beginning of 1968.

American trade position

The U.S. has been plagued with an unfavorable balance of payments, but it has enjoyed a favorable balance of trade, *i.e.*, a surplus of exports over imports. Table 1 shows that the widest margin of exports over imports in the past decade occurred in 1957 and 1964 (both $7.9 billion). But the data also show that imports increased at a much faster rate over the decade than did exports. Imports doubled, while exports increased only 30 percent. Statistics on the percentage of the world market that the U.S. claims are even more revealing. In 1956, the U.S.'s percentage share of total world trade was 18.3 percent; in 1966, its share dropped to 14.7 percent. During the same period, Japan's share doubled (from 2.4 to 4.8 percent), and most European states increased substantially (with the exception of England, which also declined). Despite this decrease in percentage of world trade, the U.S. continues to be the world's largest exporter, although the American economy sends abroad less than 5 percent of its gross national product.

TABLE 1

U.S. Exports and Imports of Merchandise[a]

Billions of Dollars

Year	Exports	Imports	Excess of Exports Over Imports
1957	20.9	13.0	7.9
1958	17.9	12.8	5.1
1959	17.6	15.2	3.4
1960	20.6	15.0	5.6
1961	21.0	14.7	6.3
1962	21.7	16.4	5.3
1963	23.3	17.2	6.1
1964	26.5	18.6	7.9
1965	27.5	21.3	6.2
1966	30.3	25.6	4.7
1967	31.5	26.9	4.6

[a] Includes "special category," or Department of Defense Shipments.

Source: *Foreign Commerce and Navigation of the United States, 1946-1963; Highlights of U.S. Export and Import Trade, December 1967.*

What is the composition of American exports and imports? The largest category of exports is machinery: industrial tools, construction equipment, electronic computers, automobiles, trucks, buses, aircraft, and railway vehicles are examples. Domestic electrical equipment, such as household appliances, are also supplied to foreign markets. Another large segment of exports are agricultural products, most of which are sold for dollars and some of which are sold under the auspices of Public Law 480 (to be discussed in the next section). The largest purchaser of American products is Canada.

The largest category of imports into the U.S. corresponds to the first category of American exports, machinery. American trading partners are also competitors in the domestic market. Foreign automobiles, trucks and vehicle parts are imported as part of the machinery category. Petroleum and petroleum products, base ores, and metals are also imported in large quantities. Foodstuff, such as coffee, bananas, and sugar, also are brought into American markets.

U.S. balance of payments

The balance of payments consists of more than exports and imports. It includes all transactions—private and public—between nations. American gold losses began in 1958, and Table 2 shows the deficit in the balance of payments since then. The U.S. government made progress toward narrowing the payments gap throughout the 1960's until 1967.

TABLE 2

U. S. Balance of Payments (Liquidity Basis)

Billions of Dollars

Year	Amount of Deficit	Year	Amount of Deficit
1958	−3.5	1963	−2.7
1959	−3.7	1964	−2.8
1960	−3.9	1965	−1.3
1961	−2.4	1966	−1.4
1962	−2.2	1967	−3.8

Source: *Statistical Abstract of the United States.*

Mr. Barr enumerates eight categories for funds which leave the U.S. and six for capital flowing in. Trade, for example, accounts for money coming into the United States when exports are sold abroad, and for money going out when foreign goods are imported. While there is a favorable balance of trade, U.S. dollars and gold have been flowing out through imbalances in the other categories mentioned by Mr. Barr: tourism, private investment, foreign grants and loans, and military expenditures abroad.

Tourism

There are more American tourists traveling abroad than foreign tourists visiting the United States. The Johnson Administration in January 1968 proposed a tax on American tourism abroad to close the gap, which totals approximately $1 billion each year.

Private investment abroad

American businessmen (and other private individuals) have sent funds abroad to invest in securities sold by foreign stock exchanges and to build branches or subsidiary firms. Over the years, a total investment of approximately $90 billion has been accumulated in foreign countries. Most of the investment has been made in developed countries, with Canada the primary recipient. The American investor has avoided the developing countries of Afro-Asia for several reasons: unstable governments, the danger of expropriation by revolutionary elites, the absence of a middle class to furnish a large market for mass-produced goods, and the lack of adequate "infrastructure" (*e.g.*, roads, railroads, harbors) to transport goods to markets in all areas of the country. Secretary of State Rusk outlines the present U.S. position on private investment. In general, the American government does not want investment halted, but it does wish to see the flow moderated. For the past several years, the outflow of private investment capital has averaged approximately $4 billion, while foreigners have invested less than $1 billion in the United States. Businessmen argue that foreign investment helps, rather than harms, by returning interest or profits totaling as much or more than the yearly outflow. Some countries encourage American investors in order to attract capital for economic growth.

Two additional problems are presented by the large amount of private investment abroad, one deals with individuals investing in a country whose foreign policy is at odds with U.S. goals, and the other concerning the dilemma of double loyalty. An example of the first problem is the Republic of South Africa, where private individuals continue to invest heavily despite American opposition to South Africa's racist policies. The second problem occurs when foreign branches owned by parent companies in the United States feel compelled to follow the dictates of American foreign policy, rather than the directives of the host country. For example, the U.S. prohibits American businessmen from trading with Communist China, while the Canadian government allows exchanges of nonstrategic goods. An American-owned firm in Canada that refuses to engage in Chinese trade in effect owes it loyalty to American, rather than Canadian, foreign policy values.

Foreign grants and loans

This category is one of the major—though by no means the only—contributors in the American balance of payments problem. While the total foreign aid bill amounts to approximately $6 billion, not all of it is considered debit. Most of the foreign grants and loans are tied to purchase of American goods and services, and thus appear as credits in the category of exports.[1] Foreign aid will be discussed in Chapter 3.

Military expenditures abroad

Government spokesmen declare that the U.S. would have no balance of payments problem were it not for the Vietnamese conflict. "Military expenditures abroad" do not include military equipment given to nations, for these statistics would appear under the "foreign grants and loans" column. The major item is the spending of military personnel who are stationed on foreign soil, primarily in Germany and Vietnam.

Exports, Communism, and tariffs

Increasing exports raises the question of trade—or lack of it—with Communist nations and of the American tariff structure. Commercial relations with Communist states have not been extensive in the post-World War II period because of the Cold War. Trade may be carried on with the U.S.S.R. and East European nations, but not in strategic goods. American trade policy toward this region will be discussed in Chapter 11. A group of four states—Mainland China, North Korea, North Vietnam, and Cuba—is subjected to a complete embargo of American goods, strategic as well as nonstrategic.

The United States today is not a "high tariff" country, although it deserved that reputation prior to World War II. After World War II, the U.S. led in reducing barriers to trade and increasing multilateral exchanges of goods and services. The General Agreements on Tariffs and Trade (GATT) was approved and has resulted in six "rounds" of multilateral, tariff-reducing conferences. The effectiveness of GATT agreements, as well as the bilateral negotiations carried on under the 1934 Reciprocal Trade Act, is attested to by the fact that American tariffs in 1962 stood at 12 percent of their 1934 levels.[2] For further reductions to occur meant a wholesale approach to Amer-

---

[1] Of $1.4 billion of foreign aid in 1967 spent for commodities, 96 percent were purchased in the United States. AID has all but stopped foreign aid "leakage," *i.e.,* the recipient government using American money to buy foreign goods.

[2] Michael Blumenthal, "The Kennedy Round," *Department of State Bulletin,* Vol. 52 (April 26, 1965), 630.

ican tariffs, especially to invade those areas that heretofore in GATT rounds were considered off-limits because of domestic politics. The Trade Expansion Act, passed in 1962, set the stage for the sixth round of trade negotiations, which was completed in June 1967. Agreements were negotiated which reduced further American tariffs an average of 35 percent on approximately 6,000 items. The tariff reductions are spread over a four year period beginning January 1, 1968, and ending January 1, 1972. During this period, American businesses affected by the tariff reductions will have an opportunity to adjust to increased foreign competition.

Conclusion

The American economic giant has exhibited a weakness which has defied strengthening for the past decade. The official concern over the balance of payments is reflected in the following policy statements, both characterized by a lack of specific solutions. The balance of payments problem is one of the most complex and persistent issues in contemporary American foreign policy. There is no easy answer. "Increase exports" is the most commonly heard solution; however, maintaining a stable domestic economy and reducing foreign commitments would have to accompany any increase in exports in order to bring the American payments position back into balance.

The Role of the Dollar

by Joseph W. Barr,

Undersecretary of the Treasury[1]

* * *

When we discuss the American dollar, I think it is important to bear in mind that the dollar serves three roles: as a national currency, as a key (sometimes referred to as a vehicle) currency, and as a reserve currency.

The Dollar as a National Currency

The first role, as a national currency, is I think obvious to everyone. The dollar in this historic role is our domestic medium of exchange, designed to meet the needs of our domestic financial transactions. Also, I think most people understand that our domestic money supply must grow over the years as our economy grows. There is some limit on how many times a year you can use a dollar for different transactions, and as the economy grows and transactions increase there is an obvious need for more dollars to keep things moving.

There is not such a clear understanding, however, of the second and third roles, and discussions of our balance of payments and world liquidity sometimes confuse the two.

The Dollar as a Vehicle Currency

We speak of the dollar as a vehicle currency, we refer to its use in financing international trade and payments. The dollar in this capaci-

---

[1] Excerpts from an address delivered before the National Association of Manufacturers, Hot Springs, Virginia, on September 21, 1965. Printed in *Vital Speeches of the Day*, Vol. 32, 18-21.

ty is held by private banks, businesses, and individuals throughout the world as a medium of exchange for their international transactions; they use it just as they use their own currencies for their domestic transactions.

To summarize, the dollar is available, it is safe, and it is enormously convenient to have one or (if one includes the British pound and French franc) two or three currencies that many countries can use, in an infinite variety of bilateral trade transactions, as a kind of common denominator.

The Dollar as a Reserve Currency

The dollar's third role—that of a reserve currency—has developed for many of the same reasons that have made it a vehicle currency.

By a reserve currency we mean that dollars are held by governments and central banks as a highly liquid and dependable asset that they can use along with gold to carry them over times of temporary imbalance—precisely the way you, as businessmen, keep reserves for contingencies. But there is an important distinction between the role of the dollar as a vehicle currency and its role as a reserve currency. I have mentioned that probably the principal factor in the dollar's role as a vehicle currency is convenience. I believe that the principal factor in the dollar's role as a reserve currency is confidence— confidence in the ability to use it quickly and at an assured price. These are approximately the criteria most businessmen use in acquiring and holding assets as contingent reserves.

Those who hold the dollar as a reserve currency, central banks and treasuries, do so in the knowledge that these dollars are freely convertible into gold at the fixed price of $35 an ounce. The fact that we have not varied from this policy and this fixed price for over 30 years plus the fact that we are the only country which stands ready to exchange gold for holdings of its currency has made the dollar second only to gold as an international reserve asset.

Foreign monetary authorities hold about $14 billion in their reserves. These dollars are used to finance their balance-of-payments deficits and surpluses and as a cushion for the future.

While these two international roles of the dollars are interdependent—dollars flow back and forth between official and private hands— changes in the world's holdings of its vehicle currency dollars can have quite different implications than changes in the world's holdings of its reserve currency dollars.

To illustrate, the amount of dollars (or any other vehicle currency) held by banks and businesses for trade and finance will probably grow as world trade grows and develops. The dollars held for reserves can vary with the judgment of central banks and governments on (a) what amount of reserves they need and (b) their judgment as to the potential value and usefulness of the dollar.

One final note on our dollar liabilities. While the large amounts of dollars which foreigners now hold represent liquid liabilities and potential claims on our gold reserves, the fact that the world is willing to hold such large amounts of dollars is testimony to their confidence in the dollar.

The program to which I refer next is designed to make sure that the integrity of—and international confidence in—the dollar are maintained.

The Twin Problems of Balance of Payments and World Liquidity

Most of the current discussions of international finance concern twin problems: our balance-of-payments deficit and world liquidity.

. . . let's make certain of our definitions. First of all let's define the balance of payments. It is not as easy as it might seem because it is an accounting of our private and Government transactions with the rest of the world. In dangerously simplified terms the major transaction would be like this:

What Funds Go Out

1. Money spent to buy imports (including shipping costs to foreign lines).

2. Money spent by tourists.

3. Money spent by the United States in maintaining troops overseas.

4. Money loaned by banks and the Government to foreign borrowers.

5. Money invested in industries in foreign nations.

6. Money given as untied grants under our foreign aid program.

7. Money sent abroad as payment of interest and principal due by U.S. borrowers.

8. Money remitted as dividend payments to foreign holders of U.S. securities, or as branch income of foreign corporations.

What Funds Come In

1. Money spent by foreigners to buy our exports.
2. Money spent by foreign tourists in the United States.
3. Money loaned by foreign banks and governments to U.S. borrowers.
4. Money invested by foreigners in U.S. industries.
5. Remittances of interest and principal payments on debts foreigners owe to U.S. lenders.
6. Remittance of dividend income and income of U.S. overseas branches to U.S. investors and corporations.

I have warned you that this is highly oversimplified accounting, but it does include the major items.

When the outgoing items exceed the incoming, we say that we have a deficit; when the reverse is true we say that we have a surplus.

* * *

Just what do we mean by liquidity? The corporate explanation of liquidity is the relation between short-term liabilities and short-term assets. It seems to me that the international economists are much less precise in their definition. When they speak of liquidity, they usually refer to the official (government and central bank) holdings of gold and convertible currencies and the credit available on a rather automatic basis in the IMF.[2] The relation of these assets to short-term liabilities is usually meaningless to most countries because their currencies are not used as a vehicle in commercial transactions or held as reserves.

However, in the United States the corporate definition of liquidity that relates liquid assets to near-term liabilities is more appropriate. It is in fact crucial because as I have pointed out $11 billion are held by private foreigners for trade and finance and $14 billion by official foreigners as reserves.

---

[2] International Monetary Fund (Editor's Note.)

Thus, the proper definition of liquidity would probably be in three parts. For most nations it could be defined as their holdings of convertible foreign currencies, gold, and their IMF position. For the United States it is more precise to define liquidity as the relation between these assets and our short-term liabilities. For the world as a whole, you would probably define liquidity as the amounts of acceptable international resources (gold, convertible currencies, and automatic credit at the IMF) available for trade, finance, and reserves.

* * *

In essence, the balance-of-payments problem is one of U. S. liquidity. Our overall financial position is good and improving but our international liquidity has been deteriorating. To illustrate, at the end of 1964 our private foreign investments alone exceeded the total of all foreign claim on us—official and private—by over $18 billion. The comparable figure in 1958, when our balance of payments first became a serious problem, was less than $7 billion. This is without taking any account of our gold stock which at the end of 1964 amounted to over $15 billion and our Government claims on foreign countries which amounted to over $23 billion. Our overall position, therefore, is obviously immensely strong.

But in the process of building up these tremendous foreign assets, most of which are long-term assets, we have incurred large short-term liquid liabilities, which, while much smaller than our long-term assets, have been large in relation to our gold reserves.

At the beginning of 1958 our holdings of gold came to almost $23 billion. They now stand at less than $14 billion. Over the same period our dollar liabilities to foreign official institutions rose from less than $9 billion to over $14 billion.

It is obvious that this process of lending long and borrowing short cannot go on indefinitely, and I think that most responsible observers are agreed that our balance of payments must be brought into equilibrium to bring it to an end. But at this point the second of our twin problems comes into focus. If the dollar outflow from the United States is ended, how will the world's needs for a key currency and a reserve currency be met?

You will remember that I have earlier indicated that net outflows of dollars have not always been turned back to the United States. Some of these dollars have been retained by foreigners to increase

55

working balances to finance an expanding level of trade and finance and some of these additional dollars have been held to build up official reserves.

On its face, it appears that we are faced with a dilemma. Actually, careful analysis leads us to believe that the ending of our deficit may not create a world liquidity problem for sometime to come.

* * *

The Administration's Approach

The administration's approach to these twin problems is to move quickly and certainly to balance-of-payments equilibrium and at the same time to move forward in discussions on improving the world's monetary system.

I have pointed out why it is imperative for us to restore equilibrium in our balance of payments. But what, it is asked, do we mean by equilibrium? Is it an exact balance or does it allow for some deficit, say $500 million, $1 billion, or even more?

Our feeling in the Treasury is that equilibrium cannot be defined solely in terms of a figure; it is importantly a matter of confidence. Whether a given figure for the overall balance of our international transactions represents equilibrium depends on the particular circumstances at the particular time. But while we may not be able to define in precise numerical terms what equilibrium is, we can say that it does not exist when the United States is continually losing gold. Perhaps, then, the best indication of what equilibrium in the U.S. balance of payments is, is what the rest of the world thinks it is. The extent to which they cash in their dollars for gold is, in short, a very useful indicator.

We are seeking the long-run, basic solution to our balance-of-payments deficit through measures which are consistent with our domestic objectives and our foreign policy objectives, and consistent with a growing volume of world trade and capital movements. In brief, our long-run approach is to:

1. Continue to minimize the balance-of-payments impact of Government expenditures abroad.

2. Strive to increase our exports and recipts from foreign tourists.

3. Encourage other developed nations to take on more international financing to relieve us of a disproportionate share.

4. Take measures to encourage more foreign investment here.

To gain the necessary time for these longer run measures, we have undertaken shorter run measures which President Johnson outlined in his message last February 10. These consist of efforts to reduce foreign travel expenditures by U.S. citizens; the extension and broadening of the interest equilization tax; and, most importantly, the request that banks and corporations curtail or adjust their activities to lessen the balance of payments impact of capital outflows.

The key to success in this program, both in the short run and in the long run, is the business community. For the short run, we must have the effective cooperation of the business community to give us the time for our longer run measures to take effect. And in the long run, the competitive position of American business in relation to the other major trading countries will be critical.

First of all, we must maintain our good record of relative price stability. Secondly, American business must become more energetic and effective in finding and exploiting foreign markets for American exports.

*　　*　　*

Trade, Investment, and United States Foreign Policy

Address by Dean Rusk,

Secretary of State[1]

* * *

The international trade and investment of American business also are important in our global strategy. . . . I should like to sketch out some of the major implications for our foreign policy of American exports, imports, and participation in foreign enterprises.

The Role of Exports

First of all, we must increase our exports—and at a faster rate than in the past. The strength of the dollar, our ability to maintain overseas military forces and installations essential to the security of the free world, and our ability to continue economic assistance rest heavily on the shoulders of American exporters.

The stability of the dollar and of the free-world monetary system will not permit indefinite deficits in the United States balance of payments. We are taking a variety of measures to meet this problem. The result has been a considerable reduction in our payments deficit. However, we still face a hard-core deficit. Theoretically we could wipe it out—and indeed create a surplus—by reducing drastically our overseas expenditures for defending and building the free world. Military defense accounts for some $3 billion a year of our dollar outflow, and foreign aid for approximately $1.3 billion. However, it would be

---

1 Excerpts from an address made in behalf of Secretary Rusk by William C. Foster, Director of the U.S. Arms Control and Disarmament Agency, before the National Business Advisory Council at Hot Springs, Va., on October 19, 1962. Printed in the *Department of State Bulletin*, November 5, 1962, pp. 684-89.

suicidal to balance our payments by weakening our deterrence to Communist aggression. And it would be short-sighted and ultimately very costly to reduce sharply our assistance to the less developed countries.

The sound, constructive way to close the remaining gap in our balance of payments is by expanding exports. In the old rhyme the kingdom was lost for want of a nail. In our case our global strategy could be undermined by failure to export.

The Government, through its trade promotion program, is attempting to stimulate greater exports, but the basic job here is one for business, not Government. I would like, however, to remind you briefly of the services the Government is providing to assist businesses increase export sales. We are building up our export promotion activities. Our Foreign Service posts are placing new emphasis on commercial services. These services now include new trade centers and increased participation in trade fairs and trade missions.

* * *

What are the prospects of increasing our exports? I think they are good for the short run, excellent for the longer run.

* * *

Looking ahead one can see many favorable factors. For example, European wages and prices are rising faster than ours. European delivery rates are stretching out as labor shortages limit production increases. Europe is demanding more and more of the labor-saving machinery typical of a mass-production, mass-market economy. And the prospective reduction of European import duties, especially on American machinery, equipment, advanced chemical products, and other products included in the special authority for negotiations with the European Common Market, should open the way for a flourishing expansion of our exports in the years ahead.

Many American firms regard the world as their market and gear their production, product design, and marketing techniques accordingly. But I fear that there are still many firms who regard exports—if they export at all—as marginal markets to be served on an order-taking basis. A long-term rapid expansion in our exports requires a basic foreign market development strategy on the part of many more American firms, large and small. This global business strategy, in brief, means that American business must think of the world as its market and must seek to maximize its long-term profits on a world, not a national, scale.

The Role of Imports

The expansion of imports does not require the same type of effort necessary for export expansion. In the long run, however, our ability to absorb increasing volumes of imports is essential both to the expansion of our export markets in advanced countries and to the development of less developed countries.

We must be prepared to open the American market wider if we are to bargain down foreign barriers to our exports. Moreover, the pressure of foreign competition may lower our production costs and increase our export potential in some industries. I probably do not have to remind many of you that foreign competition forces a number of American industries to keep a more watchful eye on customer needs as well as on costs.

* * *

The importance of imports does not end here, however. If the developing nations are ever to be able to pay for their capital equipment needs, they must progressively increase their exports to the industrialized nations. And they cannot do that simply by shipping out more primary commodities. The world's ability to absorb these commodities is limited.

During the past decade of booming world trade, exports of the industrial countries, which were high to begin with, almost doubled in value. Export earnings of the developing countries on the other hand rose by less than one-third. If we exclude petroleum, their export earnings showed only a moderate and, in terms of the needs, a very unsatisfactory rate of increase.

Prices of primary commodities tend to fluctuate widely. In the case of a few, moreover, prices have moved persistently downward, largely because of sluggish demand and chronic oversupply, with serious consequences for the development programs of the exporting countries concerned.

For this reason we are exploring a variety of devices to blunt or offset the impact of price weakness and instability in commodity markets and to create more stable conditions in the trade. Commodity agreements . . . are one of the more important of these devices. We should be under no illusion, however, that commodity agreements in themselves will solve all our problems. They may prove valuable and necessary in a number of instances to provide a breathing spell—to buy time. But the coffee agreement, and any other agreements which may be negotiated, will eventually fail unless we deal with the more fundamental problems. For many commodities the basic problem is overproduction. The only long-term solution we see is to shift resources out of production of surplus commodities into other areas— especially processing and manufacturing.

In short, the situation facing many developing countries is this: Import requirements will increase as industrialization progresses; export earnings from primary commodities cannot be expected to meet these growing needs; if development is to continue these nations must receive more aid or export more processed and manufactured goods.

The industrialized nations, and especially the United States and our chief European allies, face three choices. We can ignore the problems and aspirations of the less developed nations, at one stroke denying our faith in freedom and the dignity of man and leaving most of the world to the Communists. We can make ever larger donations of foreign aid indefinitely. Or we can progressively widen our import markets to manufactured goods from developing countries.

The third choice, increasing our imports, is the only practicable policy in the long run. This will create some difficulties—and I emphasize again that all industrialized nations must join in coping with them.

* * *

Other more intractable problems may require a common approach embracing all major exporting and importing nations. We have to face this issue directly. We must devise mechanisms which permit a continuous growth in imports of manufactures from developing nations while easing the impact on vulnerable domestic industries.

* * *

61

The Role of Foreign Investment

I turn to the role of American investment abroad. Its relationship to our foreign policy is complex. It cannot be judged merely in terms of dollars. In the long run the flows of managerial skills and attitudes, and the ties developed between American businessmen and their counterparts in other lands, may prove far more important than the flow of capital alone.

Especially in less developed areas foreign private enterprise can be of critical importance. It can demonstrate how man, by his own ingenuity, can improve his lot. It can prove the necessity for managerial as well as technical skills. It can reveal to often socialist-minded leaders that modern private enterprise can spearhead economic growth. It can refute Communist claims that foreign business feeds off, rather than builds up, the local economy.

Most of American private investment abroad is in the advanced nations. Of a total of $34.7 billion in direct investments, as of last year, $11.8 billion was in Canada and $7.7 billion in Europe—of which $3.5 billion was in the United Kingdom and $3 billion within the European Common Market. During the past decade American businessmen have seen the great investment potential in Europe. In the short run the outflow of capital has placed a strain on our balance of payments. In the longer term, however, the return flow of earnings, foreign subsidiaries' procurement from the United States, and more generally the global scope, vitality, and profitability of American firms all strengthen both the international position of the dollar and our domestic economy.

As against $19.5 billion in direct private investment in Canada and Europe, we have only $2.5 billion in Asia and $1.1 billion in Africa. And these latter investments, like the $8.2 billion we have in Latin America, are largely in the production of oil and ores.[2]

I should like to see American business expand substantially its role in modernizing the economies of the less developed countries. Admittedly, in many instances, the returns may be slower and less certain. In some countries the risks, both political and economic, may be prohibitive. Yet American firms who participate in development in

---

[2] Secretary Rusk's statistics are for 1961, but his points are still timely. Compare the following direct private investment figures for 1965 with Mr. Rusk's (all in billions of dollars): Canada, 15.2; Latin America, 9.4; Europe, 13.9; Africa, 1.9; and Asia, 3.6. (Editor's note).

62

its early stages have the prospect of securing ground-floor positions in great markets of the future.

In considering risks I shall address myself particularly to the political risks. If we can find ways to minimize political risks, I am confident that American business ingenuity will overcome the economic obstacles.

The most immediate political risk for foreign investment is, of course, expropriation. This can take either the direct form of a quick government takeover or a variety of indirect or partial forms by which the host government discriminates against foreign business or makes it possible to operate at a fair profit.

Any sovereign nation has the right to expropriate property, whether owned by foreigners or nationals. In the United States we refer to this as the power of eminent domain. However, the owner should receive adequate and prompt compensation for his property. Moreover, a legal right is not the same thing as a wise policy. Economic growth requires the expansion of capital resources. If an underdeveloped nation is to achieve self-sustaining growth in a reasonable period of time, it must, as a rule, obtain external capital. The amount of outside public funds available for investment is limited. And over the long run these public funds will tend to go to those countries which are pursuing policies that hold the prospect of achieving self-sustaining growth. We consider it extremely unwise for developing nations to alienate foreign investors, thereby stunting economic growth.

The United States Government is prepared to intercede on behalf of American firms and make strong representations to host governments in cases of economically unjustified expropriation or harassment. Various forms of investment guarantees are also available as insurance against certain political risks.

*   *   *

Despite the importance we attach to dissuading governments from expropriating foreign investments, merely to forestall expropriation is not enough. A good fire department and fire insurance coverage are indispensable, but basic prevention of fires—natural or political—stems from sound, fireproof construction and extreme care in handling flammable materials. American firms in developing nations often operate in a volatile political atmosphere. You cannot handle liquid oxygen in the same way you handle pig iron. We cannot assume that operating procedures, community relations, and governmental relations will be identical in advanced and developing nations. A primary responsibility for avoidance of political risk, therefore, rests with the firm.

I am confident that American firms can, through their own efforts, avoid a large part of the political risk inherent in operations in developing nations. They can, if they retain maximum flexibility of operations, if they focus skills and imagination on satisfying both their own imperative requirements and the imperative requirements and sensitivities of the developing country. As many of you know from experience, it is often helpful to provide for substantial participation by local partners and to employ and train as many local citizens as possible. In some cases it may be possible to work out management contracts or other arrangements which keep the essential American skills and attitudes in the plant while leaving our flag off the roof.

No matter what ingenious formulas we work out, however, difficulties do and will continue to arise between American business and foreign governments. We are seeking to make our embassy staffs from the ambassador down alertly aware of their responsibility to handle such matters expeditiously and to make necessary representations to the host governments concerned.

*　*　*

In assessing the risks and opportunities of investment in less developed areas we should try to keep a proper perspective. We must remain fully aware of the deep nationalistic, anticolonialist, often socialistic sentiment in most developing nations. Private enterprise, and particularly foreign enterprise, is often highly suspect. And yet as these new nations and their leaders realize the factors necessary for development, as they see the private sector in many instances pacing their nations' growth, their hostility is softening. In part this results from the performance of the private sector. It also results from the poor performance of the Communists. The Communist bloc economy is, of course, pallid in comparison to the West. The abysmal failure of Chinese development is evident for all the world to see. Soviet incompetence in both the aid and trade fields has led to disillusion and the search for closer ties with the West on the part of several African and

Asian nations which earlier seemed to have been taken in by the grandiose Soviet economic line.

Unhappily a few countries which previously were receptive to private foreign investment are now alienating it by expropriation and harassment. However, in many developing nations the climate for private enterprise is improving.

There are strong incentives for American firms to stake their claim now in these great potential markets. As nations develop, business opportunities are being created. Future profits will go to the firms which are enterprising and foresighted today. An American firm whose managerial skill, political sophistication, and contribution to development win the confidence of a developing nation should be in an enviable position. The risks are there; the long-term opportunities are there. The developing nations represent a classic challenge to American private enterprise.

* * *

3

Economic Development

Since the end of World War II, the United States has dispersed over $100 billion in foreign aid. The history of American aid programs is a story of early success followed by a period of groping for a rationale, a role, and an organizational framework for economic assistance in American foreign policy.

Early aid programs

Economic assistance during World War II was organized under the Lend-Lease program, which continued for a short time after the fighting stopped. For the most part, the U.S. underestimated the reconstruction needs of Europe and proposed that most of the rebuilding be financed through the United Nations Relief and Rehabilitation Agency (UNRRA) and the International Bank for Reconstruction and Development (known as the World Bank). The U.S. contributed $2.7 billion to UNRRA, which ceased operations in 1947. The reconstruction needs proved too large for the limited resources of the World Bank in 1947; thus, the U.S. attempted to supplement the Bank's efforts with *ad hoc* loans to individual countries. But loans failed to improve Europe's economic conditions. As a result, the harsh winter of 1946-47, the British abdication of power in Southern Europe, guerrilla activity in Greece, and Soviet pressure on Turkey evoked the Truman doctrine and the Marshall Plan.

The Marshall Plan (or European Recovery Program, as it was officially titled) began in April 1948 and was named after Secretary of State George Marshall, who in a June 1947 address proposed that the U.S. undertake a coordinated effort to help Europe. The European countries had to decide, first, what they could do to help themselves, and then what could be done to help each other. Finally, they presented a list of needs to the U.S. for funding. The Marshall Plan ended in January 1952, five months earlier than originally planned. Approximately $12 billion had been spent. By any criteria, the first major experience of the United States giving foreign assistance was an outstanding success.

Assistance programs since the Marshall Plan, however, have not duplicated the successes of those first years. There followed an attempt to find a workable organization for funding. Several agencies were established, each experimenting with diverse organizational structures, different combinations of types of aid (technical, military, and economic) and various relationships to the State Department. First came the Mutual Security Agency (1951-1953), followed by the Foreign Operations Administration (1953-1955), the International Cooperation Administration (1955-1961), and finally, the Agency for International Development (1961 to the present).

Types of foreign aid programs

The work done by the Agency for International Development (AID) is the best known, but not the only component of American foreign aid programs. The AID budget has been reduced to approximately $3 billion a year while the *total* foreign aid bill is twice that figure. What are the other types of foreign aid that make up the difference?

One large segment is the sale of surplus agricultural products abroad under the 1954 Public Law 480. The "sale" consists of payment by the buyers in their national currency rather than in dollars or gold. Because the national currency cannot be used for projects outside the buyer's country, Public Law 480 is in essence part of the U.S. foreign aid program. PL 480 activities have been dubbed "Food for Peace" by President Kennedy and "Food for Freedom" by President Johnson. While this program officially came of age in 1954, the U.S. government had carried on similar activities on a limited scale under the Marshall Plan. Over $14 billion of foodstuff have been distributed since 1949. Table 1 gives the amounts that geographical regions have received during this period. The Near East and South Asian region has received the largest share. In 1966, the five nations receiving the largest individual slice of Food for Freedom assistance were India ($595 million), Yugoslavia ($142 million), Republic of Vietnam ($124 million), Brazil ($119 million), and Korea ($104 million).

Another major contributor to economic development is the Export-Import Bank, which finances purchases of American exports by loans

TABLE 1

Geographical Distribution of PL 480
Funds, Fiscal Years 1949-1966

Billions of Dollars

Region	Amount
Near East and South Asia	7.0
Latin America	1.5
East Asia	2.2
Africa	0.9
Europe	2.5
Oceania	0.7
Total	14.8

Source: AID, *U.S. Overseas Loans and Grants,*
pp. 6, 26, 56, 74, 117, 143.

that must be repaid in dollars. Interest rates for the loans are high so that the Export-Import Bank does not compete with commercial sources of money. During the 20-year period, 1946-1966, the Bank loaned $9.5 billion. During that period, $6.3 billion were repaid. Two geographical regions—Latin America and Europe—account for two-thirds of the Bank's loans; from 1946-1966 France borrowed the largest share ($1.2 billion), followed by Mexico ($774 million).

Finally, the Peace Corps is considered part of the American contribution to economic development. The yearly expenditure of approximately $100 million is not large. The Peace Corps Volunteers bring teaching, engineering, and medical skills to developing countries.

Trends in foreign aid programs

Several trends can be traced through the years since the foreign aid programs were initiated. Observations on these trends will be based on the statistical data presented in Tables 2 and 3.

Trend toward smaller AID budgets

Aid and its predecessors have experienced a decidedly downward trend in the amount of money at their disposal since the high-water mark of 1953. In that year, the budget called for over $6 billion with the majority of the money going into military build-up following the Korean War. In recent years, the budget declined to half of the 1953 amount, and it appears that this trend will continue. However, the point made above should be emphasized: as the AID budget decreased, other programs such as Public Law 480 have increased. Thus, the total amount of foreign aid has not changed appreciably although AID's share has declined.

Trend from emphasis on economic aid, then to emphasis on military assistance, and finally to balance between the two

In the early 1950's economic aid was larger than military assistance, but the Korean War inverted this relationship. Beginning in 1953 and lasting through 1959, military aid was given priority over economic development; however since 1960, economic assistance has been the dominant program.

Trend from grants to loans

Economic foreign aid was largely grants or gifts until 1962, when loans become the normal vehicle for distributing assistance. In military aid, grants have always played a major role despite a slight increase in loans. The regional distribution of grants and loans is uneven, as seen in Table 2. An overwhelming majority of the capital that financed European recovery was in the form of grants. East Asia is the only other region in which grants have been larger than loans.

Trend away from European nations to developing countries

Table 3 reveals that Europe has benefited the most from U.S. economic assistance since the end of World War II. However, all but approximately $3 billion of the total was administered under the Marshall Plan. Currently, Europe is repaying loans previously made by the United States, which accounts for the minus figures for 1966. American aid has shifted to non-western countries, with East Asia the largest recipient. South Vietnam received almost 70 percent and Korea almost 20 percent of the area's $838 million in 1966. Two areas—Near East and South Asia and Latin America—received almost equal amounts in 1966, with India and Brazil the largest single-nation recipients in each region. Africa has received the smallest cut of foreign aid.

TABLE 2

Agency for International Development
(and Predecessor Agencies)
Appropriations

Fiscal Year in Millions of Dollars

Year	Economic Aid			Military Aid			Total Aid
	Loans	Grants	Total	Loans	Grants	Total	
1950	163	3,451	3,614	0	56	56	3,676
1951	45	2,577	2,622	0	980	980	3,603
1952	201	1,784	1,985	0	1,481	1,481	3,466
1953	26	1,934	1,960	0	4,159	4,159	6,119
1954	114	2,114	2,228	0	3,296	3,296	5,524
1955	197	1,624	1,821	0	3,396	3,396	5,217
1956	208	1,298	1,506	8	2,920	2,928	4,434
1957	322	1,305	1,657	7	2,078	2,085	3,713
1958	417	1,203	1,620	39	2,325	2,363	3,984
1959	626	1,291	1,916	60	2,050	2,110	4,026
1960	564	1,302	1,866	21	1,697	1,718	3,584
1961	707	1,305	2,012	30	1,344	1,374	3,386
1962	1,329	1,180	2,508	21	1,427	1,448	3,956
1963	1,343	954	2,297	44	1,765	1,809	4,107
1964	1,328	808	2,136	83	1,415	1,498	3,633
1965	1,122	904	2,026	71	1,239	1,310	3,336
1966	1,219	1,325	2,543	81	1,054	1,135	3,679
1967	n.a.	n.a.	2,415	n.a.	n.a.	n.a.	3,367

Source: *Statistical Abstract of the United States; The Foreign Assistance Program, Annual Report to the Congress, Fiscal Year 1967.*

Trend toward bilateral rather than multilateral giving

Table 3 only hints at this trend in the category of "non-regional" foreign aid. These are grants to world organizations, such as the United Nations, which in turn distribute the money according to individual criteria. The American government has preferred to distribute its funds unilaterally.

TABLE 3

Foreign Economic Assistance
Regional Distribution

Millions of Dollars

Region	Fiscal Year 1966			Fiscal Years 1946-1966		
	Loans	Grants	Total	Loans	Grants	Totals
Near East and South Asia	548.2	74.2	622.3	5,173.3	4,552.4	9,725.7
Latin America	505.4	142.0	647.4	2,435.0	1,222.9	3,657.9
East Asia (including Vietnam)	76.6	761.5	838.0	780.2	8,582.7	9,363.0
Africa	88.9	80.6	169.1	813.1	1,039.3	1,852.4
Europe	—.3	—.2	—.5	1,876.4	13,352.8	15,229.2
Non-regional	—	266.6	266.6	21.4	2,724.0	2,745.4
Totals	1,218.8	1,324.6	2,543.3	11,099.3	31,474.2	42,573.5

Source: AID, *Proposed Foreign Aid Program, FY 1968.*

Trend toward projects in health, education, and agriculture and away from infrastructive programs

This trend is not contained in either Tables 1 or 2, but it is occurring in the U.S. foreign aid program.

"Infrastructure" refers to major, long-term developmental programs, such as roads, dams, harbors, and irrigation projects. In recent years, the American government has shifted to projects that improve health, upgrade educational facilities, and increase agricultural production. These tend to be short-term, with more immediate returns on the invested capital.

Trend toward emphasis on few countries receiving more aid

Rather than attempting to support many projects in many countries, the U.S. government has begun to choose six or seven states to receive larger amounts of money for development. States are chosen that are considered vital to the American national interest, that show promise of development, and that are regional powers such as India and Brazil.

Conclusion

The U.S. commitment to foreign aid has remained stable over the years despite the downward trend seen in AID budgets. However, when considered as a percentage of the gross national product, the U.S. total commitment has declined since World War II. During the Marshall Plan days, the U.S. contributed approximately two percent of its Gross National Product. Today, however, the percentage has fallen to less than one percent, and will probably fall further.

In Mr. Bell's policy statements below, he outlines some of the more recent trends in economic assistance. Mr. McNamara discusses the relationships of economic development to security. In both statements the point is developed that foreign economic assistance is in the national interest of the United States.

Trends In Administering Foreign Aid

by David E. Bell,

Administrator, Agency for International Development[1]

* * *

I . . . will limit my remarks to three or four major aspects of the aid process which seem to me to have important consequences for aid administration.

First, I suggest that we still have much to do to adapt our arrangements for administering foreign aid to the increasingly clear view that a successful aid program must be a partnership process. Foreign aid is not something a donor does *for* or *to* a recipient; it is something to be done *with* a recipient. This is the reason for the increasingly strong emphasis on self-help performance by aid recipients. There is by now I believe a very strong consensus—although far from complete unanimity—that foreign aid in all its forms will produce maximum results only insofar as it is related to maximum self help. This is the opinion of leading public officials and leading development scholars in developing countries as well as in advanced countries.

The broad concept of partnership and self help applies to technical assistance projects, in which the purpose increasingly is to establish effective permanent institutions in the developing countries. Therefore foreign technical advice and training is made available only against appropriate commitments by those receiving aid to establish the necessary administrative and legal framework, provide necessary budget funds, make available appropriate trainees, and on a specified

---

[1] Excerpts from an address delivered to the American Society for Public Administration, Washington, D. C., on April 15, 1966. Printed in *Vital Speeches of the Day,* vol. 32, 454-56.

timetable, take over full management and support of the institution in question.

At present, with respect to technical assistance, my impression is that we need to set as our objective a general and substantial upgrading of the quality of our work. I believe aid donors and recipients need jointly to set higher standards of excellence for the targets of their joint work. I think more needs to be demanded of aid recipients by way of serious commitment, major improvements in policies, responsibility for funding, and providing personnel. And I think more needs to be demanded of aid donors—by way of higher quality resources, applied over longer periods, with persistence, imagination, and a greater sense of personal involvement and pride in the outcome.

The concept of partnership and self help applies to capital projects. In this field, I believe there is likewise increasing clarity on the objective of establishing in a developing country not simply a completed physical structure—a factory, a dam, a stretch of road—but of establishing the capacity to plan, execute and maintain capital projects, and to this end the necessity for self help action by the aid recipient to commit funds, talent, and other resources to ongoing institutions.

With respect to capital projects, I think we need more emphasis on the word development and less on the word banking in the process of assistance. I do not mean to slight banking values. Quite the contrary. Unless a project meets sound technical and economic standards it will end up as a net drain on a developing country's economy, not a net contribution to its growth.

But banking standards are in a sense the lesser part of the task. The greater part is to deal with the capital project in its broader setting, and to take full advantage of the opportunities the project presents for institutional changes—through training, through policy improvements, through the development of operational and maintenance competence—which will permit the individual project to make a maximum long-run contribution to national development.

Some of our A.I.D. people in the field feel so strongly about this point that they have suggested it is a mistake to think, as we customarily do, in the categories of technical assistance on the one hand and capital assistance on the other. They suggest that the objective invariably should be to develop institutional capacity in the developing country, to which technical and capital aid should be related in whatever combination is needed to achieve the desired results. I

75

am not ready yet wholly to accept this idea, but I believe it is very much worth thinking about as we try to improve the process of aid administration.

The concept of partnership and self help has in recent years moved well beyond a consideration of technical and capital assistance projects. Both bilateral and multilateral aid donors have increasingly expressed interest in broad questions of development policy in aid-receiving countries—questions such as whether a country's fiscal and monetary policies are inflationary; whether all of a country's foreign exchange resources, both those received from exports and from foreign aid, are applied under a sensible set of priorities; whether eduational, tax, land, and other reforms that may be needed are in fact under way. And aid recipients have increasingly recognized the propriety of such an interest by aid donors.

All these are aspects of self-help performance, and only if they are resolved satisfactorily, can external aid be fully effective. We are past the stage in most countries where an interest in matters of this type by an aid donor is considered an unwarranted invasion of an aid recipient's independence. What is involved here are not political "strings," but elements of a partnership related to the objective shared by both aid donors and recipients, namely, the most rapid possible progress toward a self-sustaining and satisfactorily high rate of economic growth.

This partnership relationship is inherently delicate but is strongly founded on mutual interest and self respect. The aid donor recognizes that the aid recipient, as an independent country, must and will make its own decisions on budget and fiscal policy, foreign exchange, educational priorities, and other national policies affecting development. And the aid recipient recognizes that the aid donor, as an independent country, must and will decide whether aid requested for a given project or purpose will in fact be likely to achieve the results desired given the policies the aid-receiving country proposes to follow. We in the United States consider that it is entirely up to an aid recipient what development policies it wishes to adopt. But it is equally up to us, as an aid donor, to decide whether the circumstances presented in a country will permit external assistance to yield significant results.

The meeting ground between these interests of aid recipients and aid donors obviously should be a broad measure of agreement on what policies in fact make the most sense for a particular country at a particular time, and it is in this area that there have been some very important developments in recent years. I would mention three, not in any particular order of importance.

First, the United States has greatly increased its competence for dealing with broad questions of development policy in aid-receiving countries. A.I.D. Mission Directors . . . , with their staffs in the field and the backstopping they can call on from Washington, are able, with a high degree of understanding and sophistication, to deal with the broad range of development issues in the countries to which they are accredited. None of us is fully satisfied with the quality of our own work, but there is no doubt it has increased very significantly over the last several years. And we see evidence of a parallel increase in the staff competence of the ministries and agencies that administer aid programs in other donor governments, such as Britain, Germany, and Japan.

Second, in Latin America an international organization—the Inter-American Committee for the Alliance for Progress, called CIAP for short—has been established specifically for the purpose of reviewing progress under the Alliance. This Committee, made up of six Latin American and one U.S. member, reviews at least annually the situation in each Latin American country, and makes judgments and recommendations concerning the improvements that aid-receiving countries should make in their policies, and the extent and nature of the assistance that aid donors should provide. The CIAP is a promising arrangement, which provides sound technical judgments from an agency in which the Latin Americans themselves play the leading role. We would hope that similar arrangements might be developed for other regions of the world.

Third, the World Bank has undertaken to expand its use of consortia and consultative groups, and to use these groups as a basis for reaching common judgments among aid donors and recipients as to the development policies that are appropriate for individual developing countries. The Bank now has set up more or less formal groups for eight countries, and several more are likely in the future. These are promising arrangements under which it should be possible to achieve three objectives at once: to increase the quality of the development policies in an aid-receiving country, to increase the understanding among aid donors as to the actual situation and the real requirements in the aid-receiving country, and to increase the quality—and if appropriate the amount—of the aid made available to that country.

In summary then on this point it seems to me that while there is much change and improvement underway, there is still far to go—for both students and practitioners—before we can legitimately think of ourselves as administering well the concept of foreign aid as a partnership involving maximum self help.

A second element in current thinking about foreign aid which seems to me to have consequences for aid administration is the growing emphasis being given to pluralism in the developing countries. I believe there is now ample evidence and a growing consensus supporting the proposition that those countries will develop fastest which rely most heavily on multiple sources of private and local initiative and energy—in general contrast to countries which hope to develop by relying most heavily on central direction and control.

We do not yet have very carefully worked out and authoritative statements on this subject, so that I would like to make clear what I mean before proceeding to discuss the consequences. I am not talking about a distinction between planned and unplanned development. National planning in a developing country seems to me essential, not only to establish national policy on such matters as fiscal and monetary policy, educational priorities, and so forth, but also to establish those policies and systems of incentives which will in fact bring forth maximum private and local initiative. A sensible national development plan in my opinion can and should be aimed at building a pluralistic society.

Furthermore, I am not talking about a simple distinction between public and private activities. There are many examples in developing countries of private activities which are centralized and monopolized to an extent which greatly hamper the growth of that country. There are at least as many examples of governments which are organized in an over-centralized fashion, stifling what could be the enormous energy of local governmental units. My point therefore relates to the great importance in *both* the public and the private sector, of establishing arrangements and incentives which will strongly encourage and call forth the initiative and energy of small units, groups, and individuals.

I think there can be no doubt of the importance of this concept, but we are only beginning in my opinion to examine its implications and build them systematically into our programs and administrative processes.

A few illustrations of the probable consequences would be as follows:

First, it is very likely that we have not given enough weight to the objective of simplifying tariffs, rectifying exchange rates, and liberalizing import control policies—because to do so will permit hundreds and thousands of private businessmen and farmers to make better decisions and take more rapid actions, resulting in quicker and sounder investment and growth. Steps of this kind have in fact had this kind of results in Greece, in Korea, in Pakistan, and in other countries. Not only is it important to simplify regulations and replace physical controls with those working through the market, but it is also important that the rules not be subject to frequent change, so that large numbers of decision-making units can act with reasonably firm expectations about the future.

Second, it is likely that we can and should learn more than we have, from such successful cases as the Joint Commission on Rural Reconstruction on Taiwan, the local-government based rural works program in East Pakistan, and the credit unions and REA co-ops in Latin America, about how to help rural communities organize and apply their latent energy to their own problems and thus achieve high rates of change not only in agricultural production but also in rural living standards.

Third, it seems likely that we can do much more to establish direct connections between private organizations and individuals in the advanced countries and problems they can help solve in the developing countries—as A.I.D. has done with considerable success in helping to establish savings and loan systems in several Latin American countries, primarily by supporting the efforts of leaders in the United States savings and loan industry.

Fourth, it seems likely that we could do more to help establish and support specialized private American organizations designed to work in the developing countries—a concept illustrated by the American Institute for Free Labor Development, established by the AFL-CIO to work with labor unions in Latin America, and the International Executive Service Corps, established by a group of private business leaders to provide American businessmen volunteers to work with individual business firms in developing countries.

These are only illustrations—of which a far longer list could be easily prepared—of ways in which it should be possible to administer assistance in more imaginative and more flexible ways to induce, encourage, and support private and local groups in developing countries to go ahead and deal with their own problems. I think this is an extremely important subject because of its potential effect not only on economic and social progress but also on the development of more democratic societies.

My last major point relates to research and evaluation. It is my impression that the organizations which carry out aid programs do not have a distinguished record of building into those programs strong elements of research and evaluation. Certainly this is true of A.I.D., the agency I know best.

This is unfortunate on at least two counts. First, foreign assistance is a relatively new activity and plainly we have an enormous amount to learn about how to conduct it effectively. We have lost much valuable time and have failed to learn from much valuable experience, because we have not had adequate research and evaluation programs in the past.

Second, the process of foreign assistance is inherently dependent on research. It is often described as a process of transferring know-how but this is plainly wrong; it is instead a process of developing know-how—a process of finding out what will work in Nigeria, not of transferring what has been found to work in Nebraska. It might well be, if we understood our own business better, that the whole process of foreign aid would be best thought of as a research process, aimed at learning how to move a particular society, with its special and unique characteristics of history and culture and physical geography, toward specified objectives.

* * *

Security in the Contemporary World

by Robert S. McNamara

Secretary of Defense[1]

* * *

Roughly 100 countries today are caught up in the difficult transition from traditional to modern societies. There is no uniform rate of progress among them, and they range from primitive mosaic societies—fractured by tribalism and held feebly together by the slenderest of political sinews—to relatively sophisticated countries well on the road to agricultural sufficiency and industrial competence.

This sweeping surge of development, particularly across the whole southern half of the globe, has no parallel in history. It has turned traditionally listless areas of the world into seething cauldrons of change. On the whole, it has not been a very peaceful process.

In the last 8 years alone there have been no less than 164 internationally significant outbreaks of violence, each of them specifically designed as a serious challenge to the authority, or the very existence, of the government in question. Eighty-two different governments have been directly involved.

What is striking is that only 15 of these 164 significant resorts to violence have been military conflicts between two states. And not a single one of the 164 conflicts has been a formally declared war. Indeed, there has not been a formal declaration of war—anywhere in the world—since World War II.

The planet is becoming a more dangerous place to live on, not merely because of a potential nuclear holocaust but also because of the large number of *de facto* conflicts and because the trend of such

---

1 Excerpts from an address made before the American Society of Newspaper Editors at Montreal, Canada, on May 18, 1966. Printed in the *Department of State Bulletin*, June 6, 1966, pp. 874-78.

conflicts is growing rather than diminishing. At the begining of 1958, there were 23 prolonged insurgencies going on about the world. As of February 1, 1966, there were 40. Further, the total number of outbreaks of violence has increased each year: In 1958, there were 34; in 1965, there were 58.

The Relationship of Violence and Economic Status

But what is most significant of all is that there is a direct and constant relationship between the incidence of violence and the economic status of the countries afflicted. The World Bank divides nations on the basis of per capita income into four categories: rich, middle-income, poor, and very poor.

The rich nations are those with a per capita income of $750 per year or more. The current U.S. level is more than $2,700. There are 27 of these rich nations. They possess 75 percent of the world's wealth, though roughly only 25 percent of the world's population.

Since 1958, only one of these 27 nations has suffered a major internal upheaval on its own territory. But observe what happens at the other end of the economic scale. Among the 38 very poor nations— those with a per capita income of under $100 a year—not less than 32 have suffered significant conflicts. Indeed, they have suffered an average of two major outbreaks of violence per country in the 8-year period. That is a great deal of conflict. What is worse, it has been predominantly conflict of a prolonged nature.

The trend holds predictably constant in the case of the two other categories: the poor and the middle-income nations. Since 1958, 87 percent of the very poor nations, 69 percent of the poor nations, and 48 percent of the middle-income nations have suffered serious violence.

There can, then, be no question but that there is an irrefutable relationship between violence and economic backwardness. And the trend of such violence is up, not down.

Now, it would perhaps be somewhat reassuring if the gap between the rich nations and the poor nations were closing and economic backwardness were significantly receding. But it is not. The economic gap is widening.

By the year 1970 over one-half of the world's total population will live in the independent nations sweeping across the southern half of the planet. But this hungering half of the human race will by then command only one-sixth of the world's total of goods and services. By the year 1975 the dependent children of these nations alone—children under 15 years of age—will equal the total population of the developed nations to the north.

Even in our own abundant societies, we have reason enough to worry over the tensions that coil and tighten among underprivileged young people and finally flail out in delinquency and crime. What are we to expect from a whole hemisphere of youth where mounting frustrations are likely to fester into eruptions of violence and extremism?

Annual per capita income in roughly half of the 80 underdeveloped nations that are members of the World Bank is rising by a paltry 1 percent a year or less. By the end of the century these nations, at their present rates of growth, will reach a per capita income of barely $170 a year. The United States, by the same criterion, will attain a per capita income of $4,500.

The conclusion to all of this is blunt and inescapable: Given the certain connection between economic stagnation and the incidence of violence, the years that lie ahead for the nations in the southern half of the globe are pregnant with violence.

U.S. Security and the Newly Developing World

This would be true even if no threat of Communist subversion existed—as it clearly does. Both Moscow and Peking, however harsh their internal differences, regard the whole modernization process as an ideal environment for the growth of communism. Their experience with subversive internal war is extensive, and they have developed a considerable array of both doctrine and practical measures in the art of political violence.

What is often misunderstood is that Communists are capable of subverting, manipulating, and finally directing for their own ends the wholly legitimate grievances of a developing society.

But it would be a gross oversimplification to regard communism as the central factor in every conflict throughout the underdeveloped world. Of the 149 serious internal insurgencies in the past 8 years, Communists have been involved in only 58 of them—38 percent of the total—and this includes seven instances in which a Communist regime itself was the target of the uprising.

83

Whether Communists are involved or not, violence anywhere in a taut world transmits sharp signals through the complex ganglia of international relations and the security of the United States *is* related to the security and stability of nations half a globe away.

But neither conscience nor sanity itself suggests that the United States is, should, or could be the global gendarme. Quite the contrary. Experience confirms what human nature suggests: that in most instances of internal violence the local people themselves are best able to deal directly with the situation within the framework of their own traditions.

The United States has no mandate from on high to police the world and no inclination to do so. There have been classic cases in which our deliberate nonaction was the wisest action of all. Where our help is not sought, it is seldom prudent to volunteer. Certainly we have no charter to rescue floundering regimes who have brought violence on themselves by deliberately refusing to meet the legitimate expectations of their citizenry.

Further, throughout the next decade advancing technology will reduce the requirements for bases and staging rights at particular locations abroad, and the whole pattern of forward deployment will gradually change.

But, though all these caveats are clear enough, the irreducible fact remains that our security is related directly to the security of the newly developing world. And our role must be precisely this: to help provide security to those developing nations which genuinely need and request our help and which demonstrably are willing and able to help themselves.

Security and Development

The rub comes in this: We do not always grasp the meaning of the word "security" in this context. In a modernizing society, security means development.

Security is not military hardware, though it may include it. Security is not military force, though it may involve it. Security is not traditional military activity, though it may encompass it.

Security is development. Without development, there can be no security. A developing nation that does not in fact develop simply cannot remain "secure." It cannot remain secure for the intractable reason that its own citizenry cannot shed its human nature.

If security implies anything, it implies a minimal measure of order and stability. Without internal development of at least a minimal degree, order and stability are simply not possible. They are not possible because human nature cannot be frustrated beyond intrinsic limits. It reacts because it must.

Now, that is what we do not always understand, and that is also what governnments of modernizing nations do not always understand. But by emphasizing that security arises from development, I do not say that an underdeveloped nation cannot be subverted from within, or be aggressed upon from without, or be the victim of a combination of the two. It can. And to prevent any or all of these conditions, a nation does require appropriate military capabilities to deal with the specific problem. But the specific military problem is only a narrow facet of the broader security problem.

Military force can help provide law and order but only to the degree that a basis for law and order already exists in the developing society: a basic willingness on the part of the people to cooperate. The law and order is a shield, behind which the central fact of security—development—can be achieved.

Now we are not playing a semantic game with these words. The trouble is that we have been lost in a semantic jungle for too long. We have come to identify "security" with exclusively military phenomena, and most particularly with military hardware. But it just isn't so. And we need to accommodate to the facts of the matter if we want to see security survive and grow in the southern half of the globe.

Development means economic, social, and political progress. It means a reasonable standard of living, and the word "reasonable" in this context requires continual redefinition. What is "reasonable" in an earlier stage of development will become "unreasonable" in a later stage.

As development progresses, security progresses. And when the people of a nation have organized their own human and natural resources to provide themselves with what they need and expect out of life—and have learned to compromise peacefully among competing demands in the larger national interest—then their resistance to disorder and violence will be enormously increased.

Conversely, the tragic need of desperate men to resort to force to achieve the inner imperatives of human decency will diminish.

Military and Economic Spheres of U.S. Aid

Now, I have said that the role of the United States is to help provide security to these modernizing nations, providing they need and request our help and are clearly willing and able to help themselves. But what should our help be? Clearly, it should be help toward development.

In the military sphere, that involves two broad categories of assistance.

We should help the developing nation with such training and equipment as is necessary to maintain the protective shield behind which development can go forward. The dimensions of that shield vary from country to country, but what is essential is that it should be a shield and not a capacity for external aggression.

The second, and perhaps less understood category of military assistance in a modernizing nation, is training in civic action. Civic action is another one of those semantic puzzles. Too few Americans—and too few officials in developing nations—really comprehend what military civic action means.

Essentially, it means using indigenous military forces for nontraditional military projects, projects that are useful to the local population in fields such as education, public works, health, sanitation, agriculture—indeed, anything connected with economic or social progress.

It has had some impressive results. In the past 4 years the U.S.-assisted civic action program, worldwide, has constructed or repaired more than 10,000 miles of roads, built over 1,000 schools, hundreds of hospitals and clinics, and has provided medical and dental care to approximately 4 million people.

What is important is that all this was done by indigenous men in uniform. Quite apart from the developmental projects themselves, the program powerfully alters the negative image of the military man as the oppressive preserver of the stagnant *status quo*.

But assistance in the purely military sphere is not enough. Economic assistance is also essential. The President is determined that our aid should be hardheaded and rigorously realistic, that it should deal directly with the roots of underdevelopment and not merely attempt to alleviate the symptoms. His bedrock principle is that U.S. economic aid—no matter what its magnitude—is futile unless the country in question is resolute in making the primary effort itself. That will be

86

the criterion, and that will be the crucial condition for all our future assistance.

Only the developing nations themselves can take the fundamental measures that make outside assistance meaningful. These measures are often unpalatable—and frequently call for political courage and decisiveness. But to fail to undertake painful, but essential, reform inevitably leads to far more painful revolutionary violence. Our economic assistance is designed to offer a reasonable alternative to that violence. It is designed to help substitute peaceful progress for tragic internal conflict.

The United States intends to be compassionate and generous in this effort, but it is not an effort it can carry exclusively by itself. And thus it looks to those nations who have reached the point of self-sustaining prosperity to increase their contribution to the development and, thus, to the security of the modernizing world.

* * *

4

The United Nations

The "balance of power," which traditionally has regulated nations' behavior in the international system, has been regarded with suspicion by U.S. leaders. In his 1824 State of the Union message, James Monroe stated that the U.S. was not concerned about wars among European governments. "The balance of power between them, into whatever scale it may turn in its various vibrations, cannot affect us," he wrote. In more modern times, President Kennedy in his Inaugural Address in 1961 invited the U.S.S.R. to "join in creating a new endeavor, not a new balance of power, but a new world of law, where the strong are just and the weak secure and the peace preserved." Other presidents similarly spoke disparagingly of the balance of power. The American position was that the balance of power did not halt wars, but, in fact, caused them by its shifting alliance systems, by ignoring the rights of small states, and by its secret and unprincipled way of making foreign policy.

In the place of the balance of power, American officials proposed a new concept—the "community of power"—popularized by Woodrow Wilson. In his 1917 State of the Union message, Wilson declared that future world peace depended on a "community of interest and of power" rather than the balance of power. The League of Nations gave structure to the community of power concept. But the U.S. after World War I failed to join in building a community of power. This mistake was not repeated in 1945 when the United Nations was born.

In policy statements since World War II, presidents have pledged generous support to the United Nations. For example, President Truman in his 1952 annual message labeled the U.N. "the world's great hope for peace." In his 1961 Inaugural Address, Mr. Kennedy went further by referring to the U.N. as "our last hope in an age where the instruments of war have far out paced the instruments of peace." How have these glowing words of praise for the U.N. been translated into policy? In general, two phases of U.S.-U.N. policy can be read in the history of the post-World War II period.

1945-1955: The U.N. as an instrument of U.S. policy

During the first phase of U.S.-U.N. relations, the General Assembly was a "safe" place to bring policy matters. Since the United States and its allies (primarily the Latin American and Western European states) constituted a majority in the U.N., the American government usually could muster enough votes to support its policy initiatives. In the Security Council, the Soviet veto effectively blocked most policy initiatives; thus, the U.S. encouraged a larger role for the General Assembly. Also, the growth of the Secretary-General's power was supported by the American government. From the American viewpoint, the U.N. was a reliable instrument of foreign policy. The actions of Communist states could be condemned and U.S. policy could be made "legitimate" by U.N. approval. In June 1950, for example, the U.N. approved the use of American force to halt North Korean aggression.

1955-present: U.N. as an international arena

The end of the first phase of U.S.-U.N. relations may be dated from December 14, 1955, when 16 new members were admitted. Previously, U.S.-U.S.S.R. differences did not permit *en bloc* additions to the U.N. The December 1955 decision broke the membership dikes and the western complexion of the General Assembly gradually changed. No longer could the U.S. count on a favorable vote in the General Assembly. Issues which were embarrassing to American allies, such as colonial and disarmament questions, now were brought to the U.N. and debated. The U.S. could not put off debate and voting on the "seating" of the Peoples Republic of China.

The U.N. has become more of an international arena for debate on political issues of concern to the smaller states. While the U.N. possesses little power to sanction actions by the large states, it has encouraged the "give and take" of multilateral diplomacy. In addition, the U.N. involvement in Middle Eastern and African problems has provided an alternative to East-West intervention into areas of secondary importance in Soviet and American foreign policy. The U.N. also contributed to world stability through non-political and less controversial activities which have brought about East-West cooperation when deep-seated ideological and strategic issues were divisive. The U.N.'s functional commissions (*e.g.,* on population, status of women) and specialized agencies (*e.g.,* Universal Postal Union, World Health Organization) have performed services to the international community without regard to political alignment.

Organizations for U.S. policy

The structure for implementing U.S. foreign policy through the U.N. is a twofold organization. One component is the State Department's Bureau of International Organization, which functions to give guidance to all U.S. diplomacy occurring through multilateral conferences. The U.S. attends over 600 conferences a year and belongs to 75 international and regional organizations. The Bureau must prepare delegations for each conference and organizational meeting; thus, its charge is much broader than providing policy guidance to the United States Mission to the United Nations, which is the second component of the structure.

The U.S. Mission to the U.N., which is the only American embassy on American soil, is approximately the same size as the Bureau of International Organization (140 employees). The U.S. Mission is led by a permanent representative with the rank of ambassador. The men who have been appointed ambassador since the United Nations' inception have brought increased prestige to a post that ordinarily would not be considered outstanding. Edward Stettinius, while Secretary of State, and Bernard Baruch served for brief periods. Warren R. Austin (1946-1953), a Republican Senator from Vermont, resigned his seat and served during the bipartisan era in U.S. foreign policy. Henry Cabot Lodge (1953-1960) was also an ex-senator, but he had been defeated for re-election. Beginning with Lodge, the President invited the United Nations ambassador to cabinet meetings. James J. Wadsworth served briefly after Lodge resigned to seek the Republican Presidential nomination. Adlai Stevenson (1961-1965) brought to the position the prestige of twice leading his party in presidential campaigns. Arthur Goldberg (1965-1968) resigned from the Supreme Court to accept the ambassadorship. George Ball, former Under Secretary of State, replaced Goldberg in June 1968.

Conclusion

The United States has adjusted well to internal changes within the U.N. Despite changes, American decision-makers continue to heap praise on the organization. There is now a sense of realism about what the U.N. can—and cannot—do. In Mr. Rusk's look into the 1970's, the U.N. will better serve as a "clearing house" for multilateral diplomacy and as a stabilizer during periods of vast scientific and technological changes. Arthur Goldberg's speech in the following chapter discusses the relationship of international law to the United Nations. What is missing from both of these addresses is the expectation, voiced earlier in the history of the U.N., that the United Nations could solve the political problems of the international system.

The First Twenty-five Years of the United Nations—From San Francisco to the 1970's

by Dean Rusk,

Secretary of State[1]

* * *

I believe that the influence of the United Nations will be even greater in the 1970's than it is today.

I believe also that the executive capacity of the United Nations to act in support of the purposes of the charter will be greater in the 1970's than it is today.

I hold these convictions despite valid cause for concern and some necessary reservations. I shall try to explain why.

The U.N. a Necessity for Our Times

Let me begin by observing that it means little to study the performance of an institution against abstract standards without reference to the realities—and even the illusions—of the total environment in which it must operate. In that context the first thing that strikes one about the United Nations is that international organization is a plain necessity of our times. This is so for both technical and political reasons.

The technical reasons stem, of course, from the headlong rush of scientific discovery and technological advance. That process has overrun the hypothetical question as to whether there is to be an international community that requires organization. It has left us with the

---

[1] Excerpts from the Dag Hammarskjöld Memorial Lecture, prepared for delivery by Secretary Rusk and read by Harlan Cleveland, Assistant Secretary for International Organization Affairs, at Columbia University, New York, N.Y., January 10, 1964. Printed in the *Department of State Bulletin,* Jaunary 27, 1964, pp. 112-19.

practical question of *what kind* of international community we have the wit to organize around the scientific and technical imperatives of our time.

* * *

World community is a fact
—because instantaneous international communication is a fact;
—because fast international transport is a fact;
—because matters ranging from the control of communicable disease to weather reporting and forecasting demand international organization;
—because the transfer of technology essential to the spread of industrialization and the modernization of agriculture can be assisted by international organizations;
—because modern economics engage nations in a web of commercial, financial, and technical arrangements at the international level.

The advance of science, and the technology that follows, create an insistent demand to build international technical and regulatory institutions which lend substance to world community. Few people seem to realize just how far this movement has gone. The United States is now a member of 53 international organizations. We contribute to 22 international operating programs, mostly sponsored by these same organizations. And last year we attended 547 international intergovernmental conferences, mostly on technical subjects. We do these things because they are always helpful and often downright essential to the conduct of our national and international affairs.

It is obvious that in the 1970's we shall require more effective international organization—making for a more substantial world community—than we have today. We already know that in the next decade we shall become accustomed to international communication, including television, via satellites in outer space. We shall travel in aircraft that fly at speeds above a thousand and perhaps above two thousand miles per hour. Industrialization will pursue its relentless course. Cities and their suburbs will keep on growing. The world economy will become increasingly interdependent. And science will rush ahead, leaving to us the task of fashioning institutions— increasingly on the international level—to administer its benefits and circumscribe its dangers.

So, while nations may cling to national values and ideas and ambitions and prerogatives, science has created a functional international society, whether we like it or not. And that society, like any other, must be organized.

Anyone who questions the *need* for international technical organizations like the United Nations agencies dealing with maritime matters, civil aviation, telecommunications, atomic energy, and meteorology simply does not recognize the times in which we live.

In a world caught up in an urgent drive to modernize areas containing two-thirds of the human race, there is need also for the United Nations specialized agencies dealing with health, agriculture, labor standards, education, and other subjects related to national development and human welfare. A massive effort to transfer and adapt modern technology from the more to the less advanced areas is a part of the great drama of our age. This sometimes can be done best through, or with the help of, the institutions of the international community.

And the international organizations concerned with trade and monetary and financial affairs are important to the expanding prosperity of the world economy.

Adjustment to Reality of Political World

The need for political organs at the international level is just as plain as the need for technical agencies.

You will recall that the decision to try to form a new international organization to preserve peace grew out of the agonies of the Second World War. The United States took the lead in this enterprise. President Franklin D. Roosevelt and Secretary of State Cordell Hull sought to avoid repeating what many believed to have been mistakes in political tactics which kept the United States from joining the League of Nations. They consulted at every stage the leaders of both political parties in both Houses of Congress. They insisted that the formation of this organization should be accomplished, if possible, *before* the end of the war.

Most of our allies readily endorsed this objective and cooperated in achieving it. You will recall that the charter conference at San Francisco convened before the end of the war against Hitler and that the United States Senate consented to ratification of the charter in July

1945, before the end of the war in the Pacific. The vote in the Senate was 89 to 2, reflecting a national consensus bordering on unanimity. The significance of that solemn action was especially appreciated by those of us who were in uniform.

The commitment of the United States to the United Nations was wholehearted. We threw our best efforts and some of our best men into getting it organized and moving. We set about binding the wounds of war. We demobilized our armed forces and drastically reduced our military budget. We proposed—not only proposed but worked hard to obtain agreement—that atomic energy should be put under control of an agency of the United Nations, that it should be devoted solely to peaceful purposes, that nuclear weapons should be abolished and forever forbidden.

What happened? Stalin refused to cooperate. Even before the guns were silent, he set in motion a program of imperialistic expansion, in violation of his pledges to the Western Allies and in contravention of the principles of the United Nations.

You will recall that the United Nations was designed on the assumption that the great powers in the alliance destined to be victors in the Second World War would remain united to maintain the future peace of the world. The United Nations would be the instrument through which these powers, in cooperation with others, of course, would give effect to their mutual determination to keep the peace against any threats that might arise from some future Mussolini or Hitler. World peace was to be enforced by international forces carrying the flag of the United Nations but called into action and directed by agreement among the major powers. Action without big-power agreement was not ruled out by the charter, but such agreement was assumed to be the prior condition of an effective peace organization. Indeed, it was stated repeatedly by early supporters of the United Nations that the organization could not possibly work unless the wartime Allies joined in collective action within the United Nations to exert their combined power to make it work.

That view of the postwar world rapidly turned out to be an illusory hope. One might well have expected—as many good people did—that when the conceptual basis for the United Nations fell to the ground, the organization would fall down beside it.

But all great institutions are flexible. The United Nations adjusted gradually to the political and power realities of the quite different world that came into being. In the absence of major-power agreement in the Security Council, it drew on the charter's authority to balance that weakness with a greater reliance upon the General Assembly.

By adapting to political reality the United Nations lived and grew in effectiveness, in prestige, and in relevance. It could not act in some of the ways the founding fathers intended it to act, but it went on to do many things that the founding fathers never envisaged as being necessary. The most dramatic reversal of its intended role is seen in the fact that, while the United Nations could not bring the great powers together, it could on occasion keep them apart by getting between them—by becoming the "man in the middle"—as it did in differing ways in the Middle East and in the Congo.

In short, the political organs of the United Nations survived and did effective work under the shadow of a nuclear arms race of awesome proportions, despite the so-called cold war between the major powers whose unity was once presumed to be its foundation.

This was not bound to happen. It is evident that in the political environment of the second half of the 20th century both technical and political reasons dictate the need for large-scale and diversified international organizations. But it does not necessarily follow that the United Nations was destined to work in practice—or even to survive. Indeed, its very survival may be more of an achievement than it seems at first blush. That it has steadily grown in its capacity to act is even more remarkable.

It has survived and grown in effectiveness because a great majority of the nations of the world have been determined to make it work. They have repulsed those who sought to wreck or paralyze it. They have remained determined not only to keep it alive but to improve and strengthen it. To this we owe in part the peace of the world.

Preserver and Repairer of World Peace

Indeed, it is difficult to avoid the conclusion that the existence of the General Assembly and the Security Council these past 18 years was a plain necessity for the preservation and repair of world peace. The failures would still have been failures, but without the U.N. some of the successes might not have been possible.

In the world of today any breach of the peace could lead to the destruction of civilization. In the thermonuclear age any instrumentality with a potential for deterring war can hardly be described as

97

less than indispensable to mankind. In 18 brief years the United Nations has helped to deter or to terminate warfare in Iran and Greece, in Kashmir and Korea, in the Congo and the Caribbean, and twice in the Middle East and twice in the Western Pacific. It is not fanciful to speculate that any or all of us may owe our lives to the fact that these dangers were contained, with the active and persistent help of the processes of the United Nations.

With half a dozen international disputes chronically or repeatedly at the flash point, with forces of change bordering on violence loose in the world, our very instinct to survival informs us that we must keep building the peacekeeping machinery of the United Nations—and keep it lubricated with funds and logistical support.

And if we are to entertain rational hopes for general disarmament, we know that the U.N. must develop a reliable system for reconciling international conflict without resort to force. For peace in the world community—like peace in smaller communities—means not an end of conflict but an accepted system of dealing with conflict and with change through nonviolent means.

"Switchboard for Bilateral Diplomacy"

Traditional bilateral diplomacy—of the quiet kind—has a heavier task today than at any time in history. But with the annual agenda of urgent international business growing apace, with the birth of more than half a hundred new nations in less than two decades, an institution that can serve as an annual diplomatic conference becomes almost a necessity. As a general manager of our own nation's diplomatic establishment, I cannot imagine how we could conduct or coordinate our foreign affairs if we were limited to dealing directly through bilateral channels with the 114 nations with which we have diplomatic relations tonight.

At the last General Assembly representatives of 111 countries met for more than 3 months to discuss, negotiate, and debate. Two more countries became U.N. members, to make it 113. When the tumult and the shouting had died, the General Assembly had adopted, curiously enough, 113 resolutions. This is what we have come to call parliamentary diplomacy.

But outside the formal agenda the General Assembly also has become the world's greatest switchboard for bilateral diplomacy. For many of the young and small nations, lacking a fully developed diplomatic service, the United Nations is the main, sometimes the only, general mechanism available for the conduct of their diplomacy.

Without formal decision the opening of each new Assembly has turned into something like an informal conference of the foreign ministers of the world community. In New York last fall, in a period of 11 days, I conferred with the foreign ministers or heads of government of 54 nations.

I believe that too many items are placed on the agenda of the General Assembly. Too many issues are debated and not enough are negotiated. I feel strongly that members should take more seriously article 33 of the charter which pledges them to seek solutions to their disputes "first of all . . . by negotiation, enquiry, mediation, conciliation, arbitration, judicial settlement, resort to regional agencies or arrangements, or other peaceful means of their own choice" before bringing disputes to the U.N. at all.

But the point here is that it is hard to imagine the conduct of diplomacy throughout the year without a meeting of the General Assembly to deal in one forum and, in a more or less systematic manner, with subjects which demand widespread diplomatic attention among the members of the world community.

The need for an annual diplomatic conference, the need for a peacekeeping deterrent to wars large and small, and the need for an international monitor of peaceful change are plain enough. They seem to me to warrant the conclusion that the political organs as well as the technical organs of the United Nations have been very useful to the world at large for the past decade and a half. Common sense informs us that they can be even more useful in the years ahead.

Recognizing the Peacekeeping Capacity of U.N.

I suspect that the near future will witness another period of adjustment for the United Nations. Some adjustments are, indeed, required—because the political environment is changing and so is the structure of the U.N. itself.

For one thing the cobweb syndrome, the illusion that one nation or bloc of nations could, by coercion, weave the world into a single pattern directed from a single center of power, is fading into limbo.

That other illusion, the bipolar theory, of a world divided permanently between two overwhelming centers of power with most other nations clustered about them, is fading too. The reality of a world of great diversity with many centers of power and influence is coming into better focus.

Meanwhile, a first brake has been placed on the nuclear arms race, and the major powers are searching for other agreements in areas of common interest. One is entitled to hope that the major power conflicts which so often have characterized U.N. proceedings in the past will yield more and more to great-power cooperation; . . .

* * *

As long as a member possessing great power was intent on promoting conflict and upheaval—the better to coerce the world into its own image—that member might well regard the United Nations as a threat to its own ambitions. But suppose it is agreed that all members, despite their deep differences, share a common interest in survival and therefore a common interest in preventing resort to force anywhere in the world. Then the peacekeeping capacity of the United Nations can be seen realistically for what it is: an indispensable service potentially in the national interest of all members—in the common interest of even rival states.

If this reality is grasped by the responsible leaders of all the large powers, then the peacekeeping capacity of the United Nations will find some degree of support from all sides, not as a rival system of order but as contributor to, and sometimes guarantor of, the common interest in survival.

It would be a great service to peace if there could develop common recognition of a common interest in the peacekeeping capacity of the United Nations. That recognition is far from common now. My belief that it will dawn is based on the fact that it would serve the national interests of all nations, large and small, and because sooner or later nations can be expected to act in line with their national interests.

Peace will not be achieved by repeating worn-out propaganda themes or resetting rusty old traps. But if our Soviet friends are prepared to act on what Chairman Khrushchev says in part of his New Year's message—that war over territorial questions is unacceptable, that nations should not be the targets of direct or indirect aggression, that we should use the United Nations and every other means of

The United Nations

peaceful settlement—then let us together build up the peace-keeping machinery of the United Nations to prevent even small wars in our flammable world.

For small wars could too easily, too quickly, lead to nuclear war, and nuclear war can too easily, too quickly, prove fatal to friend and foe alike.

Problems Affected by Growth

Meanwhile the internal structure of the United Nations has been changing radically over the past several years. The United Nations began life with 51 members. When its headquarters building was designed, United Nations officials believed they were foresighted in planning for an eventual membership of 75. This year major alterations will be undertaken to make room for the present 113 members and more. It is a fair guess that membership of the U.N. will level off during the next decade at 125 to 130 members.

This more than doubling of the U.N.'s membership is proud testament to the tidal sweep through the old colonial areas of the doctrine of self-determination of peoples. It is a triumph of largely peaceful change. It is a tribute to those advanced countries which have helped bring dependent areas to self-government and independence and made possible their free choice of their own destiny. It is a striking and welcome result of the greatest wave of national liberation in all time. It also has important implications for all U.N. members—the new members and the older members too—and for the U.N. itself.

The most prosaic—but nonetheless important—implication is for methods of work in the General Assembly. With more than twice as many voices to be heard, views to be reconciled, and votes to be cast and counted, on a swelling agenda of business, there is obvious danger that the General Assembly will be swamped.

I already have suggested that the agenda may be unnecessarily bloated, that in many cases private discourse and real progress are preferable to public debate and symbolic resolution and that the U.N. might well be used more as a court of last resort and less as a forum of original jurisdiction.

But I think still more needs to be done. If the expanded Assembly is to work with reasonable proficiency, it must find ways of delegating some of its work to units less cumbersome than committees of 113

101

members. The General Assembly is the only parliamentary body in the world that tries to do most of its business in committees-of-the-whole. The Assembly has, in fact, moved to establish several subcommittees, including one to consider financing peace-keeping operations, and perhaps more thought should now be given to the future role of such committees in the work of the organization.

The radical expansion of the membership raises problems for the newer and smaller nations. They rightly feel that they are under-represented on some organs—notably the Security Council and the Economic and Social Council—whose membership was based on the U.N.'s original size and composition.

The growth of membership also raises problems for the middle-range powers, who were early members and have reason to feel that they are next in line for a larger voice.

And it raises problems—or potential problems—for the larger powers too.

The rapid and radical expansion of the General Assembly may require some adaptation of procedures if the U.N. is to remain relevant to the real world and therefore effective in that world.

Theoretically, a two-thirds majority of the General Assembly could now be formed by nations with only 10 percent of the world's population, or who contribute, altogether, 5 percent of the assessed budget. In practice, of course, this does not happen, and I do not share the dread expressed by some that the General Assembly will be taken over by its "swirling majorities."

But even the theoretical possibility that a two-thirds majority, made up primarily of smaller states, could recommend a course of action for which other nations would bear the primary responsibility and burden is one that requires thoughtful attention.

There are two extreme views of how national influence should be expressed in the work of the United Nations. At one extreme is the contention that no action at all should be taken by the United Nations without the unanimous approval of the permanent members of the Security Council. This is a prescription for chronic paralysis. The United Nations was never intended to be kept in such a box. The rights and duties of the General Assembly are inherent in the charter. The United Nations has been able to develop its capacity to act precisely because those rights were not blocked by the requirement of big-power unanimity.

At the other extreme are those few who feel that nothing should matter except the number of votes that can be mustered—that what a majority wants done must be done regardless of what states make up the majority. This notion flies in the face of common sense. The plain fact of the matter is that the United Nations simply cannot take significant action without the support of the members who supply it with resources and have the capacity to act.

Some have suggested that all General Assembly votes should be weighed to reflect population, or wealth, or level of contributions, or some combination of these or other factors. I do not believe that so far-reaching an answer would be realistic or practical. The equal vote in the General Assembly for each member—however unequal in size, wealth, experience, technology, or other criterion—is rooted in the idea of "sovereign equality." And that idea is not one which any nation, large or small, is eager to abandon.

I do not pretend to have the final answer, nor is it timely or appropriate for any member to formulate the answer without wide and careful consultations with others in the world community. However, extended discussions lie ahead on such questions as expanding the councils, scales of payment for peacekeeping, and procedures for authorizing peacekeeping operations.

I shall not discuss U.N. finances in detail tonight. But let me say that the first principle of a healthy organization is that all its members take part in its work and contribute their proper shares to its financial support. Two years ago more than half the U.N. members were behind in their dues—some because of political objections but many simply because they were not paying. I am glad to see that most members are now beginning to act on the principle of collective financial responsibility. But there remains a serious problem of large nations that have not been willing to pay for peacekeeping operations.

I would hope that the discussions which lie ahead will not only strengthen the financial underpinnings of the U.N. but, among other things, develop an acceptable way for the General Assembly to take account of capacity to act, of responsibility for the consequences, and of actual contributions to the work of the U.N. Such a way must be found if the United Nations machinery is to be relevant to the tasks that lie ahead—in peacekeeping, in nation building, and in the expansion of human rights.

All adjustment is difficult. Adaptation of the U.N. to recent changes in the environment may take time. It will require a shift away from some hardened ideas and some rigid patterns of action and reaction—perhaps on all sides. It will require—to come back to Hammarskjold's words—"perseverance and patience, a firm grip on realities, careful but imaginative planning, a clear awareness of the dangers. . . ."

To ask all this may seem to be asking a great deal. But I am inclined toward confidence because the U.N. already has demonstrated a capacity to adapt under the flexible provisions of the charter to the realities of international politics.

I am further persuaded that all, or most, of the smaller members are realistic enough to know:

—that their own national interests lie with, not against, an effective United Nations;

—that the U.N. can be effective only if it has the backing of those who have the means to make it effective;

—that the U.N. is made less, not more, effective by ritualistic passage of symbolic resolutions with no practical influence on the real world;

—that only responsible use of voting power is effective use of voting power;

—that true progress on behalf of the world community lies along the path on which the weak and the strong find ways to walk together.

These are some of the reasons, derived from analysis of the current state of world affairs, why I expect the United Nations to evolve and to grow in executive capacity to act in support of its goals.

* * *

5

International Law

International law is one concept that the Official Voice has discussed since the inception of the American state both as a means and an end to foreign policy. U.S. decision-makers have made a world ruled by law an objective (or end) of policy, and have advocated the use of legal techniques, such as arbitration, as instruments (or means) of solving issues of conflict. Unlike other concepts—such as international organization and alliances—international law appears in the earliest pronouncement of the Official Voice. Indeed, it is possible to identify three trends that appear chronologically in the development of American foreign policy and international law.

Law and neutral rights

The first period dates from 1789 to the Civil War. The infant United States government attempted to remain impartial during the Napoleonic wars, but it insisted on the right to trade with both belligerents, England and France. At the same time, it had the duty, as a neutral, to discourage U.S. citizens from meddling in European conflicts and from exporting the American revolution to other countries (or British dependencies, such as Canada). In his 1792 message, President Washington declared that it "would be wise ... to guard against those acts of our own citizens which might tend to give that satisfaction to foreign nations which we may sometimes have occasion to require of them." In 1851, President Fillmore echoed Washington's theme when he wrote in his second State of the Union message that no citizen had the right to "hazard the peace of the country or to violate its laws" when motivated by "vague notions" of changing neighboring states for the better. He justified his objections on the basis of the "public law" which had been "ingrafted into the codes of other nations as well as our own."

Law and settling disputes

Following the Civil War, and lasting until World War I, U.S. policy-makers invoked international law as the answer to disputes which divided nations. A legal solution, rather than a forceful solution, best answered political and economic differences of national interest. The optimism and confidence in international law was fed by the use of arbitration to settle claims arising from the Civil War, and lasted until 1914 shattered all hopes. Andrew Johnson, in reference to the claims against British breach of neutrality, declared that the United States had a "higher motive" than monetary gain: ". . . it was in the interest of peace and justice to establish important principles of international law."[1]

In particular, arbitration with its binding judgment on both parties was singled out as the answer to disputes. Rutherford B. Hayes in his 1877 Inaugural Address referred to arbitration as "a new, and incomparably the best, instrumentality for the preservation of peace. . . ." The establishment of the Permanent Court of Arbitration, as well as bilateral agreements between states to arbitrate differences, was hailed by Taft as setting "the highest mark of the aspiration of nations toward the substitution of arbitration and reason for war in the settlement of international disputes."[2]

The Rule of Law

During the third period, the dominant theme was the Rule of Law concept. The emphasis on arbitration did not survive World War I, even though isolated references to it continue in policy statements. While neutral rights was the emphasis for a weak and growing nation, and arbitration for a middle-range power developing world-wide interests, the Rule of Law became the emphasis for a Great Power. The Rule of Law concept was more nebulous than either neutrality or the peaceful settlement of disputes, and American decision-makers were prone to describe rather than define it. During the interwar period,

---

[1] Andrew Johnson, First State of the Union Message, December 4, 1865.
[2] Rutherford B. Hayes, Third State of the Union Message, December 3, 1912.

the Rule of Law took on a moralistic or even religious hue. In his 1925 Inaugural Address, President Coolidge said: "Peace will come when there is a realization that only under a reign of law, based on righteousness and supported by the religious conviction of the brotherhood of man, can there be any hope of a complete and satisfying life." This theme does not appear in the post-World War II period except for occasional references by Secretary of State Dulles.[3]

The Rule of Law since 1946

What does the Rule of Law mean in contemporary American foreign policy? Four motifs appear, some of which are found in the statement by Ambassador Goldberg reprinted below.

Settlement of disputes without resort to force

This theme harks back to statements made after the Civil War with one important change: The contemporary emphasis is on adjudication rather than arbitration. In both cases, the award is binding on the parties, but the composition of the decisional boards is different. In arbitration, the parties to the dispute each appoint one, two, or three members to the board, and then the board members agree on an "odd" or "swing" member of the panel. In adjudication, the panel is already in existence as is the case with any court of law. Since 1945, adjudication has been linked with the International Court of Justice. Adjudication was embodied in Secretary of State Herter's definition of the Rule of Law as "a set of arrangements wherein states can settle their unresolved differences by peaceful means and without resort to force."[4]

The Rule of Law and changes in the status quo

The U.S. has not held the post-war status quo sacrosanct. In fact, one statement by Mr. Herter indicates that changes will be encouraged

---

3 "World order, in the long run, depends not on men but upon law—law which embodies eternal principles of justice and morality." John Foster Dulles, "U.S. Constitution and U.N. Charter: An Appraisal," *Department of State Bulletin*, Vol. 29 (September 7, 1953) , 310.

4 Christian Herter, "The Self-Judging Aspect of the U.S. Reservation on Jurisdiction of the International Court," *Ibid.*, Vol. 42 (February 15, 1960) , 227. It should be noted that the Connally Amendment, which withheld complete American commitment to the International Court of Justice, is not part of the Official Voice. Executive spokesmen have consistently opposed the reservation and urged its repeal.

in American foreign policy.[5] Forces such as nationalism, economic development, and technology have brought about changes in the international system and American spokesmen felt that the Rule of Law should govern these transformations. "If change is to be peaceful and not destructive," Mr. Dulles said in 1958, "then human conduct and national conduct must be based on principles of law and justice."[6]

The Rule of Law and the Soviet Union

The primary threat to the Rule of Law concept throughout most of the Cold War period has been the Soviet Union. The U.S.S.R. was viewed as possessing a code of conduct described variously as a "rule of force"[7] and a "rule of terror."[8] While international changes were permitted within the framework of the Rule of Law, a U.S. spokesman early stated that we cannot overlook a unilateral gnawing away of the status quo.[9]

U.S. military force and the Rule of Law

Obviously, the United States possesses military force; its use is justified under the Rule of Law rubric. In 1946, Secretary of State Byrnes said: "Our tradition as a peace-loving, law-abiding democratic people should be assurance that our force will not be used except in the defense of law."[10] At the signing of the North Atlantic Treaty, Mr. Truman asked, "What does this rule of law mean?" His answer was not a definition, but a description of the frontier days of the Wild West when the gun was law until citizens banded together for self-protection. He then pointed to the North Atlantic Treaty as a present-day analogy to those earlier bands of citizens who united to battle lawless men.[11]

---

[5] ". . . we must seek to promote peaceful change which will lay the basis for a just and lasting peace." Christian Herter, "Peaceful Change," *Ibid.*, Vol. 41, (October 5, 1959), 469.

[6] John Foster Dulles, "Foundation of Peace," *Ibid.*, Vol. 39, (September 8, 1958), 37.

[7] Harry S. Truman, "A Strong Defense to Achieve Peace," *Ibid.*, Vol. 26, (June 2, 1952), 848.

[8] Dwight D. Eisenhower, "Security in the Free World," *Ibid.*, Vol. 40, (April 6, 1959), 469.

[9] James Byrnes, ". . . we have pinned our hopes to the banner of the United Nations," *Ibid.*, Vol. 14, (March 10, 1946), 357.

[10] *Ibid.*

[11] Harry S. Truman, "Address of the President of the United States," *Ibid.*, Vol. 20, (April 17, 1949), 482.

Conclusion

In the following statement Mr. Goldberg argues that international law is much broader than the use of military power to attain political goals. He employs examples from domestic situations which show that law is present when police power is not. As evidence that international law is operative in the international system today, he points to agreements in the technical field where law is "made" and observed by most nations, large and small. In the political arena he contends that the United Nations creates embryonic international law by its decisions on controversial issues. Because these issues are controversial, there will be occasions in which one or both disputants will not obey them. Mr. Goldberg's analysis is balanced, neither overly optimistic nor pessimistic, and presents the American government's cautious view of the role of international law in the world community.

The Rule of Law in an Unruly World

by Arthur J. Goldberg

U.S. Representative to the United Nations[1]

* * *

My purpose in this discussion . . . is to suggest in what sense and to what extent the rule of law is today a fact among nations and how, in our own American interest, we should seek to widen the areas of international relations that are susceptible to it.

* * *

I am well aware that there are other views of this subject, even among people who have wide experience of diplomacy and world politics. We hear it said that what nations really respect is not law but political power. Besides, we are told, this is an age of revolutions, of deep splits of values between East and West and between North and South. And since law derives from values, this revolutionary era is said to be going through what one distinguished critic calls "a withdrawal of the legal order," in which sheer power is more decisive than ever in international affairs and law, especially that of the United Nations, has become little more than a mockery.

Law and Power

My own reading of the facts leads me to a very different conclusion, as I shall explain in a moment. But before specifically discussing international law, I would first like to make three observations about law in general.

---

[1] Excerpts from the Adlai Stevenson Memorial Lecture at the School of International Affairs, Columbia University, New York, N.Y., on May 18, 1966. Printed in the *Department of State Bulletin,* June 13, 1966, pp. 936-44.

First, we must beware of framing the argument in such a way that law and power become antithetical. In real life, law and power operate together. Power not ruled by law is a menace, but law not served by power is a delusion. Law is thus the higher of the two principles; but it cannot operate by itself.

This is true particularly of the United Nations, whose charter is lofty in purpose but realistic in method. It recognizes the facts of power, as all good law does. But as far as possible, it subjects power to law: to an agreed rule of conduct and to procedures for putting that rule into effect in particular cases. And we Americans should not forget that since the rule is embodied in the charter, which is a treaty to which we are a party, it is thus a part of the supreme law of the United States under our Constitution. Our fidelity to it is therefore not a matter of convenience but of binding commitment, to continue even when it is inconvenient.

My second broad point is that law cannot be derived from power alone. Might does not make right. On the contrary, law springs from one of the deepest impulses of human nature. No doubt the contrary impulses to fight and dominate often prevail, but sooner or later law has its turn.

* * *

My third point flows from the second. Because law responds to a human impulse, it rests on much more than coercion. Law must have the police power, but it is by no means synonymous or coterminous with police power. It is much larger in its conception and in its reach. It builds new institutions and it produces new remedies: It tames the forces of change and keeps them peaceful. People obey the law not only out of fear of punishment but also because of what law does for them: the durability and reliability it gives to institutions, the reciprocity that comes from keeping one's word, and the expectation, grounded in experience, that the just processes of law will right their wrongs and grievances. All the police power in creation could not long uphold a system of law that did not meet these affirmative expectations.

Examples in Our Domestic Scene

With these thoughts in mind, I turn now to the contention of the distinguished critic just referred to, that there has been a withdrawal of the legal order in this chaotic and revolutionary age. He has sought to bolster his case by citing two aspects of our domestic life—with both of which I have had considerable experience. Before turning to the world scene, let me therefore discuss these two examples briefly.

The first example given is the inadequacy of police forces to solve the problem of crime and violence in our cities. But this argument, if I may say so, contradicts itself, for good law, as we have seen, does not manifest itself solely in police forces and jails but also in just and equitable provision for the righting of wrongs. Any judge knows that the great majority of juvenile crimes are committed not by spoiled children of rich or middle-class parents but by the young victims of longstanding and deep-rooted evils: poverty, racial discrimination, and the rejection of society's values that these conditions so often breed. Any prison warden in a big city knows how high a proportion of his cells are filled with the poor, semiliterate youth of our racial ghettos. These evils were not created yesterday; they will not all be cured tomorrow; and even when they are cured the destructive attitudes they have generated are likely to persist for years. In the back lots of city slums, we are reaping the weeds that have germinated during generations of complacent neglect.

Much of the answer to such conditions as these lies in the law: not the law of the police blotter, inescapable though that may be, but the laws that govern education, jobs, housing, and public facilities of all kinds. It is up to the law promptly to create these facilities where they are lacking and promptly to secure equal access to them where race prejudice has customarily denied such access. Such an affirmative body of law is being written and applied today. In it lies much of our hope for domestic peace and stability in future decades.

The second example given was in the field of United States labor-management relations, in which the role of law was pictured as being of minor importance. Actually, the last 30 years have seen a remarkable growth of labor law, and indeed it is my experience in precisely that area that gives me confidence in the possibilities of a comparable growth of the rule of law in the international realm. For in the affairs of labor and management also, revolutionary forces are at work: rapidly changing technology and working conditions, and the dying out of obsolete jobs. Moreover, as in international disputes, the stakes are often large and the contending forces are powerful.

In our free enterprise system, the law is properly reticent about the actual terms of labor contracts, which the parties are expected to settle freely. But our laws do not allow freedom to the contending parties to menace the national health and safety. The powers of government in such cases include factfinding, mediation, conciliation, mandatory "cooling off" periods—and finally, coercion.

All through the Second World War, the War Labor Board enforced its orders, where necessary, by both legal and military means. Few of us old enough to remember will forget the heavy fine imposed on the Mineworkers' Union and John L. Lewis, or the picture of a major industrialist being carried out in his office chair by soldiers in uniform.

Nor is this power confined to wartime. In recent years we have seen Congress pass an arbitration law to prevent a crippling national strike of railroad firemen; and that law was upheld in the courts. And more than 95 percent of labor contracts contain an arbitration clause under which arbitral awards are enforcible in the courts. This is scarcely a picture of the breakdown of law in labor-management relations.

These domestic examples contain clues to the nature and value of law among nations. First, good law involves the necessary minimum of coercion and a maximum of affirmative, creative action—political, social, and economic—to correct the wrongs that underlie much of the violent conflict of our time. Second, where disputes threaten to get out of hand and injure the entire community, the community must possess the machinery to contain the dispute and prevent the injury.

Functions of Law Among Nations

When we study the functions of law among nations, we find both these propositions repeated on a larger scale. The international institutions that exist to give effect to them are much weaker and less cohesive than those of a national government. But we cannot afford not to use them to the full, because the consequences of international war, under modern circumstances, are even more unacceptable than those of civil insurrection. Our hope for world peace depends on our ability to extend to the international sphere a dual concept of law, both creative and coercive.

This extension of law into the international realm is not going to be achieved in one great utopian stroke of the pen. In the United Nations Charter, and in age-old norms of international law, the community of nations already has a set of fundamental rules which do not need to be rewritten so much as they need to be observed. Our task, therefore, is to make greater use of existing machinery and existing norms—to build on them and to broaden out the areas of international relations that are susceptible to them.

To keep the matter in perspective, let us first recall that the areas of international law and order are already very broad—and they are constantly broadening to fit the emerging common interests of nations. Without law, international mail would not be delivered; short-wave broadcasts would drown each other out; ships, or aircraft, would collide in the night; international business contracts could be violated with impunity; travelers would lack the protection of their governments; infectious diseases and insect pests would cross frontiers all the time; and even we diplomats—who are supposedly fulltime practitioners of power politics—would be unable to carry on our business.

These many functions of the international order are so familiar as almost to be taken for granted. Many of them long antedate the United Nations. But it would be a great mistake to underrate them or to dismiss them as merely "technical" and "nonpolitical." They are bridges of common interest among nations, and the sum of these common interests is one of the great unseen inhibitors of political conflict and international violence. The specialized agencies of the U.N., and all its economic, social, and technical programs, continue to extend these bridges year by year. They are defended not by forcible sanctions but by an incentive just as powerful in its own way: the long-term self-interest of each member.

The United Nations and its agencies, through their economic, technical, and social programs, continue to add to this system of bridges. In doing so, they serve not only the technical convenience of nations but also their desperate need to cure the evils from which lawless action springs: poverty, illiteracy, hunger, disease, and deprivation of human rights. I believe that this multilateral system must be strengthened further wherever possible.

U.N. System of Peace and Security

Now I turn to the most difficult area, where law directly confronts political conflict and violence among nations.

The basic law here is in article 2, paragraph 4, of the United Nations Charter: "All members shall refrain in their international relations from the threat or use of force against the territorial integrity or political independence of any state." As the charter embodies this law, so the United Nations as an organization should be, ideally, the court of last resort in seeing that it is adhered to. I say "last resort" because the charter itself imposes on member states the prior duty to seek peaceful settlement of disputes through "negotiation, enquiry, mediation, conciliation, arbitration, judicial settlement, resort to regional agencies or arrangements, or other peaceful means of their own choice."

The framers of the charter did not assume that even when these remedies had been exhausted the Security Council would always be able to meet its responsibilities. By providing for a great-power veto, they recognized the divisions of power and the paralysis that these divisions might cause. For situations in which the U.N. was unable to act, they reaffirmed in article 51 the inherent right of individual or collective self-defense against aggression. The U.N. is certainly the preferred policeman, but where it cannot act, individual states must accept the responsibility—as the United States and others are doing in Viet-Nam today.

This United Nations system of peace and security, then, depends upon the individual actions of states as well as the collective actions of the organization. It is a fragile system, to be sure, but the record of its achievements in the past 20 years proves it far from impotent. In Korea it successfully met open, full-scale aggression. In the Middle East, in Kashmir, in Cyprus, it has kept smoldering conflicts under control—and when they leapt out of control, it has created new instruments to put out the flames. In the Congo it prevented a newborn nation, lacking most of the practical essentials of nationhood, from being torn apart, recolonized, or turned into a great-power battle-ground in the heart of Africa. And right now in Rhodesia, in a most complex and dangerous situation, the United Nations is exerting its influence for a lawful transition to self-government by all the people—which is the only possible and just basis for Rhodesian independence.

* * *

"International Law in Embryo"

In addition to these innovations in the working of the organization itself, the United Nations contributes to the growth of law in another way. Some of its resolutions have turned out to be international law in embryo. This is true of a number of famous resolutions in the field of human rights, which—most notably the Universal Declaration of Human Rights—laid down principles later incorporated and refined in binding conventions.

* * *

Other General Assembly resolutions on peace and security questions, even though they have no binding legal force, may provide a basis for peacekeeping operations, and in any event, carry with them the weight of world opinion. If a party to a dispute acts contrary to such a U.N. resolution, it thereby assumes a considerable political burden to justify its action. How great that burden is depends very much on how many members, and which members, voted and spoke for the resolution in the General Assembly.

The U.N. has had to learn the hard way that words on paper can have force and effect only if there lies behind them the requisite political commitment. The World Court duly rendered an advisory opinion that peacekeeping costs incurred in the Middle East and the Congo were "expenses of the Organization" and that a member's failure to pay its share was therefore subject to the loss of vote under article 19. The General Assembly gave its verbal acceptance of this opinion in a resolution overwhelmingly adopted. Yet this very provision, having been accepted in words, proved for political reasons to be unenforcible in fact.

Nor can the Assembly force the growth of law beyond the realities of the time. Attempts to recodify the law of the charter have not thus far borne much fruit, chiefly because what is needed most is not a new statement of law but better compliance with the law that already exists.

Sometimes a proposal made in the Assembly is couched in legal terms but is essentially political in content and purpose. Last fall, for instance, the Soviet Union introduced a resolution on "nonintervention" as a platform from which to attack United States policy in Viet-Nam. This maneuver failed of its purpose when other delegations added language condemning many forms of intervention, including indirect aggression and subversion by proxy. The amended resolution passed by 109 votes to 0, and it is a good political document.[2] But because of the tactical necessities of political com-

---

[2] For text, see *ibid.*, January 24, 1966, p. 164.

promise, its text was too imprecise and inconsistent to be adequate as a statement of international law.

Maintaining the Integrity of the U.N.

Before closing, I want to turn for a moment from the U.N.'s actions themselves—successful or not, as the case may be—to the procedures by which those actions are taken. I must report candidly that a real danger to the U.N. as an organization, and to the rule of law of which it is the highest embodiment, arises from a recent tendency to jettison normal parliamentary procedure for the sake of short-term political gains.

This was especially apparent last December at the end of the 20th General Assembly. Certain delegations, understandably impatient with the pace of decolonization, presented a draft resolution calling for strong measures against colonialism. One of its provisions concerned military bases, a subject clearly and undeniably related to international peace and security, which under the charter is explicitly classed as an important question subject to the two-thirds majority requirement. Yet the General Assembly declared this resolution, including the part on military bases, adopted by a simple majority.

What primarily disturbed us was not the substance of the resolution—with much of which we could agree—but the flouting of due process. When procedures laid down in the charter are not adhered to, the charter's integrity is impaired. Rules of procedure may seem to be dull things, but they are not: They are dikes against the flood of disorder. The observance of them, as I said in the Assembly at the time, is of the essence of liberty. It was my duty to point out to the Assembly the danger not just to some members but to all members, and to the organization itself, if the rules are not followed. And I announced that the United States would regard the resolution in question as having been illegally adopted and therefore as null and void.[3] In taking this position, we were not repudiating an action of the Assembly; on the contrary, we were following a familiar principle of law; namely that unconstitutional action is no action.

It is clear that this impatience with rules arises from a passionate desire to achieve certain political objectives without delay—in this

---

[3] For text of Ambassador Goldberg's statement in the General Assembly on December 17, 1965, see U.S. delegation press release 4762.

case, to make a declaration against colonialism; and I can readily understand the impatience with the vestiges of that system shown by those who have lived under it. This, as well as the fact that no constitution or laws, including our own, command universal observance, should teach us a measure of modesty and patience. But we cannot let patience deteriorate into a habit of laxity, or modesty into a condoning of clear violations of the charter; for what is at stake is the integrity of the world institution that serves us all.

Such, then, is my report on the extent of the rule of law today in the international realm, and specifically in the affairs of the United Nations. The daily headlines from every quarter of the globe are sufficient reminder of how tenuous that rule is.

* * *

6

Disarmament and Arms Control

Disarmament and arms control are recent interests in American foreign policy and can be dated from Woodrow Wilson. Pre-World War I presidents approved of attempts to curtail weapons of war, but they also believed that the U.S. should not be involved. President McKinley expressed the opinion that disarmament was an acceptable technique, but should not be applied to the U.S. for her "active military force" was "so conspicuously less than that of the [other] armed powers. . . ."[1] Theodore Roosevelt, on the other hand, argued that it would be a mistake for the U.S. to disarm. As a "righteous" or "enlightened" nation, the U.S. could not afford to be stripped of its power and world problems left for less righteous and less enlightened nations to solve.[2]

Woodrow Wilson was the first American President who committed the U.S. to seek ways of limiting armaments. While Wilson's views on international organization were not accepted by his successors, his policies on disarmament were. The period between the two world wars saw the U.S. involved deeply in arms control agreements, such as those reached at the Washington Naval Conference in 1922, and the 1928 Kellogg-Briand Pact. In the former agreement, the American government pledged to adhere to a tonnage limit on certain naval vessels and in the latter it pledged to foreswear war as an instrument of national policy.

The main characters in the post-World War II disarmament drama have been the two superpowers: the U.S. and U.S.S.R. The authors of one study argue that both nations have engaged in gamesmanship in disarmament and arms control negotiations, calling them "one form of

---

1 William McKinley, Second State of the Union message, December 5, 1898.
2 See President Roosevelt's Fifth State of the Union message, dated December 5, 1905.

the arms race itself, the aim of each nation being an increase in its relative power position."[3] Thus, each disarmament proposal has "inevitably contained at least one element—the "joker"—that the other could not possibly accept. This joker has served a dual function: to compel a rejection of the whole plan and thus place the onus for deadlock on the other side, and to protect the vital interests of the proposing side."[4] Why did the two superpowers keep up the constant dialogue on disarmament when it was obvious that no agreement was forthcoming? Several answers are suggested: first, the U.S. and U.S.S.R. had little else to negotiate in the Cold War; such issues as Berlin were so vital to both sides that there was little room to maneuver in negotiations. Secondly, one side might gain a military advantage if it could get the other to agree to a plan with a "joker" in it. But neither side was a simpleton, and never signed a disarmament contract without reading the fine print. Finally, the non-nuclear neutrals brought pressure on both the American and Russian governments to reduce the threat of a nuclear war.

The first plans

The first plans submitted by the U.S. and U.S.S.R. in June 1946 established patterns for future proposals from each nation. The U.S.'s Baruch Plan called for a U.N. agency to own, operate, and inspect all plants and mines producing nuclear fuel. Once control and inspection of nuclear production had been established, nuclear stock-piles would be destroyed or converted to peaceful uses. Ceilings also would be placed on conventional armies so that both states would have equal numbers of men in uniform. The Soviet approach took a different tack: first the destruction of nuclear weapons, then the establishment of control agency with limited functions under the oversight of the U.N. Security Council (and hence subject to the Soviet Union's veto), and finally, a percentage reduction of conventional armies. Each plan protected the strengths of the proposing country. Soviet conventional forces outnumbered the American counterparts; therefore, the Russian proposal calling for reductions on a percentage basis of troops insured the American disadvantage. In American plans, the U.S. atomic monopoly was protected until effective controls were established.

3 John W. Spanier and Joseph L. Nogee, *The Politics of Disarmament: A Study in Soviet-American Gamesmanship* (New York: Frederick A. Praeger, Inc., 1962), p. 15.
4 *Ibid.*, p. 5.

Since the Baruch Plan was the first disarmament proposal, the U.S. achieved a propaganda victory over the U.S.S.R. American initiatives continued until the mid-1950s. On December 8, 1953, President Eisenhower proposed the establishment of the International Atomic Energy Agency and suggested that both the U.S. and U.S.S.R. contribute nuclear fuel for its beginning. At first the U.S.S.R. refused, then relented and the Agency became a reality in 1957. In March 1955, Mr. Eisenhower appointed Harold Stassen as Special Assistant to the President for Disarmament; hence, the U.S. became the first large nation to have a major official who concentrated on disarmament and arms control proposals. In July 1955, Mr. Eisenhower unveiled his "Open Skies" plan at the Geneva conference, which would have permitted overflights to determine if a surprise attack were in preparation. The U.S.S.R., as a closed society, had more to lose, and rejected the Open Skies proposal.

Nineteen fifty-five also marked the end of the American initiative in disarmament and arms control proposals. In May 1955 before the summit conference, the U.S.S.R. reversed itself and accepted the traditional pattern of Western disarmament plans, with their ceilings on conventional forces, inspection, and control of nuclear weapons. The move was dramatic and appeared to herald a major change in policy, but the Soviet Union insisted on several conditions that were unacceptable to the U.S., such as the dismantling of overseas bases and the disbanding of all alliance systems. In 1958, the U.S.S.R. announced a unilateral ban on nuclear testing, and again caught the U.S. government unprepared.

Thus, the 1940's and 1950's were filled with many propaganda victories for both sides. The initiative was held by the Americans during the first half of the period and the Russians during the second. One treaty was signed: the Antarctic Treaty of 1959 in which both nations agreed to keep arms out of that area of the world. It was hardly a major accomplishment and was little to show for the extensive negotiations of the previous fifteen years.

The 1960s

Compared to the dearth of arms control agreements in the first fifteen years of the postwar period, the 1960's have witnessed significant progress: the August 1963 treaty to ban testing in the atmosphere, on land and water; prohibition on nuclear weapons in outer space; nonproliferation of nuclear weapons treaty (negotiated by the U.S. and U.S.S.R. in July 1968); and the "Hot Line" agreement. What accounts for progress after 1960? Several reasons are suggested:

First, the Kennedy Administration gave a higher priority to arms control than previous administrations. Upon taking office, President Kennedy declared in his 1961 State of the Union message that arms control would be "a central goal of our national policy." He later told the United Nations General Assembly that "the weapons of war must be abolished before they abolish us." In 1961, the Arms Control and Disarmament Agency was established.

Secondly, the U.N. began to take a more active role in the disarmament talks. In 1960, the Ten Nation Disarmament Committee was established, with five nations from each bloc; in 1962, eight nations were added and the group met in Geneva as the Eighteen Nation Disarmament Committee.

Finally, an apparent reduction of tension-levels between the U.S. and U.S.S.R. presented an opportunity for the two nations to agree on problem areas which were not central to their national security.

Conclusion

The first years of the disarmament debates were characterized by propaganda battles in which the U.S. and then the U.S.S.R. emerged as the victors in their gamesmanship. The 1960's, however, have seen progress between the two superstates, but the "nuclear club" has now been enlarged to include other nations. Mr. William Foster's statement sketches current American policy on arms control and outlines areas of possible future agreement. It is typical of government pronouncements on this subject in two respects. First, there is pride in the Baruch Plan. American spokesmen feel that Soviet rejection of this plan was one of the missed opportunities in the Cold War. They fail to see the "joker" in it for Soviet policy, *i.e.,* it prohibited the Soviet Union from developing an atomic weapon while the U.S. was allowed to retain its nuclear monopoly until adequate safeguards were erected. Second, it shows the American reluctance to progress beyond agreements that can be inspected. If adequate testing equipment is developed to identify underground detonations, then the U.S. would agree to expand the 1963 Test Ban Agreement.

Arms Control—A Serious Business

by William C. Foster

Director, U.S. Arms Control and Disarmament Agency[1]

* * *

At that time [1946], the United States held a world monopoly of the atomic bomb—and did not know quite what to do with it. The Western Powers had drastically demobilized their conventional forces, but how can you demobilize a secret, a secret which others are bound to learn?

The United States Government took the course which seemed wise and possible: It offered to destroy its atomic bombs and turn its atomic energy establishments over to an international authority. Henceforth that international authority would control all atomic facilities throughout the world. This plan, as you may recall, was known as the "Baruch plan"[2] (named after the American delegate at the U.N., Bernard Baruch, who presented it). Perhaps we were overly optimistic in presenting such a plan and perhaps the plan itself was less than perfect. But it has always been my belief that it could and should have been a subject of negotiation—instead of which the Soviet Union rejected it out of hand.

All that is ancient history, of course, though I think it is worth remembering for the lesson it offers: that when a great opportunity is allowed to slip by, it takes a long time afterward to pick up the pieces. For the past 20 years we have been trying to do just that. We have been trying to keep nuclear weapons within bounds, while seeking arrangements for their eventual elimination.

---

[1] Excerpts from an address made before the Belgo-American Association at Brussels, Belgium, on June 20, 1966. Printed in the *Department of State Bulletin*, July 11, 1966, pp. 50-55.
[2] For background, see *ibid.*, June 14, 1946, p. 1056.

123

We have made an appreciable degree of progress. Moreover, in spite of a very bad beginning, the Russian approach to this problem has not been entirely negative. On the contrary, it has undergone a considerable evolution over the years.

In the early days following 1946 the Russian position was essentially propagandistic.

* * *

The Soviet position in those early days called for immediate "banning" of the bomb by declaration—as if such a thing could be done by a pious statement of good intentions. But gradually, under the pressure of British, Canadian, French, and American negotiators, and perhaps most of all under the pressure of reality, the Soviet position began to evolve. I would say that it crossed the threshold of reality when it recognized the following basic fact: By the mid-1950's there was so much fissionable material on both sides of the Iron Curtain that not even the most alert international inspectorate could have been able to prevent a nuclear power from retaining hidden stocks and secretly making nuclear weapons. This meant that in any disarmament process some nuclear weapons would have to be retained by each side until the end—as a cover in case the other side cheated. With time, as I say, the Soviet Government has come, at least tacitly, to admit this principle.

Another reality which the Soviets came to accept was that a disarmament process would have to be balanced so that neither side would gain a temporary advantage and would have to take place in stages, with the setting up of controls and inspection at each stage.

By 1961 the Soviet and American positions were close enough for the two countries to submit jointly to the U.N. General Assembly a Joint Statement of Agreed Principles on disarmament.[3] This was definitely a turning point, as it provided an agreed framework within which future negotiations could take place.

Which is not to say that we have enjoyed smooth sailing since 1961. On the contrary, there are in particular two aspects of the Russian approach which have caused immense difficulties.

The first has been an evident desire to bring about an imbalance in their favor during the early stages of any arms control or disarma-

---

[3] For text, see *ibid.*, October 9, 1961, p. 589.

ment process (despite the joint statement). An example of this is their constant insistence on early withdrawal of American troops from foreign bases—which of course wouuld leave Russia with a considerable superiority in conventional arms on the continent of Europe.

Secondly, while the West has placed paramount importance on inspection and control, the Russians, with their ancient fixation about secrecy, have insisted that we are more interested in control than in disarmament, that our real purpose is espionage.

Steps Toward Disarmament

Thus we are still a long way from our goal. But while everyone agrees that the ultimate goal, that of general and complete disarmament, is perhaps very far off, there are a number of steps which we can take in the meantime and some which we have already taken.

Of the gains made to date, the most striking has been the partial nuclear test ban of 1963,[4] in accordance with which both the United States and the Soviet Union have refrained since then from conducting nuclear explosions in the atmosphere, under water, or in outer space. There has also been the "hot line," establishing a communications link between Washington and Moscow, which could prove vital in an emergency. There has also been the U.N. resolution against the placing of nuclear weapons in orbit, subscribed to by both the United States and the Soviet Union.

Another important achievement, in my opinion, has been the establishment of the 18-Nation Conference itself. Since its creation in 1962, this body, which to many seemed far too large and unwieldy when it was set up, has acquired a remarkable degree of realism and expertise. It has also provided focus and momentum to a subject which otherwise could bog down all too easily into inaction.

At the present time at the 18-Nation Conference in Geneva, our most urgent preoccupation is with preventing the further spread of nuclear weapons. Our feeling, of course, is that if more countries go nuclear, we will find ourselves in an extremely perilous situation, with nuclear weapons in so many and perhaps such irresponsible hands that a country could be attacked without even knowing who the attacker was. I believe the Russians recognize as well as we do

---

[4] For background and text of the treaty banning nuclear weapon tests in the atmosphere, in outer space and under water, see *ibid.*, August 12, 1963, p. 239.

that putting a halt to this drift is in the interests of everyone, including, incidentally, the Chinese.

Now, one way of heading off this danger is to conclude a non-proliferation treaty specifically aimed at stopping the further spread of nuclear weapons; and we have been attempting to do just this.[5]

Another way would be to close the gap left by the partial nuclear test ban treaty of 1963, prohibiting underground testing in addition to the prohibition of testing in the three other environments. For obviously a nation which could not test at all would find it exceedingly difficult, if not impossible, to develop nuclear weapons.

Identifying Underground Testing

We can detect and identify tests in the other three environments, but how well could we monitor an agreement not to test underground?

In the United States we have been conducting extensive research in the identification of underground nuclear blasts, and we have made considerable progress. But we have found, so far at least, that there are certain levels of seismic disturbance below which it simply is not possible to distinguish between a nuclear explosion and an earth tremor. With an international network of seismic instruments, we could now identify a very high percentage of earth disturbances which take place in the Soviet Union, but there would still remain a few which would require on-site inspection to make sure that they were not of nuclear origin.

We have suggested to the Soviets that international inspectors could be blindfolded and transported in Russian planes with blackened windows, under the surveillance of Russian guards, to make certain that they saw nothing except what they were specifically sent to check on; namely, whether or not a nuclear explosion had taken place at this or that point in the great expanse of Russia. But they have refused to lift the veil of secrecy even this much.

It seems almost quaint and old-fashioned that anyone today should insist so much on privacy, with all those satellites streaking across the sky. Perhaps the real reason is that the Russians simply are not yet ready to stop underground nuclear tests, and therefore are posing

---

5 For background, see *ibid.*, September 20, 1965, p. 466, and April 25, 1966, p. 675.

impossible—and meaningless—conditions. Whatever the case, we are continuing to perfect our identification technology, preparing for the time when such an agreement may become possible.

I alluded a moment ago to the research program which we have been carrying out in the United States. Much of our research is devoted to finding out whether this or that measure of arms control would really be practicable and could be effectively guaranteed against evasion.

Working with the American Armed Forces, for example, we have carried out a number of field tests under hypothetical arms limitations agreements, to see just how successful a team of inspectors would be in detecting hidden military equipment within a given area of the country when faced with deliberately evasive action. Other projects have sought to develop foolproof ways of monitoring the destruction of nuclear weapons, of monitoring a cutoff in the production of fissionable materials, and so on.

Impact of Disarmament on U.S. Economy

* * *

It is now rather widely understood that the Federal Government can sustain demand on a national scale—which is the essential thing—either by stimulating the private sector or by increasing public expenditures, or both. Moreover, the acceptability of these public expenditures has now been established.

You can see, then, that cutbacks in defense spending under a disarmament process would no longer be widely regarded as posing serious problems for the national economy as a whole.

In fact, a number of shifts and cutbacks in defense spending have already occurred. In 1964 military spending in the United States leveled off and actually declined slightly. The fact was given much attention at the time and there was considerable discussion of the probabilities of further declines. Although some concern was indicated by certain areas which were rather heavily specialized in defense, as in California, it is significant that the general reaction was remarkably unruffled. There were no crises of confidence, and the economy continued to make the same sustained gains that it had been making since 1961.

These various developments have done much, I believe, to remove the fear that disarmament would be followed by an economic depression, national in scope.

* * *

7

Educational and Cultural Diplomacy

Although the United States' involvement in educational and cultural (E&C) diplomacy is three decades old, dating from July 28, 1938, when the State Department's Division of Cultural Relations was established,[1] the most commonly referred to "birthday" is the 1946 Fulbright Act. Since then, over 100,000 individuals have engaged in one form or another of cultural diplomacy. Approximately 70 percent were foreign nationals who came to the United States, and the balance were Americans going abroad. By modern budgetary standards, E&C diplomacy is not an expensive program. During the fiscal year 1967, $50.3 million were obligated. Most of the money came from the 1961 Mutual Educational and Cultural Exchange Act (or the Fulbright-Hays Act).

Types of exchanges

The best known E&C activity is study abroad for American students and study in the U.S. for foreign nationals. This program is only one of seven E&C activities. During the fiscal year 1967, 5,264 grants were made under the seven programs listed in Table 1 with more than 130 countries represented in the exchanges.

The largest program for both groups of recipients was academic study; in both cases, it accounted for almost one-half of the individuals participating in educational and cultural exchanges. For foreign grantees, educational travel and observation and consultation accounted for another one-third of the participants. Under these two

---

[1] Francis J. Colligan, "Twenty Years After: Two Decades of Government Sponsored Cultural Relations," *Department of State Bulletin*, Vol. 39 (July 21, 1958), 112-120.

TABLE 1

Educational and Cultural Programs

Fiscal Year Data

Program	Foreign Grantees in U.S.		U.S. Grantees Abroad	
	1967	1949-67	1967	1949-67
University Study	1,824	34,845	868	15,354
Advanced Research (postdoctoral)	496	7,927	174	3,318
University Lecturing	188	2,205	514	6,064
Specialized Programs	421	5,222	273	3,410
Teaching or Teaching Development	652	10,787	276	6,031
Observation and Consultation	1,023	17,029	0	0
Educational Travel	660	6,570	9	78
Totals	5,264	84,585	2,114	34,255

Source: Department of State, *International Exchange, 1967.*

programs, foreign nationals are brought to the U.S. for tours that, will contribute to their understanding of American culture. One of the uses of "observation and consultation" is to acquaint foreign national elites, such as religious leaders, labor union organizers, and newspaper editors with American society. Hopefully, these people will return to their countries, share with others the experiences of their visit, and influence their views on American foreign policy positions.

On the American side, "observation and consultation" is not an active program, and "educational travel" has been financed for only a handful of U.S. citizens going abroad. Most of the American grants were for graduate and post-doctoral study. "University lecturing" and "teaching and teaching development" have received approximately the same emphasis: both programs are aimed at improving the educational expertise in foreign countries, the former by providing American experts in school administration and curriculum development and the latter by furnishing university professors to fill visiting positions in foreign institutions. The "specialized programs" are staffed by authorities in different aspects of American civilization who are recruited to travel abroad and lecture. Usually their tours are much shorter than university lecturers, and their audiences tend to be more varied.

Regional representation

Table 2 depicts the regions of the world which supply foreign nationals who participate in E&C diplomacy, and the regions chosen by American recipients. The region that has benefited the most in both respects has been Western Europe. Although there appears to be a trend toward non-western nations in bringing foreign nationals to the United States, the predominant preference for Western European nations among American grantees continues. There is an element of irony here, for the most often heard rationale for E&C diplomacy is that exchanges break down prejudice and ignorance among nationalities. However, nationalities best known and most accepted to the United States are the ones that benefit from E&C diplomacy. East European states have provided the least number of grantees, but they are the most recent to be added to E&C exchange agreements.

TABLE 2

Regional Selections

Fiscal Year Data

Region	Foreign Grantees in U.S.		U.S. Grantees Abroad	
	1967	1949-67	1967	1949-67
Latin America	1,413	16,064	306	2,967
Africa	432	3,965	49	662
Western Europe	1,651	40,225	1,116	22,559
Eastern Europe & Yugoslavia	165	884	71	389
Near East and South Asia	717	10,389	286	3,728
East Asia and Pacific	886	13,058	266	3,487
Multiarea	0	0	20	463
Totals	5,264	84,585	2,114	34,255

Source: Department of State, *International Exchange, 1957.*

Because of the American balance of payments problems, joint financing agreements were worked out with ten nations in 1966: United Kingdom, France, Netherlands, Denmark, Federal Republic of Germany, Sweden, Iceland, Ireland, and Australia.[2] All but one of the nations is in Western Europe where the bulk of exchanges occurs and where PL 480 counterpart funds from the sale of surplus farm products are not available. The signatories of joint financing agreements share the expense of E&C exchanges.

Academic Fields of Grantees

What academic fields of study do the foreign national and American grantees represent? Table 3 provides the answer.[3]

TABLE 3

Fields of Study

Arrivals Only, 1952-65

Field	Foreign Nationals	U.S. Citizens
Science and Engineering	17,986	4,356
Social Science	27,703	7,495
Humanities	8,211	11,746
Education	12,416	3,078
Miscellaneous	144	17
Totals	66,460	26,692

Source: *Educational and Cultural Diplomacy, 1965.*

For foreign nationals, the largest field is social science, followed by science and engineering, with education in third place. This rank-order reflects the needs of the developing countries. In the social sciences most students are studying political science, government, international relations, and attending law schools. One of the contin-

---

[2] *International Education Exchange: The Opening Decades, 1946-1966* (Washington D.C.: Government Printing Office, 1967) , p. 39.

[3] Note that Table 3 covers the years 1952 through 1965. Consequently, the totals for Table 3 do not correspond to the totals of Tables 1 and 2.

uing demands by developing nations is for public administrators who can make government operate.

For U.S. grantees, the largest group is found in the humanities (literature, language, and fine arts), followed by social science (history) and then science and engineering (medicine, mathematics, and physics). Among U.S. citizens going abroad, the popularity of the humanities as a field of study correlates with Western Europe as the most popular region in which to study. Most of the Americans receiving grants to West European countries study literature, language, and the fine arts. Also, U.S. science and engineering scholars tend to choose universities in the same region.

Conclusion

Other executive agencies are engaged in E&C diplomacy besides those activities of the State Department's Bureau for Educational and Cultural Affairs. The United States Information Agency provides films and publications, establishes libraries abroad, and staffs most embassies with the Cultural Affairs Officer. The Peace Corps, in addition to being an instrument of foreign assistance, can be considered part of E&C diplomacy.

In the midst of billion dollar budgets, $50 million for E&C diplomacy appears quite small. Nonetheless, the U.S. is committed to E&C diplomacy in a time which Mr. Frankel characterizes below as an era of educational and cultural relations.

The Era of Educational and Cultural Relations

by Charles Frankel

Assistant Secretary for Educational and Cultural Affairs[1]

* * *

Educational and cultural affairs . . . are not simply instruments of foreign policy. If the considerations I wish to put before you have any validity, they are an essential part of what foreign policy today is all about. They enter into the definition of its ends and purposes and are not simply instruments for the achievement of ends that have been defined without regard to them. For we are in an era which has been fundamentally affected by certain new phenomena on the human scene, which have propelled educational and cultural relations to the forefront of international relations.

If I am right, we are entering an era that can properly be called "the era of educational and cultural relations."

* * *

Broadly speaking, I venture to suggest, we may distinguish three great stages in the history of cultural exchange.

In the first stage, which covered the longest period in human history, cultural exchange was simply an accidental byproduct of the contact between different groups. It was not usually sought, and it was frequently resisted.

In the second stage, cultural exchange—or, at any rate, the triumph of one's own culture over the culture of others—was not accidental but was deliberately sought and promoted. It was a motive as well as

[1] Excerpts from the Edward L. Bernays Foundation Lecture at the Fletcher School of Law and Diplomacy, Tufts University, Medford, Mass., on April 25, 1966. Printed in the *Department of State Bulletin,* June 6, 1966, pp. 889-97.

a consequence of war, of commerce, of imperial organization and imperial rivalry, and the preponderant influence over it was exercised by government or government-sponsored activities or by churches. This is the period of the great explorations and of colonization, which came to its climax in the 19th century.

Characteristics of the New Era

The third stage is the one in which we have now entered. It is marked by an extraordinary flow of cultural traffic—of people, news, ideas, ideologies, fashions, machines, and passions—between almost all the human groups in the world. This cultural exchange, a good part of which is not deliberately planned or intended, goes farther and penetrates more deeply than any kind of cultural exchange known in the past. And while efforts can and have been made to resist the flow of this traffic, it is probably not fundamentally resistible but is an almost automatic consequence of changes in the character of human thought and work and in the conditions of human travel and communication. Most of us in most parts of the world simply live in a physical, psychological, and moral neighborhood that has an international color and dimension, and we live in such a neighborhood whether we know it or not, or like it or not.

Moreover, this is not all that characterizes this third, relatively new, stage in the history of cultural relations. What also characterizes it is that organized social institutions—churches, universities, foundations, voluntary associations, and governments—also play a heavier role than ever as initiators and regulators of the cultural traffic. In brief, in this third stage cultural exchange is the accidental but at the same time the inexorable consequence of the accelerating contact of different human groups, and it is also deeply affected by deliberately adopted social policies, official and unofficial.

Finally, this cultural exchange has a new quality. Not only do the powerful nations impose themselves on the attention of the less powerful, but the less powerful impose themselves on the attention of the more powerful. A century ago, an untutored inhabitant of an Asiatic city was likely to be made sharply aware every day that there really was a Europe, but a worker in a European factory might well not have the fact that Asia existed clearly in focus in his mind. That is not likely to be the case today. The flow of information, attention,

135

and trouble is in both directions, and the flow is between cultures and peoples which have in the past regarded themselves as remote in history, experience, and destiny.

* * *

. . . the most decisive characteristics of the new era of cultural relations have emerged only recently. In the present century, and particularly in the last 20 years, we have entered a period in which the internal history of every nation and the intimate daily experience of growing numbers of individuals have been vitally affected by certain radical changes. Among them are the revolution in knowledge and in the place that the man of knowledge occupies in society, the extraordinary revolution in the technology of travel and communication, the advent of the school as a major instrument of social development and social control, and the rapid and now almost universal acceptance of the egalitarian language and moral outlook of democracy. Whatever the practice of a people or a government may be and however various or even bizarre their interpretations of democracy may seem, there is hardly a people or a government in the world today which would not try to explain and justify its behavior in what it presents as democratic terms.

In these factors we have the major sources of the new era of cultural relations. They are of such magnitude that they imply a new era in international relations as well. They have changed the nature and conditions of national power, the character ₐnd function of diplomacy, and the very terms, I believe, in which the conception of "national interest" must be defined.

The Revolution in Knowledge

The revolution in knowledge, which is the first of the factors that affect the present scene, has had a number of significant consequences that are relevant to our present scene. In the first place, the massive development of science as a social institution—as a set of arrangements for acquiring, communicating, and assessing information—has advanced and solidified the growth of an international community of coworkers whose standards and temper of mind and, not infrequently, whose loyalties transcend purely parochial barriers. Given the existence of science, even if of nothing else, international affairs are not simply an arena for rivalry, disagreement, and misunderstanding. They are also an arena in which some men speak the same language, seek the same goals, and have worked out a procedure for the rational resolution of differences of opinion.

Moreover, these men of science have new prestige and influence. For in the last few decades, the traditional relationship between science and technology has been altered. In the past, major technological innovations—like the wheel, the compass, or the steam engine—were often developed without the immediate support of any large body of basic theoretical research. Often, these technological innovations themselves provided instruments and analogies which were used by scientists.

Today, however, basic theoretical research is the indispensable prerequisite for the overwhelming proportion of technological inventions. Research and development is a major component of a modern industrial establishment. The power of the American industrial establishment, for example, probably turns more than anything else on our capacity to devote large numbers of people and large amounts of capital to basic research and development.

Science more than ever before, therefore, is an engine which drives human history along its imperfectly charted road. And with this change there has also come, quite naturally, a new role and influence for scientists and for their typical institutions like the laboratory and the university.

It is no longer possible, therefore, for any country that desires to prosper, and understands the conditions for such prosperity that must now be met, to ignore the peculiar demands and the peculiar mores of the learned community. And under the pressure of scientific standards of workmanship, these demands and these mores are becoming increasingly alike in all countries, increasingly transnational and international. Indeed, not the least of these demands is that the scientific communities of the different nations, if only in their own self-interest, must remain in touch with each other.

Moreover, we must not imagine that the changes which science has brought are only in the field of physical innovation. It is more than evident that the application of new technologies involves great changes in human behavior and the organization of society and that they demand a degree of flexibility and a capacity for quick adaptation on the part of the human animal beyond anything that has been demanded of this animal in the past. Indeed, many technical innovations are actually innovations in the field of human organization. The assembly line and traffic controls are only more obvious examples. And these changes in the ways in which human beings organize their joint ventures have come to be influenced increasingly by fundamental research in the social sciences.

It is true that we continue to depend much more on hunch, on ingenuity, and on folk wisdom in arranging our social affairs than we do in the physical sciences. Nevertheless, it is reasonably plain, I think, that just as the complexities and pressures of modern life have been generated very largely by organized research, the answers to these complexities and pressures, if we find them at all, are also likely to come in large part from organized research. And because organized research is increasingly international in its methods and practical consequences, this means, in effect, that we have systematized and galvanized the process of cultural exchange.

I do not take this, however, to be an optimistic utterance. It defines a problem; it does not offer a solution. For we have a natural interest in maintaining diversity in the world. A great many people in a great many nations resist such changes. A large number of them, given the preeminence of the United States in science and technology, blame these changes on us, even though they are rather the products of a secular change in human knowledge and in the relation of man to his environment. Not least, technology makes trouble because it makes trouble so visibly and noisily and communicates its impact so quickly and so far.

Ease of Communication

The revolution in the technology of travel and communication, indeed, is in itself a second major factor in the emergence of the new era in international affairs that I am attempting to describe. It has made the reporting of news itself a major influence on what actually happens. It has made foreign places realities at the breakfast table every morning. It has put the decisionmakers under extraordinary pressure to make decisions fast and to make half a dozen at once. It has placed a premium on planning and on the capacity to deliberate carefully about hypothetical problems, because the chance to deliberate about real ones is generally likely to be short and not very sweet. And not least, it fosters the impression that we know what is going on and why in other places because we see so much and hear so much about them.

* * *

Role of the School in Social Development

The job of teachers, students, and educational institutions is per· haps even more evident when we turn to the developing nations. For it is plain, to begin with the most elementary fact, that if we are to have fruitful and mutually beneficial relations with the people of these nations, we must know more about them. Not enough of us know very much, and too many of us know nothing at all. It is in response to this simple fact that a basic element of the President's new program in international education is the International Education Act of 1966, a proposal whose intention is to strengthen the intellectual capacity and cultural imagination which we Americans can bring to any of our activities overseas.

But an even more powerful imperative stands behind the steps that the United States Government is now taking to sharpen and increase its efforts in international education. It is the imperative presented by a secular change in social structures of the greatest significance. The family, traditional religious organizations, and the neighborhood community have in the past been the most powerful social agencies with regard to the formation of human attitudes and the control of human behavior.

In both modern and modernizing societies, however, the power of these agencies must now be supplemented. They cannot by themselves cope with the pace of change or the disturbances of industrialization and urbanization. Neither are they capable of training people in the skills a modern economy requires or in the attitudes and national perspective which spell the difference today between a viable and unviable society. The school—primary, secondary, or advanced—has in consequence been projected to the forefront of contemporary history. It has become an indispensable agency of social development and control.

The school is fundamental in our foreign relations because investment in human beings is an indispensable investment for development. It is fundamental because education is not only a capital investment but provides a consumer's good which a mounting number of people everywhere are demanding with greater and greater urgency for themselves or their children. It is fundamental because only the school can provide individuals with the means to understand and control their experience with all the elements it contains that signal the existence and importance of distant places in the world.

Last but not at all least, the school is fundamental because close association between the schools of different countries is a primary means for creating, for the long run, patterns of mutual respect and forbearance on the international scene. The close relation of education to development has been emphasized by the President in his recent message to the Congress, and is reflected in the greater emphasis which the Agency for International Development is going to give to education, along with health and food production, in its programs.[2] But beyond the recognition of education as an instrument of development, there is an additional feature of the President's program that is equally important. Educational cooperation with other nations is conceived as part of the enduring national interest of the United States, a necessity for us and for others in building a firmer structure for peace.

* * *

Advent of Democracy

These considerations take me to the final characteristic of the present international scene which has pushed educational and cultural relations to the foreground. It is the advent of democracy and of the language of liberty, equality, and fraternity as the fundamental legitimation, real or professed, for contemporary government and for the struggles and aspirations of the inhabitants of this planet.

International affairs can no longer be conducted and no longer are conducted as affairs between the high and mighty, the crowned heads and elected presidents, alone. The heads of government speak over the heads of their fellows to the citizens who are the presumed source

---

[2] For text of President Johnson's message on foreign aid, see *ibid.*, February 28, 1966, p. 320.

of authority. Every important move in foreign policy involves an effort not only to move another government but to move public opinion. And distant though public opinion may seem from the councils where the decisions are made, it has its effect, if not immediately then in the long run.

In the long run, international educational and cultural relations play a decisive role in the flow of public opinion. They work perhaps less dramatically than the more rapid techniques for effecting changes in opinion, and these latter, of course, cannot be neglected. But opinion is generally a reflection of character and outlook, of long training and education, and not simply of the most recent information that one receives. If public opinion in our nation and in the world is to be consistent with the interests of peace and of mutual tolerance between diverse systems and cultures, a substantial effort must be made in the field of mutual education and cultural exchange.

It is, of course, possible to adopt alternative approaches to this state of affairs. At least once before, the nations of Europe were faced by a secular shift in the conditions of national security and power. This occurred when improvements in navigation made it possible for them to move out into the open seas. They met this test by establishing a system of commercial rivalry and warfare with whose effects we are still struggling. In the emerging era of educational and cultural relations, the solidification of a system of educational and cultural warfare and ideological recrimination is of course a possibility. The school systems of the world, past and present, have made their contributions to chauvinism and insularity.

But there is an alternative. In an era in which men demand equality, in which the citizens of nations long subject insist on looking you in the eye, it is possible—and it is necessary—to seek cultural exchange on a basis of equality and in the spirit that each nation has as much to learn as to teach. It is possible—and it is necessary—to act on the principle that, where education is concerned, where a people's deepest values are at issue, the ear as well as the mouth should be brought into play.

Educational and cultural relations today, if they are to serve the common causes of humanity and if they are to serve our most enduring national interest, require a delicate touch and a cooperative international approach. They cannot rest on the presumption that our nation or any nation has a mission to educate the world.

Guidelines for the New Era

*　*　*

What are the basic guidelines for educational and cultural policy in this emerging era of educational and cultural relations? They are implicit, I think, in what I have said.

Educational and cultural programs should be bilateral or multilateral wherever possible, not unilateral.

They should rest on the established principle in all free educational systems that there is a difference between education and propaganda, and they must exemplify this principle in practice.

Their success should be measured against long-term goals, not short-term ones.

They should be geared, for practical reasons as well as for reasons of policy, to the needs, interests, and modes of behavior of the people most immediately concerned: scholars, teachers, artists, students.

They should be conceived and implemented as continuing programs, as responses to imperatives that are now permanent on the human scene. They should not be viewed primarily as a means for the achievement of passing objectives.

Finally, the educational and cultural programs of the Federal Government, though they are indispensable, should properly be viewed only as elements in a larger national enterprise. They should not be and cannot be substitutes for nongovernmental efforts. Their main purpose, properly, is further to release and stimulate the energies of the non-Federal and private sectors of our country, which are already leading the effort in international education and cultural exchange.

*　*　*

8

Science and Technology

The voices of the scientific and technological community are the most recent to be heard in the American foreign policy-making process. The scientists and technicians have been invited to offer their expertise on a variety of national security questions, such as weapon systems and disarmament. They also have demanded a voice in the way that their contributions to national power are used. In addition, a "diplomacy of science" is emerging in American relations with other countries.

Development of channels for the voice of science and technology

The United States was abruptly introduced to the importance of science and technology on October 4, 1957, when the Russian Sputnik was launched. There followed a rash of activity to introduce the scientific community into the decision-making process more effectively. Also, there was a need to coordinate the science offices of the different executive agencies and branches. Prior to 1957, the State Department's Office of International Scientific and Technological Affairs (established 1951) and the National Science Foundation (established 1950) existed but proved inadequate. The National Science Foundation had failed to perform one of its major duties—to develop and coordinate national policies on science. In the State Department, Secretary Dulles showed less interest in science than did Secretary Acheson.[1]

---

1 Eugene Skolnikoff, *Science, Technology and American Foreign Policy* (Cambridge: MIT Press, 1967) , pp. 256-57.

Thus, Sputnik spurred the U.S. government to action and in 1957 the President's Science Advisory Committee and an office of Special Assistant to the President for Science and Technology were established. The Special Assistant, who came to be known by the shorthand label of "Science Advisor," was chairman of the committee. Other executive agencies created or upgraded their own science offices.

If 1957 was a year for creating, 1958 was a year for coordinating. The National Aeronautics and Space Council was added to the Executive Office of the President. It was primarily concerned with space exploration, and was to be chaired by the President, although Mr. Kennedy turned over the chairmanship to Vice-President Johnson. Its members included the Secretaries of State and Defense, and heads of NSF, National Aeronautics and Space Administration, Atomic Energy Commission, and the National Academy of Science. Also founded in 1958 was the Committee of Principals to coordinate disarmament policy—a subject in which scientific expertise played a large role. In 1959, the Federal Council for Science and Technology was established, composed of officials of each department (usually Assistant Secretaries) responsible for research programs in science and technology. Finally, the importance of science in policy-making was further underscored in 1962 when President Kennedy established the Office of Science and Technology as a unit in the Executive Office of the President with the President's Science Advisor in charge.

As U.S. interest in science and technology has matured, and as the national organization has developed since 1957, two general areas of issues emerge: one is the application of science to national power and the other is the relationship of science to building a world community of peace and stability.

Science and national power

The development of weapon systems, of instruments for intelligence gathering, and of space exploration are three examples of the contribution of science to national power.

Development of weapon systems

It is in the development of new families of weapons—not simply the revision or updating of present weapons in the field—that scientists have been called upon most often by the U.S. government. Hence, the

144

military establishment has tended to be the largest user of scientific and technological expertise.[2]

The impetus from new weapons most often results from the military establishment's concept of future wars. The scientist is instructed to design a practical weapon to fulfill a specified mission envisioned by the military establishment.

Intelligence gathering

The advent of U-2 airplanes and "spy in the sky" satellites have been part of a trend in intelligence gathering toward the use of sophisticated electronic surveillance equipment. The National Security Agency, established in 1952, has specialized in this type of intelligence gathering and evaluating, as well as the service agencies and the Defense Intelligence Agency. The scientist has been called upon to design and perfect equipment needed by the intelligence community.

Space exploration

The exploration of space relates to national power because of its military potential and its prestige factor. In an attempt to overtake the Soviet space lead and to defend against new Russian military developments (such as the fractional or partial orbit weapons system), the scientist has been called upon to make a large contribution.

Science and international community

Dean Rusk, in the policy statement below, describes many of the world's problems which are susceptible to solution by the combined knowledge of many nations' scientists. The United States has introduced science into bilateral relations with other states for purposes of building goodwill. For example, in 1961, President Kennedy and Premier Ikeda agreed to set up a joint Japanese-American committee of scientists. Also, in 1961, Mr. Kennedy proposed to Ayub Kahn that the U.S. help Pakistan solve the problems of waterlogging and salinity in West Pakistan. The U.S. and U.S.S.R. have cooperated in areas of scientific exploration while they have not in the political arena.

---

[2] See Burton Sapin, *The Making of United States Foreign Policy* (New York: Frederick A. Praeger, Inc., 1966), pp. 217-45.

Conclusion

Science and technology are late-comers to the decision-making process in the post-World War II period, and most often they entered in at the military level. Secretary of State Rusk describes the role of science in foreign policy-making and stresses the importance of science in helping to build a world community of nations and its contributions to national power.

Science and Foreign Affairs

by Dean Rusk,

Secretary of State[1]

The uncharted region where the interests of science and foreign policy meet is of great import in a world increasingly devoted to understanding and control of our total physical environment. The United States is one of several nations trying to chart that region, and until it is mapped we cannot intelligently choose our routes. In foreign affairs we pool our knowledge of history, politics, economics, science, and technology to arrive at new syntheses.

Science and technology are, in the United States today, a part of the fabric of life itself. We have, in the past 20 years, entered a new phase of the great American adventure. Throughout the world, technology and the science which supports it have provided new means of education, new sources of power, new ways of processing data, and fast, reliable transportation and communication. Man is extending his reach beyond this earth and into the vast reaches of space. The new knowledge and concepts, even the very tools of the new technology, promise ever more intensive investigations in the years ahead. We have learned how to pool our resources in coordinated efforts to develop new devices and to exploit new fields. We are supporting science and technology on a scale undreamed of even two decades ago.

We are all familiar with the so-called culture gap between science and the humanities and, more recently, with the "technological gap" between the United States and Europe. Last year Vice President Humphrey said to this committee:

---

[1] Excerpts from an address made before the eighth annual Panel on Science and Technology of the House Committee on Science and Astronautics on January 24, 1967. Printed in the *Department of State Bulletin*, February 13, 1967, pp. 238-42.

Contemporary American Foreign Policy: The Official Voice

> I think there is danger of another gap—a gap between public policy
> and advancing science and technology. It is in government that we must
> face the task of closing that gap. . . . It is only in recent years that we
> have really understood the close relationship between public policy at
> the governmental level and science and technology.

In the interest of closing that gap, the Department of State began a
program at the Foreign Service Institute in 1965 designed to equip
Foreign Service officers with some competence to handle science as a
part of foreign affairs. For the most part, we selected officers who will
be assuming the foreign affairs burdens over the next decade. We
followed this with a program for the exchange of officers with the
scientific agencies to provide direct experience in scientific programs.

For any American involved in public affairs today, scientific literacy
is a must; and that is particularly so in foreign affairs. We are firmly
convinced that the Foreign Service officer should be familiar with the
ways, the concepts, and the purposes of science. He should understand
the sources of our technological civilization. He should be able to
grasp the social and economic implications of current scientific discoveries and engineering accomplishments. I think it is feasible for
nonscientists to be, in the phrase of H. G. Wells, "men of science"
with real awareness of this aspect of man's advance.

But the burden is not all on one side. Scientists and engineers must,
of course, recognize very real progress in many fields outside their
own specialties, and they should be conscious of the difference between the values of society and the verifiable truths of the natural
sciences. For such men there is a role in the foreign policy process. I
think that perhaps scientists have been a little more willing to wade in
the turbulent pond of foreign policy and that we in foreign affairs
must be more willing and better prepared to dip in the waters of
science. That science is international in character has come to be
regarded as a truism, but it is no more true of science than it is of the
humanities or the social sciences. The larger truth is that billions
must live together successfully on this planet and that we are making
common cause in vast areas of human competence and search for
knowledge.

* * *

We have in the State Department a small group of scientists and
Foreign Service officers working with the science agencies and with

148

the scientific community on policies and programs for international scientific and technical cooperation. We do not administer those programs, but we guide them and retain the foreign policy decisions. The Department's International Scientific and Technological Affairs Bureau has the resources of the Government at its disposal in the United States and a network of scientific attachés in 17 capitals on the other end. At some major posts, our science agencies support their own representatives to assist in specialized cooperative programs. It is not a question of preparing to move in new dimensions; science and technology are already important elements in our international relations and, indeed, have emerged as instruments of foreign policy.

Scientific and Technological Forecasting

To some extent, we can extrapolate from politics, economics, and science in projecting future policy. In a way, science is the least predictable of these three major fields. There are few "breakthroughs" in politics and economics; these are evolutionary fields. Broad patterns, such as a United Nations Organization, the rise of nationalism in Africa, and the movement of Europe toward economic integration, are discernible far in advance. To a lesser degree this also holds for the products of known technology. We foresee the wide use of nuclear electric power and satellite communications, and we can predict some of the uses to which computer technology will be put, for example.

However, we cannot foresee the breakthroughs in basic understandings to come. Let me illustrate this point.

Thirty years ago President Roosevelt established a blue-ribbon science committee to look into "technological trends and their social implications." The committee was accurate in predicting increased development and use of helicopters and conventional aircraft. Autogiros and dirigibles were reported as on the way out. The committee predicted color television (and commercials), stereo FM radio, our modern high-speed highway system and urban traffic congestion. Air conditioning, plastics, frozen foods, infrared and radio air navigation, microfilm, and accounting card machines were also predicted. All of these extrapolations were based upon then-known technology.

But where were the microcircuit, the computer, radar and sonics, the jet engine and rocketry, radioactivity, and underwater breathing gases? The top three scientific and technical fields of major foreign

149

policy interest today were almost completely ignored by that eminent committee. Space technology or even rudimentary investigations of our solar system were not mentioned. In oceanography mention was made only of the possibility of extracting minerals from sea water. In spite of predicted future needs for oil, none of these experts considered the continental shelves as new sources. Investigation of the sea as a source of fresh water, for fish protein, or simply because of man's native curiosity, was not considered. The sole reference to the third area, nuclear energy, was by a chemist of some vision, in these words:

> Much has been said and written about releasing atomic energy and utilizing the vast forces that it represents. While we see no immediate possibility of doing this economically, who shall say that it will not be achieved, and once achieved, how shall we estimate the social implications resulting from the use of such energy?

How indeed? This same man of vision advised that:

> It is the unexpected turn, when some little detail has been perfected after long search, that brings such things to pass, just as occasionally a promising development must be dropped when some unexpected defect develops. These are what make prophecy difficult.

And so they do. The year after that report was written, nuclear fission was discovered; and in 4 years more the world's first nuclear reactor reached criticality in Chicago, opening the nuclear era. In our turn, we cannot now predict if we will harness the thermonuclear reaction nor would we be able to gauge its social and economic implications.

* * *

International Efforts Needed in Science

Although scientific prediction seems to me to remain a chancy business, we can usefully examine some aspects of the changing modern environment which are of direct concern to foreign affairs, many of which can only be dealt with internationally.

The increasing pollution of our atmosphere, particularly in large urban complexes, is of common interest to the advanced nations. The industrialization and urbanization of the developing nations will further contaminate the atmosphere. An international cooperative effort to cure our air, followed by international conventions to keep it clean, would be a long step toward meeting our responsibilities to our own future.

Population pressures can be relieved by means more civilized than war, disease, or famine. Recent discoveries make possible effective population control, and information and assistance for family planning are widely available. The barriers are those of conviction and communication. The governments of the world must first be convinced of the necessity for a program of concerted and immediate action. They must act in time to prevent the mass starvation predicted within the next 15 years. We shall need more food, but more food is not the long-term solution. We must continue development of better instrumentalities for population control; we need better means for reaching billions of people; and we must recognize that a crisis is at hand. Changes in mores are in process in many parts of the world, and the approach is becoming international.

*   *   *

The spread of nuclear power reactors requires reliable and credible safeguards over the use of nuclear fuels and equipment to prevent their diversion to military uses. The further proliferation of nuclear weapons programs not only increases the hazard to peace but diverts material and human resources from more constructive goals. We have a good beginning on effective international safeguards, but much remains to be done. Some of the remaining tasks are political and some are technical. We must act in good faith and with resolution to try to assure the world that the doorway to nuclear warfare can be locked.

A cooperative assault on the treasure chest of the seas would prevent the waste of talent and money through unnecessary duplication.

The challenges of our space environment require a truly international response. It is already clear that there are benefits to be derived from the use of space which are worldwide in application. The agreement last month on a draft treaty on the peaceful use of outer space[2] makes this a propitious moment to consider again whether we cannot respond even more effectively to this challenge.

All of these possibilities for cooperative programs with other na-

---

[2] For background, see *ibid.*, December 26, 1966, p. 952, and January 9, 1967, p. 78.

151

tions call for an advanced technology. But we have not forgotten our own growing pains.

Most of the world's population lives in the developing nations, and not all of these are making sufficient material progress. There is an ever-widening gap between the advanced and those struggling to keep their heads above water. The advanced nations must assist the developing countries in building a base for technological competence. We cannot overlay advanced technology on an insufficient base. That base must first be prepared through intelligent planning toward rational goals.

Alliance of Natural and Social Sciences

Our world has acquired a new orientation over the past 20 years. Science and technology are advancing the clock of civilization at an ever-increasing rate. Science has become accustomed to its place at the frontiers of man's knowledge. But we do not forget the older frontiers where man meets man, and we welcome the alliance of the natural sciences with the social sciences in meeting new facets of old problems in the world laboratory.

The political significance of strong national programs in science and technology expands steadily. Political-scientific areas such as disarmament, nuclear safeguards, ocean exploitation, space technology and communications, and water management are areas in which the natural and the social sciences meet, and they offer major opportunities for international programs. Wider use of forums such as this today to bring the international problems of science and technology before learned men from both broad areas can assist in finding the solutions.

As to our approach to this kind of international cooperation, my points were three. We can make better use of new techniques for technological forecasting as an input to foreign policy judgments. New understandings and mutual respect between the physical sciences and the social sciences are prerequisites if the gap between them is to be completely closed. We must have programs of international scientific and technical cooperation on two levels: with the advanced nations in understanding and controlling the total environment, and with those nations in assisting the material progress of the developing nations.

* * *

9

Population Policy

Several minor themes appear from time to time in U.S. policy pronouncements, and most of them have not been developed in detail to warrant consideration in this volume. For example, no concise statement exists on maritime policy, overseas territories, or aviation policy. U.S. policy on population has been late in forming. Mr. Gaud's statement represents the only comprehensive declaration of American policy on this subject.

The population explosion

The "population explosion" is a recent concern for the United States, as well as other industrialized nations. Even the developing nations are divided on their view of its seriousness. For example, the South American nations, unlike the Afro-Asian states, tend to be underpopulated.

For the developing countries, a 2 to 3 percent a year population growth rate is not uncommon. Hence, a country with a 4 or 5 percent a year economic growth rate has its per capita gross national product reduced by one-half because of population increases. Reducing population growth by one or two percentage points each year would enable a developing nation to add to its economic well being.

But how is population growth decreased? The answer to this question is yet unknown, and this explains Mr. Gaud's emphasis on study and research. As a country becomes urbanized and industrialized, the population growth rate slows down. City-dwelling families evidently do not possess the same incentives to have large families as rural folk who need many hands for farm work. But how can population growth

153

among developing yet unindustralized countries be reduced? This question has no simple answer.

Developmental assistance coming from industralized nations often increases the population growth rate by introducing simple measures of hygiene. In the past, population increases in developing nations have been held down by high infant mortality rates and diseases which take younger and middle-aged people. (Cancer and coronaries are diseases of old age found in Western, industrialized societies and little known in the developing nations.) Health measures that lower the infant mortality rate and extend the average life span are easily introduced into developing societies, while corresponding success in agricultural production has been harder to achieve.

U.S. attitude toward population programs

The U.S. has been one of the few countries to have no domestic population policy, either to increase or decrease its population growth. Most major nations have had one or the other of these policies. Fascist Italy and Germany and Soviet Russia have encouraged population increases by outlawing abortions, taxing bachelors, and giving state funds to support large families produced by "hero mothers." But the contemporary problem is limiting growth, not encouraging it. The U.S. government has never possessed a population policy because of the influence of domestic religious groups and because the official policy position has been that family planning is a private, and not a national affair.

A similar attitude had characterized foreign policy until 1967. Prior to 1967 AID funds were not allotted for attempts to limit population growth. Mr. Gaud describes his actions in March of that year when AID established its Population Service. A major change in policy occurred in May when AID allowed contraceptives to be financed by foreign aid funds and in November, AID gave population control the same priority as food production.

Conclusion

American decision-makers were reluctant to prescribe solutions to the population explosion before 1967. Currently, AID is spending over $4 million for family planning and population programs, a surprising "about face" for the American government, who in fiscal year 1964 spent no money for this activity.

AID Policy on Family Planning and Population Growth

by William S. Gaud

Administrator, Agency for International Development[1]

Mr. Chairman and Members of the Committee:

I am happy to appear before you to discuss a subject of the highest importance to the Agency for International Development—the rapid growth of population in the developing nations.

*   *   *

The problem

The population of the world is now growing at the unparalleled rate of 2% a year. This is a new problem for the world. It took us from the beginning of time until 1830 to reach our first billion of world population. One century later, in 1930, we had two billion. Only thirty years later, by 1960, we had the third billion. Currently, we are adding something like 65 million more people annually, more than the equivalent of a new West Germany or United Kingdom each year. At this rate, the present world population of 3.5 billion will double in the next 35 years.

This adds a radically new dimension to a host of problems which are already difficult enough: how to feed and house the world's people, how to educate them and find jobs for them, how to deal with the problems of urban growth, how to get on with the business of economic development and—above all—how to secure and maintain a lasting peace. President Johnson put it plainly when he said that:

---

[1] Excerpts from a statement made before the Subcommittee on Foreign Aid Expenditures of the Senate Government Operations Committee on February 1, 1968. Released as a pamphlet with no date and publisher listed.

Next to the pursuit of peace, the really greatest challenge to the human family is the race between food supply and population increase.

The greatest and most immediate pressure will be felt by the two-thirds of humanity living in the less developed areas of Asia, Latin America and Africa. These are already areas of need and want. Yet they enjoy—if that is a proper use of the word—the fastest population growth in the world, and they cannot afford it.

A.I.D.'s Population Policy

In November 1967 I issued to all A.I.D. offices here and abroad a formal Policy Determination directing them *to give the highest priority*—along with food production—to encouraging, supporting and strengthening family planning programs in the developing countries (P.D. 39, November 3, 1967) .

Our population policy is based on four fundamental principles.

The first principle is that overpopulation and underdevelopment go hand-in-hand. This tie is both biological and economic. Overpopulation in the less developed countries leads to malnutrition, which cuts energy and kills initiative. Malnutrition also shortens the life span and saps productivity. These personal deprivations add up to national failures in development. We have evidence, too, that infant and maternal malnutrition can cause mental retardation—again, personal tragedies which hobble national growth. Finally, national resources used to care for weak, ill, overcrowded, under-employed people are resources diverted from development.

In sum, when a country's production gains are matched by population gains—*nothing is gained.* The country is not moving ahead. It is treading water, and it is in trouble. The progress of the poor nations will depend largely upon their success in slowing down their rates of population increase. They will not be able to offer their people better lives and opportunities until their resources and populations are in proper balance.

The second principle is that the government of every nation with a population problem—whether developed or developing—should do its utmost to increase the knowledge and practice of family planning among its citizens. Our role is to encourage and help the developing nations with this task.

157

The third principle is respect for the sovereignty and the sensibilities of the nations we assist. The population question is as delicate as it is urgent. Over half the people in the developing world now live under governments that have policies of reducing birth rates. But some countries, even though they are aware of the seriousness of the problem, and are working on it, either do not welcome outside help in this field or do not want it on a large scale. Our work in the population field must be carried on in such a way as not to raise political problems. The family planning programs we assist must be host nation programs—not our programs. They should avoid labels marked "made in the USA."

This principle is based upon Section 291 of the Foreign Assistance Act of 1967. It declares that "every nation is and should be free to determine its own policies and procedures with respect to problems of population growth and family planning within its own boundary." Consistent with this, we will not assist any program unless we are asked to do so.

The fourth principle is that A.I.D. will support no family planning or population program unless it is voluntary. This means several things. For one thing, each developing country must decide for itself what types of programs best suit its requirements and its people. We will not force a particular type of program on any country. For another, we will assist only those programs in which individuals are free to participate or not as they see fit, and where they have a choice of means. In short, Mr. Chairman, we want no part of either international coercion or individual coercion. We do not make family planning a condition of aid.

Guided by these principles, and acting in accordance with our determination to give programs relating to population growth the highest priority, A.I.D. is determined to do everything it can to help the developing countries face up to and overcome their population growth problems.

Program Expansion

The Agency for International Development has financed population and family planning programs in some 30 countries.

* * *

In the main, our contributions have been modest. This is so for several reasons. For one thing, some nations do not want outside help in dealing with this problem. Others, while tentatively exploring the problem and sniffing at it around the edges, are not yet ready to embark on large-scale programs. Also, as I have already mentioned, A.I.D. has only recently reached a stage of substantially expanding its activities in this area.

Our dollar obligations for family planning and population programs over the past few years were as follows:

FY 1964 .... $	None
FY 1965	2,292,307
FY 1966	5,487,192
FY 1967	4,252,988

In the current fiscal year, FY 1968, our obligations will be far higher. Section 292 of the Foreign Assistance Act provides that $35 million of economic aid funds may be used only for programs relating to population growth. This year's Authorization Act did not become effective until November 14, 1967, the Appropriation Act did not become effective until January 2, 1968, and we operated through much of the fall without benefit of a continuing resolution. Nevertheless we have obligated or committed $8.7 million for dollar projects.

* * *

The Agency has taken great pains to see that these policy changes are recognized and enforced by our entire staff both here and abroad. This is done through staff meetings, published guidelines and policy determinations, airgrams and cables. The Regional Administrators, in particular, devote considerable time and effort to this undertaking. In a future effort to keep the Agency's employees up-to-date and informed on developments in this field, I propose to reprint this statement and see that it is distributed to all A.I.D. employees with the request that they read it and be guided by it in carrying on the Agency's business.

In April 1966, when this Committee last heard from A.I.D., there were 8 people in the Agency spending all or a major part of their time on population matters. Today there are 52. Twenty-five of these are in the Population Service. The rest are either in our Regional Bureaus or are serving overseas. For example, there are 10 American

159

professionals in the Health and Family Planning Division in our India Mission, and 7 in the comparable office in our Pakistan Mission. Every overseas Mission has at least a part-time Population Officer.

Research Expansion

The entire field of population problems and family planning in developing countries is still largely uncharted. We have a great deal to learn about motivating people to practice birth control, about how best to administer family planning programs and about other problems. More research is vital.

* * *

Country Programs

I would like to refer briefly, Mr. Chairman, to our programs in a few of the countries which are making substantial efforts to deal with the problem of population growth.

Pakistan

Pakistan has 118 million people and is the fifth most populous nation in the world. Its population is growing at an extremely high rate.

Pakistan has an active, expanding and well-administered population program. To the best of my knowledge there is no head of state in the developing world with a greater awareness of the importance of this problem—or more determined to do something about it—than President Ayub. The head of his Family Planning Program told me when he visited Washington some time ago that President Ayub has given family planning such high priority that he has no trouble getting all the funds, people and material that he needs. I wish the United States foreign aid program could get this kind of blank check.

Pakistan's goal is to reduce its birth rate from 50 per 1,000 to 40 per 1,000 by 1970. I believe this goal can be met. More than 1 million IUD's[2] had been inserted by the end of 1967, 40,000 were taking oral

---

[2] Intrauterine device, which is a contraceptive device. (Editor's note)

contraceptives and voluntary sterilization of males was increasing. There were 23,000 of the latter during last September alone.

Pakistan is bearing most of the cost of this program. Sweden has been giving some support since 1961. Since 1966 this has consisted of $1 million worth of contraceptives a year. Since 1964 A.I.D. has provided technical help, training and commodities in the aggregate amount of approximately $500,000. We have also made a Cooley loan of $168,000 in rupees to a Pakistan subsidiary of G. D. Searle of Chicago which will make and market contraceptives and other drug products in Pakistan.

Our A.I.D. Mission in Pakistan includes a seven man Health and Family Planning Team. This year we plan to finance training in the United States in population work for about 40 Pakistanis, and provide pills, clinical supplies, training equipment and other commodities. All told, in FY 1968 we expect to obligate more than $6 million—$750,000 in dollars and $5.3 million in rupees—for family planning work in Pakistan. We estimate that from its own budget, Pakistan will spend approximately $12 million on its program during this fiscal year.

India

India's population problems are clear and pressing. There were 340 million Indians in 1947. In 1967 there were more than 515 million. Population is growing by more than 1,000,000 people monthly—a new Netherlands every year.

The Indian Government has had a national family planning policy and program since 1951. It has not been a dynamic or effective program. But now, under vigorous leadership from a new Family Planning Minister, the program appears to be moving.

India's family planning budget for this year is about $41 million—2% of the total Indian budget and five times the size of the 1965-1966 budget. The Government has opened 5,400 rural Family Planning Centers and 8,500 subcenters. Approximately 25,000 people are now working on family planning. More and more Indian couples now use conventional contraceptives. More IUDs are being inserted and more voluntary sterilizations are taking place. Plants for the manufacture of condoms are being set up and modernized.

In addition, there is legislation pending to raise the minimum age for marriage in India. This could be most significant.

161

All this is a start. But much more is required if India's population problem is to be brought under control. The number of couples in the child-producing age groups, practicing contraception, must increase ten-fold. Some 95,000 existing family planning jobs have to be filled. Enormous problems of supply and administration must be solved. Family planning information must be effectively circulated over a vast country. It is the view of the Indian Government that couples must be motivated not only to practice contraception but to plan smaller families—many who presently practice contraception already have four or more children.

A.I.D. is helping in a number of ways. This year we will obligate $1.9 million to finance contraceptives, research, organizational help and advanced training in the United States. We have already obligated $4 million worth of rupees, generated by P.L. 480 sales, for family planning projects. We are also providing resident experts. Our A.I.D. Mission in New Delhi now has a Health and Family Planning Team which includes ten American and four Indian professionals.

So much for what is already under way in India. Looking to the future, our Mission in New Delhi is currently discussing with the Government of India new assistance which would more than double currently planned U.S. dollar aid to the Indian family planning program. Less than a month ago, when the new Indian Family Planning Minister, Mr. Chandrasekhar, was in Washington, we discussed what additional assistance A.I.D. might usefully provide to quicken the pace of India's program. The Minister showed us a list of possible projects which are the subject of the current discussion in New Delhi.

The new package totals $4 million in dollars and $22 million in rupees. It would provide condoms and pills in addition to the quantities I announced last year, as well as equipment for packaging condoms, jeeps for family planning workers, and visual aid and printing equipment for the Indian education and advertising effort.

Our preliminary review gives us confidence that mutual agreement on the bulk of this additional assistance will be reached quickly.

Korea

South Korea, with 30 million people, is conducting a substantial population program at a cost of around $2 million a year. There are now more than 2,200 Korean paid family planning workers, over

28,000 family planning volunteers, 1,100 IUD clinics, 700 vasectomy (male sterilization) clinics and 11 mobile clinics. The Koreans are doing well. It is estimated that over 20% of all Korean families are now practicing family planning of one kind or another. Since 1963 the population growth rate has been cut from 3% to $2\frac{1}{2}$%. The Koreans intend to reduce it to 1.9% before the end of 1970.

In FY 1966 A.I.D. helped the Korean Government equip ambulance-type vehicles for IUD insertions and vasectomy operations. In the next year we provided approximately $100,000 to finance vehicles, health centers and central family planning expenses. This year, under an A.I.D. contract with the Population Council, $235,000 will be granted to the Planned Parenthood Federation of Korea for field workers, evaluation teams, data processors and oral contraceptives for some 900,000 women—women who are expected to be "drop-outs" from the IUD program over the next two years. We have also made a $40,000 grant through the Population Council to a Korean university for a study which we hope will indicate how family planning services can be offered most effectively throughout the country.

Latin America

Latin America's population growth rate of 3% is the highest in the world. There is an awareness of increasing food shortages, malnutrition, unemployment and overcrowding, but family planning is a very sensitive subject and Latin America leaders have been cautious and slow in developing effective programs.

Underlying much of this reluctance to take action has been the notion that Latin America has the room to accommodate larger and larger populations. This view of the problem mistakes room for resources.

Today, however, Latin American leaders are becoming increasingly concerned with the problems of uncontrolled population increase. Eight countries in Latin America now have official programs to lower birth rates: Barbados, Chile, Costa Rica, the Dominican Republic, Honduras, Jamaica, Nicaragua and Venezuela.

Last April, the Eighth World Conference of the International Planned Parenthood Federation was held in Chile, the first meeting of this kind in Latin America. President Frei attended. Latin American response to the Conference was encouraging, suggesting new attitudes in leadership and new initiatives in the making.

163

A.I.D. has provided over $1.9 million for the Latin American program of a number of private international organizations such as the International Planned Parenthood Federation, the Latin American Demographic Center, the Latin American Center for Studies of Population and Family, and the Pan American Health Organization. Our A.I.D. Regional Office for Central America and Panama provides help for country population programs and for the population programs of the Organization of Central American States and the Central American Institute for Economic and Social Development.

This work must go forward on a vastly expanded scale. It is my view that there are some countries in Latin America in which the goals of the Alliance for Progress will be most difficult to achieve unless and until their governments and people face up to the problem of rapid population growth.

Aid to Private Organizations

In October 1967 A.I.D. granted $3 million to the International Planned Parenthood Federation. $1 million of the grant will finance contraceptives, medical supplies, vehicles and other materials for family planning programs. $500,000 will support IPPF work in Latin America. The remainder will finance enlarged family planning training, demonstration and other activities in Asia and Africa.

In FY 1967 A.I.D. provided $375,000 to the Population Council for expansion of its family planning activities in East Asia, plus $300,000 for study and expansion of the Council's highly successful postpartum family planning program. This program now operates in 27 hospitals in 15 countries around the world. It offers family planning information, contraceptives and practical instruction to obstetrical patients during the lying-in period. About 40% of the women in the program hospitals have accepted family planning. What's more, by their word-of-mouth advertising, an equal number of other women have been introduced to family planning. These women are relatively young and have small families, another important consideration. This fiscal year A.I.D. plans to provide the Population Council with $500,000 for a three year expansion of this program in many developing countries.

PART 2

American Foreign Policy Toward World Regions

10

Western Europe

A study of U.S. foreign policy towards Western Europe includes three regions, not one. Western Europe as a geographical region encompasses eleven nations: Austria, Belgium, France, United Kingdom, Ireland, Liechtenstein, Monaco, Netherlands, Luxembourg, Federal Republic of Germany, and Switzerland. Often the northern European or Scandinavian nations (Denmark, Finland, Iceland, Norway, and Sweden) are included, as well as the countries of southern Europe (Albania, Greece, Italy, Malta, San Marino, Spain, plus Andorra and the Vatican). The tendency in American thinking is to lump these three Europes into one "homogeneous" grouping and draw general conclusions that somehow apply to all 25 entities. It is an area of diversity, which sometimes borders on the extremes, rather than a stereotype of a monolithic region. There are "neutrals," such as Ireland, Yugoslavia, Switzerland, Sweden, Austria; very young states (*e.g.*, Malta) and very old (*e.g.*, San Marino); large regional powers and "ministates," such as Liechtenstein.

Despite the diversity, trends since 1946 can be recognized and analyzed. A threefold heading will be used to serve as a background for the two policy statements reprinted below: the Soviet threat and the American response, the trend toward integration, and finally, problems presented by French leadership of the New Europe.

The Soviet Threat

The beginnings of the Cold War are not found in Eastern or Western Europe, but the first conflicts occurred in Southern Europe and the Middle East. The presence of Soviet troops in Iran

169

in 1946, Russian pressure on Turkey, and Communist guerrillas in Greece were the curtain raisers for the Cold War. The traditional Great Power "protector" of this area was England, but in early 1947, the British government informed the Truman Administration that the United Kingdom could no longer support Greece and Turkey financially and militarily. Mr. Truman on March 12, 1947, in an address to the joint session of Congress, called for economic support of the Greek and Turkish nations. His address was dubbed the "Truman Doctrine."

In the same month, Britain and France signed the Treaty of Dunkirk, a defensive alliance primarily against Germany, but also aimed at any nation which would act in concert with German aggression. This treaty was the first of three western alliances. One year later, the Brussels Pact united Britain, France, Netherlands, Belgium, and Luxembourg; and in April 1949 the North Atlantic Treaty was signed by the Brussels Pact countries and the U.S., Canada, Norway, Denmark, Portugal, and Iceland. Later Greece, Turkey, Federal Republic of Germany, and Italy joined. The North Atlantic Treaty was a mutual agreement to give military assistance to the attacked nation. Two years later, in 1951, at the Lisbon meeting of the North Atlantic Council the treaty members, with American persuasion, agreed to the joint command structure and coordinated strategy which are now hallmarks of NATO.

Not only was the Soviet threat during this early period perceived by American decision-makers in terms of military aggression, but the possibility of internal subversion also was considered likely. The extremely harsh winter in 1946-47 in Europe and the deteriorating British financial position led the U.S. government to re-evaluate the economic instruments, such as the World Bank, that had been established for Europe's reconstruction, and to decide that more drastic and more massive assistance was needed. In June 1947 Secretary of State George C. Marshall spelled out the new American policy in a famous speech which gave the effort his name—the Marshall Plan. The strategy of the Marshall Plan was, first, for the European countries to coordinate their efforts and, then, present the U.S. with a "once-for-all bill." By the time the "bill" (which ranged from $12 to $17 billion) was presented to Congress, the February 1948 *coup d'etat* had occurred in Czechoslovakia and the Italian elections were to be held with a strong possibility that the Communist Party might win a majority of the seats. Consequently, Congress quickly passed the Marshall Plan. Europe, hopefully, was made "safe" from both external aggression and internal subversion.

One last U.S. policy objective was yet to be realized: the re-arming of Germany within a framework of effective safeguards. After the European Defense Community was defeated by the French Assembly in 1954, Germany became a signatory to the Brussels Pact, and hence, was brought into NATO in May 1955.

The structure to contain the U.S.S.R., a goal of American foreign policy enunciated in the March 1947 Truman Doctrine, was completed in 1955. Observers writing later have argued that the Russian threat perceived by American policy-makers either did not exist in the late 1940s and early 1950s, or if it did exist, had diminished by 1955 when the final touches were put on the containment structure.[1]

European integration

Unlike American policy on the Soviet threat, where the United States played an active—at times, a heavy-handed—role, the U.S. assumed a policy of benign encouragement on European integration. American policy-makers *did* want a Europe united but felt that the decision for integration would have to come from the Europeans themselves. However, some of the more aggressive American policies contributed to integration. The Marshall Plan's call for a coordinated effort (later institutionalized in the Organization for European Economic Cooperation) pushed the Europeans toward integration. Also, the search for a suitable formula to rearm Germany gave birth to the European Defense Community. Finally, the decision in 1951 to institutionalize the North Atlantic Treaty was another stimulus for European federation.

Still, the impetus did come from the Europeans, and the Americans were content to support these initiatives.[2] In May 1950, the European Coal and Steel Community was established, and in March 1957,

---

[1] See, for example, William A. Williams, *The Tragedy of American Diplomacy* (New York: Harcourt, Brace & World, Inc., 1948) ; and John Lukacs, *A History of the Cold War* (Garden City, New York: Doubleday & Company, Inc., 1963) .

[2] Max Beloff writes that in the early days of the European integration movement "...there was a general sense...that movements toward the reshaping of Europe must come from Europeans, as indeed eventually it did, and that American pressure should be limited to supporting such initiatives." *The United States and the Unity of Europe* (Washington, D.C.: The Brookings Institution, 1963), p. 36.

the Rome Treaty which formed the European Economic Community (EEC) or Common Market, was signed. Much to the disappointment of the U.S. government, a bipolar Europe emerged, rather than a single-knit region. In 1959, a rival economic bloc, the European Free Trade Association (EFTA), was established, led by the United Kingdom. The U.S. government favored EEC and encouraged the hastening of the day when its six nations (France, Federal Republic of Germany, Italy, Belgium, Luxembourg, and the Netherlands) and the seven EFTA countries (United Kingdom, Denmark, Norway, Sweden, Switzerland, Austria, and Portugal) would cease their rivalry.

EEC has come to be associated with French leadership in the 1960s. In January 1963, the French vetoed the admission of England into the Common Market. As the policy statement by Mr. Popper illustrates, French foreign policy has presented new problems and challenges to American foreign policy.

Problems of French foreign policy

The French Fifth Republic was founded in 1958 with Charles de Gaulle elected as its first president. However, it was not until January 1961, when the burden of the Algerian war was jettisoned, that France began to assume a more dominant position in Europe. What are the areas of conflict in Franco-American relations?

Disagreements on the Soviet threat

Evidently, De Gaulle feels that the Soviet Union remains a threat to Europe, but he perceives a threat of lesser intensity and magnitude than that seen by the Americans. The threat can be countered effectively by the North Atlantic Treaty—but not the Organization. The "O" in NATO has a built-in American hegemony which France as a sovereign nation will not tolerate.

Disagreements on uniting Europe

To De Gaulle, the present division of Europe between East and West is a remnant of the Cold War brought on by the bitterness of the Soviet-American conflict. The danger is that the Cold War perpetually will separate Europe into antagonistic camps. The decision to divide Europe into East and West was an arbitrary action taken by the United States and Soviet Union. The American position is that unity will come only by withstanding Soviet aggression long enough to permit a weakening of the Communist Empire. De Gaulle, on the other hand, thinks that unity can be achieved only when American presence (and therefore the American threat to the Soviet Union) has been removed from Europe. The New Europe should include both Eastern and Western Europe.

Disagreements on the French independent nuclear strike force

The French have undertaken to build an independent nuclear strike force which American spokesmen have either treated lightly or warned that it possesses the potential to trigger World War III. The Americans have argued that the French should concentrate on conventional weapons rather than duplicate the U.S. nuclear forces. The Gaulist argument, on the other hand, is that an independent nuclear strike force is needed for those issues which the Americans might decide are not worth a nuclear exchange with the Russians. These issues may be of vital importance to French national interest, but could be viewed as minor consequences to American national interest.

Other differences between American and French foreign policy are evident in Mr. Popper's statement below.

Conclusion

Contemporary American policy appears to be based on the assumption that President De Gaulle is a temporary obstruction to Europe's inexorable trend toward integration. Once De Gaulle removes himself from the political scene, NATO will return to its normal position and peace will be made between the two European factions. Mr. Ball declares that part of the problem is the emergence of the old-style nationalism which divided rather than united Europe. Thus, in American eyes, De Gaulle represents this divisive nationalism.

U.S. Policy Toward NATO

by George Ball,
Under Secretary of State[1]

* * *

There are two questions that demand our first attention:

Are the interests of the United States and Western Europe still basically parallel?

If so, how should we pursue those interests?

Common Interests of the Atlantic Nations

The answer to the first question seems to me quite clear. We and our European allies are in the same boat and we shall sink or navigate together.

—The security of the United States depends on the security of Western Europe; and Western European countries still count on us for their security. The words of the North Atlantic Treaty are as valid as ever: An attack on one is an attack on all.

—Economic well-being is also indivisible. Prosperity on both sides of the North Atlantic depends on what happens in the area as a whole.

—We have great tasks that we must achieve together. The most difficult is to settle the obdurate problems left over from the Second World War, the problems between East and West. We shall make little progress toward a lasting settlement of these problems without common purpose and common action.

---

[1] Excerpts from a statement prepared for delivery before the Senate Committee on Foreign Relations on June 30, 1966. Mr. Ball's statement was entered into the committee's record but was not read during the hearing, which was devoted to questions and answers. Printed in the *Department of State Bulletin*, July 25, 1966, pp. 143-48.

—But our common responsibilities extend far beyond our own boundaries, for the Atlantic nations have a common duty also to assist the peoples of the developing areas toward peace and progress.

We should, therefore, answer the first question in the affirmative. Recent changes have not diminished but expanded our common interests. In the light of these changes, how can we best fulfill those interests, not merely today but tomorrow?

Progress Toward European Unity

The answer, it seems to me, is that we must first form a clear concept of relationships among Atlantic nations and stick to it. Only in this way can we build an enduring structure. For the broad lines of that structure we should consult both history and common sense.

The first lesson of history is clear. The world should never again have to live with the dangers of a Europe in which each individual nation-state seeks to advance its own interests at the expense of its neighbors or to gain ascendancy over its neighbors by shifting coalitions or balance-of-power politics. For 300 years, such a system produced one bloody and senseless war after another. To return to a Europe of 1914 or 1939 would be folly beyond belief.

Our European friends have fully recognized this. One of the most hopeful developments of the postwar world has been their determination to substitute unity for national rivalry and to break forever with the pattern of the past.

They have expressed this determination by action. Through the Treaty of Rome, six European nations have established common institutions which are applying common principles and practices to serve a common economic purpose. In a few brief years the European Economic Community has made remarkable strides toward the integration of the separate economies of the member nations. Not only has it helped to create a prosperous Europe and to raise the standard of living of the European peoples to unprecedented heights, but that prosperity has reinforced the well-being of the whole Atlantic world.

Yet the building of a stable Europe will require something more than economic integration. It can be achieved only by progress toward political unity. For, until the Western European peoples can be drawn together on a basis of equality and under common rules and institutions, there can be no assurance that the nationalistic quarrels of the past will be permanently put aside.

Serious obstacles, of course, now block progress toward political unity in Europe. But in a great affair such as this it is a grave mistake to judge the future on the basis of day-to-day events. For political unity responds to a compelling logic that, in the longer term, can hardly be avoided. In Western Europe there are more than a quarter of a billion of the most highly educated, trained, skilled people in the world. It is their tradition to play a significant role in world affairs. But today they are facing the hard fact that, in spite of their intellectual and material resources, they will not again play such a role unless they organize their affairs to accord with the needs of the modern age.

For the postwar world has been marked by a new and decisive political reality: the predominance of two nations, the United States and the Soviet Union. Each is organized on a continent-wide basis; each commands vast resources of men and material equal to, or surpassing, the combined resources of all the Western European nations. The emergence of these two powers reflects the needs and consequences of an age of technology. And it has transformed the whole structure of world politics. European states which a quarter of a century ago occupied the center of the stage now find themselves only medium powers, with a limited capacity to influence world events.

I do not think that the European peoples will be content for very long to stand aside from a major participation in world affairs. Yet, so long as Europe remains in its present form, their participation will be severely limited. If Europeans are to play a role worthy of their resources and their abilities, it is clear what they must do. They must build their political arrangements on a scale commensurate with the requirements of the modern world.

Building an Atlantic Partnership

This question of size has a special significance in our transatlantic relations.

During the past few years some have suggested that the proper policy was to forget European unity and try to move directly to some form of Atlantic political structure. This proposal, it seems to me, creates a false choice between the steps toward unity in Europe and the establishment of a closer partnership across the ocean. There is no contradiction between these ideas; they go hand in hand. A healthy relationship between Europe and America can be fully established only when the principle of equality is solidly grounded in the facts of relative power.

For, so long as there remains the great disparity in size and resources between the United States and the nations of Europe acting individually, there will be awkwardness in any Atlantic arrangement. The Europeans will be concerned by what some regard as the undue weight of American influence in our common counsels. Some European industrialists will be concerned by fear of the disproportionate power of American enterprises.

Something can be done to meet these concerns even within the present structure. Our Government can make a greater effort to improve consultation, although our initiatives in that direction have not met much response. But, in the long pull, equality between Western Europe and America is not something that the United States can grant or create merely by avoiding unilateral actions. It springs from the fact that we Americans can act through a single set of institutions and can thus apply the full resources of our continent to a single purpose, while the Europeans cannot. For they are not yet organized, as President Kennedy said, to speak with one voice and act with one will.

The efforts to build the basis of Atlantic partnership cannot, of course, await the emergence of a united Europe—and they need not. There is much that we can and should do. For some years, in OECD[2] and NATO, the Atlantic nations have been seeking to perfect instruments for common action for defense, economic policies, and foreign policy, and we should get on with this work. But we should have no illusions as to the limits of possible progress. So long as Europe remains disunited the essential goal of equality will be more a matter of manners than reality.

Achieving Permanent East-West Settlement

European unity and Atlantic partnership have a meaning beyond the stability of the West. They are essential for the achievement of a

---

[2] Organization for Economic Cooperation and Development. OECD was established in 1960 and is composed of the United States, Canada, Japan, and all European countries with foreign aid programs. (Editor's note)

secure settlement of the great unfinished business left over from the war. This point cannot be too strongly emphasized. A permanent East-West settlement will not be achieved by fragmenting Europe or by loosening the institutional bonds that tie the West together but only if the Western Powers, acting from a base of unity, bring about a situation in which a settlement is possible.

The obvious preconditions to a settlement are changes in the attitude of the Soviet Government. Such changes as have already occurred have not come through the independent action of individual Western states. They have occurred in part because of internal shifts and movements within the Soviet system. But equally as important, they have occurred because the Western Powers, acting together, have created conditions to which the Soviet Union has had to adjust.

The common action of the West has blunted Soviet hopes for expansion.

The stability and prosperity that followed economic integration in Western Europe have created new aspirations and have stimulated new thinking in Eastern Europe.

By sublimating nationalistic ambitions, Western cohesion has dampened traditional fears among the Eastern European peoples.

In short, Western unity does not conflict with the serious pursuit of a East-West settlement, it opens the only effective route to it.

We should not, of course, seek any settlement as an end in itself. What we must achieve is a settlement embodying condition that will assure stability and lasting peace for all of Europe, a settlement that will endure. This means that it must be free from built-in stresses and tensions. The essential condition of such a settlement is that it must be fair to all. It must embody the same basic principle that is essential to enduring relations within the West—the principle of equality.

This point is central. No secure settlement of Europe can leave the German people divided. Nor can a lasting settlement place the German people under permanent discrimination. This was tried before, and, as we all know, it did not work. We must aim for something better and not for improvisations that are inherently unstable.

U.S. Has a Constructive Role To Play

In working toward a lasting settlement, a sense of both security and unity in the West is needed to set in motion the process of ending the partition of Europe.

We have a constructive role to play in that undertaking. Our purpose is to create conditions that will make it possible for Europe to be reunited, with neither the United States nor the Soviet Union seeing in that happy event any threat to themselves.

That is why the United States is committed to a policy of peaceful and intimate engagement toward the countries of Eastern Europe and the Soviet Union. Ours is not an effort to subvert their governments nor to make those states hostile to the Soviet Union or to each other. No one would benefit from an Eastern Europe that is again balkanized. We wish to build bridges to the East so that the Soviet Union and the Eastern European states can begin to see a genuine interest for themselves in moving toward ending the partition of Europe and Germany.

All of us—Americans, Russians, Europeans—can benefit from drawing closer together. In that way we can reduce the risks of war, minimize the bitter legacies of national conflicts, and increase the tangible fruits of economic cooperation so that the wealth and the talent which Europe, the United States, and the Soviet Union have in such abundance can serve the cause of humanity. What we thus desire for Europe, we firmly believe, is what most Europeans want, and that is why America remains so relevant to Europe's future.

This kind of peace and stability in Europe will not be achieved by any sudden or dramatic gesture. The difficulties are many and the obstacles great. The road to the eventual ending of the partition of Europe and of Germany will be long. But a start has been made.

There are already many contacts between East and West. These must be expanded. That is why the President has asked the Congress for authority to extend most-favored-nation privileges to Eastern European states.[3] Cultural contacts must also grow, and it may be pertinent to note that it was American foundations that took the first major initiative in developing such East-West cultural exchanges.

It is also important to expand multilateral ties. Existing multilateral institutions, such as OECD, can and doubtless will respond to these emerging opportunities.

If we can help in all these ways to narrow the existing differences in European standards of living, to develop East-West communications systems, and to facilitate trade, we can create some of the preconditions for solving basic political and security issues. The

---

[3] For background and text of the proposed East-West Trade Relations Act of 1966, see *Bulletin*, May 30, 1966, p. 838.

United States is prepared to share in this effort, for we believe that it represents a serious and a constructive way of working to end the partition of Europe.

We believe that just as peace and stability in Western Europe have been advanced by reconciliation between the Germans and their Western neighbors, so too in the East a reconciliation between the German people and particularly the Poles, the Czechs, and the Russians is in the interest of all of us. The German Federal Republic recently reaffirmed its desire to develop friendly relations with the East, and the United States will do everything it can to promote that desirable end. The continuance of old hatreds, however real and bitter may be their causes, is not in the interest of Europe, and in the nuclear age they are dangerous to all of us.

These, then, are the general principles that define our policy. Changed conditions have not impaired their basic validity. Yet this does not mean that their application need not be reexamined in the light of changing conditions or that all of the institutional arrangements established since the war are perfect or may not need to be adapted.

Certainly, some changes in the structure of the North Atlantic Treaty Organization will be required as a result of the recent actions of the French Government. The alliance has weathered those actions and stayed remarkably well on course.

Our first common task was to maintain a solid defense and an effective deterrent. We made good progress toward this end at the recent Brussels meeting.[4] The 14 members other than France agreed to relocate the North Atlantic Organization military headquarters and will probably move in a few months to relocate the North Atlantic Council. They laid the basis for negotiation with France about French forces in Germany.

But defense and deterrence are not NATO's sole objects. It must also provide the unity of purpose that will facilitate a lasting settlement between East and West.

This does not mean, of course, that we should think of NATO as a negotiating instrument. But it can help to insure that individual Western nations, if dealing with the East, will work toward a common purpose rather than toward competing national advantage. Only on this basis will there be any chance of success.

---

4 For background, see *ibid.*, June 27, 1966, p. 1001.

Elements of U.S. Policy Toward Europe

I have tried in this brief statement to outline the main elements of United States policy toward Europe. Those elements briefly are three in number:

First, to encourage the nations of Western Europe to submerge their old national rivalries in the achievement of a new political unity based on principles of equality;

Second, at the same time to continue to build the institutional arrangements that can result in a more effective partnership between the United States and a Europe moving toward unity; and

Third, to continue by every means available to create the conditions that will make possible a secure and lasting settlement of the division of Europe.

These principles form a broad framework for United States policy. Obviously, no one of them can be realized by U.S. efforts alone. We cannot, solely by American efforts, bring about the unification of Western Europe; that is a task primarily for Europeans.

We cannot by ourselves create an effective working relation with the Western European peoples; it takes more than one to make a partnership.

Finally, we cannot alone bring about a settlement of the fundamental issue of a divided Europe; that will come to pass only when the conditions are created that will influence the Soviet Union to take the necessary decisions to make that possible.

But we can, by a loyal adherence to these principles, prevent their frustration and encourage their achievement. For we have a great deal running for us: good sense, logic, the lessons of history, and the desire of peoples to contribute their full share to a peaceful world.

* * *

The United States, France, and NATO: A Comparison of Two Approaches

by David H. Popper

Director, Office of Atlantic Political and Military Affairs[1]

* * *

In the past, United States relations with the French have sometimes been calm and sometimes delicate, but they have almost never been dull. France was our first ally. Over almost 200 years we have had numerous altercations, some quite serious; and we have had our common ventures, in war and in peace. It has been a long, if occasionally troubled, friendship.

Today—let us admit it—there are elements in the international scene which, if not carefully watched, could jeopardize our good relations. We are determined not to have this happen. We intend to work our way through our difficulties by careful analysis and thorough discussion of our common problems, always with due regard for the interests of other states. These interests are important, and they are closely affected by our actions vis-a-vis the French.

France and the United States seldom stand alone on opposite sides of an issue. Clustered in their respective neighborhoods—perhaps more often in ours than in theirs, for the range of problems on our agenda today—are our NATO partners and other states.

The United States and France, that is to say, are not ranged against each other in a great, bipolar confrontation. Thus the issues we shall discuss are not in the same class as those which divide us from the Russians or the Chinese Communists. We are not talking about absolutist, ideological extremes. France is and will remain a part of

---

1 Excerpts from an address made at the University of Utah, Salt Lake City, Utah, on January 21, 1965. Printed in the *Department of State Bulletin*, February 8, 1965, pp. 180-87.

the free world. As long as French governmental institutions are stable—and no one alive can remember when they have been more stable than they are today—the French will not embrace Communist doctrine. No one is more stanch than President de Gaulle in his opposition to Communist world domination. In the last great test of Soviet adventurism—the Cuban missile crisis of October 1962—the French stood as firmly at the side of the United States as any country.

France, a Key Factor in Europe

* * *

Like other Europeans, the French have been deeply scarred by the ravages of 20th-century conflict in Europe. In 1918 they were among the victors, but their manhood and their substance were bled white. In 1940 they suffered a cataclysmic defeat. Recovering sturdily from that setback, they were plunged into frustrating colonial wars in Southeast Asia and in Algeria. During all this period their actions were hampered by the governmental structure of the Third and Fourth Republics. This saddled the French with a system of weak and short-lived executives—a system tolerated in the interest of preserving a more secure democracy. In the end, the system proved inadequate to meet the harsh tests of the times.

It is not surprising, then—it is only natural—that this able, proud, energetic, and logical French populace should rally round the great historical figure who led their resistance in war and restored their status in peace. And he has not disappointed them. He liquidated the French colonial problem; restored the morale, the effectiveness, the loyalty, and the respectability of the French armed forces; presided over a great national economic and financial revival; brought to fruition a Franco-German reconciliation which should cement the peace in Western Europe; and gave France a vigorous and important role in the leadership of the West. It is a supremely impressive catalog of accomplishment, one which secures President de Gaulle's place in the firmament of French history.

France's friends in NATO—not least, the United States—can only rejoice in this modern French renaissance. We never forget that France is a key factor in Europe. Its size, its human and material strength, its resources, its geographical position make it a virtually indispensable element of any Western European or Atlantic area association. It would be very difficult even to think of NATO or an integrated Europe without it. Stability and strength in France are a matter of primary importance to us.

NATO at a Crossroads

We are examining the French and American attitudes toward a North Atlantic world which stands at a crossroads. NATO, the institutional embodiment of that world, is thought by some to be in dire straits; by others, more realistically we believe, to be in a phase of significant change.

NATO was organized in 1949 not only for the common defense against an imminent danger of Communist aggression, but also, as the North Atlantic Treaty states, to preserve the freedom and civilization of its members and to promote stability and well-being in the North Atlantic area. The problem of defense it has tackled directly, and with remarkable success. NATO nuclear deterrence, almost completely provided by the United States, has held in check any Communist aggressive tendencies; and NATO's powerful general-purpose forces, including large American contingents, have curbed any desires there might have been for military adventures along NATO frontiers. No NATO territory has been lost. The NATO countries feel more secure today than ever before. The very credibility of a large-scale war in Europe has dwindled.

Behind this shield, free Europe, originally assisted by Marshall Plan aid, has provided a dazzling display of the recuperative powers, the energy, and the skill of its people. From an exhausted and depleted subcontinent with highly uncertain political and economic prospects, it has been transformed into a stable, dynamic, and highly prosperous area. And as the Soviet bloc loses its monolithic unity and is subjected to the mellowing influences of a more sophisticated and stable society, the sense of imminent military and social peril that existed in 1949 has all but vanished.

But people are prone to forget that only the maintenance of NATO strength can insure its members against a recurrence of cold-war threats. NATO is not immune from the time-honored phenomenon which afflicts all alliances—that, while they hang together in times of crisis, they tend to fall apart in fair weather. In this sense, NATO could become a victim of its own success.

Not that NATO is on the point of disintegration. Responsible leaders in NATO countries are quite aware that the basic circumstance which brought it into being—the Communist threat to the free world—continues to exist. Communist methods have changed but not Communist objectives. There was a Berlin crisis in 1961 and a Cuban crisis in 1962. There could be another crisis in 1965 or in subsequent years.

Every NATO government recognizes that its security still rests on the Atlantic alliance. This applies not only to Europe, including the French, but equally to the United States. Our postwar policy has been predicated on the recognition that a strong and free Europe is essential to our own safety. That is why we maintain close to 400,000 men in and around Europe and why we are in fact the strongest military power in Europe today.

Nevertheless, changing circumstances in both the North Atlantic and the Communist worlds do have an impact on NATO itself. The 15 NATO nations can if they wish exploit the growth potential which lies in the alliance and can adapt it to the requirements of the Atlantic partnership of the future. Or they can, though we would hope they would not, take a static view toward NATO. In this case its utility and its relevance to changing conditions would gradually decline and its future might be one of diminishing importance.

We are approaching the time when some great decisions will need to be made in this area. The North Atlantic Treaty has no terminal date; it continues in effect indefinitely. But in 1969, 20 years after the treaty was signed, any member may denounce it and withdraw from NATO 1 year thereafter. The remaining members would of course continue to be bound by the treaty unless they followed suit.

One might conclude from French official statements that they might conceivably withdraw, or that they would at least call for a thorough review of the NATO system, as they are quite entitled to do under the terms of the treaty. Whether they would actually do so is in the realm of conjecture. Unfortunately, while the French have made clear their dissatisfaction with certain aspects of the system, they have not yet furnished a bill of particulars indicating the specific changes they might desire to make.

The French decision in this matter will be linked with the development of French policy toward the organization of Europe. For a primary question for any emerging European association of nations must be its relationship to the United States.

France's Stress on Nationalism

To survey the French approach toward Atlantic area problems in relation to our own, let me make a few points as to the attitudes of the two countries and discuss them in some detail.

The first point is that, in comparison with its principal allies, France has tended in recent years to lay increasing stress on nationalism and less on interdependence. We are talking here, of course, in relative terms. All countries are to some degree interdependent in the close-knit world of today; none would willingly submerge its national identity or fundamental purposes.

Yet France under De Gaulle makes no secret of its strongly nationalist orientation. Whether in NATO or in the area of European union, the French are cool to proposals involving new steps toward integration or suggestions of broader supranational authority.

As we shall note, they seem to want to reverse the progress so far made in NATO toward military integration. It is also true that they have recognized that their interests are advanced by fulfillment of the provisions of the 1957 Treaty of Rome, through the mechanism of the European Economic Community—provisions which will produce an economically integrated Europe of the Six when they have been fully applied. These were negotiated before President de Gaulle returned to power. But as regards political integration, other Europeans complain of French unwillingness to move forward. A French veto in 1963 cut short efforts to bring Britain into the EEC. And French indifference seems to becloud the prospects for steps toward further integration which, in varying ways, are advocated by the Germans, Italians, Belgians, and Dutch.

I mention these matters with some diffidence, for it is not for Americans, even by implication, to seek to tell Europeans of any nationality how to manage their own affairs. We do not, however, conceal our conviction that the influence of free Europe in a world dominated by aggregations of great power will depend on closer integration in Europe, rather than on the jealous safeguard of every exclusive national prerogative on the part of any state. And we have a direct stake in the decisions which Europeans may make in this regard. For an Atlantic partnership is certain to be more soundly based if it rests on a footing of dealings between an American and a European unit of comparable importance, than if—as is the case today—there is no effective voice to speak for Europe.

The President put the case most succinctly in his address at George-town University on December 3—an address which charts America's course in the Atlantic community during the years ahead:[2]

> The United States [he declared] has no policy *for* the people of Europe, but we do have a policy *toward* the people of Europe. . . .
>
> First, we must all seek to assist in increasing the unity of Europe as a key to Western strength and a barrier to resurgent and erosive nation-alism.
>
> Second, we must all work to multiply in number and intimacy the ties between North America and Europe. For we shape an Atlantic civilization with an Atlantic destiny.

Recent French official statements would lead one to doubt that the French Government would address the problem from a similar stand-point. When French officials refer to unity in Europe, they stress the independence of Europe, in military and in other matters, rather than the interdependence of Atlantic welfare and defense. From this stand-point what seems to us to be realistic cooperation can be represented as domination from outside and as somehow denaturing the Europe-an ideal. Other NATO governments have not embraced this thesis.

Question of Military Integration

I turn now to my second point with respect to French views. It can be stated as follows: There are clear indications that the French, far more than any other NATO member, wish to modify the existing NATO system so as to move it in the direction of the classical-type alliance of an earlier period.

A bit of background is perhaps necessary to understand what is involved here. Very properly, the French make a sharp distinction between the Western alliance and the organizational structure of NATO. The North Atlantic Treaty, as negotiated in 1949, is a general agreement for the collective defense of its signatories within a prescribed area, in accordance with provisions of the United Nations Charter. It mentions a permanent council, but apart from that it is silent as to the way in which the parties should organize themselves to carry out the defensive purposes of the treaty.

---

2 For text, see *Ibid.*, December 21, 1964, p. 866.

The NATO political and military structure we have today was created step by step by the members of the organization, including the French. While the treaty itself is an expression of the underlying unity of its members, its effective organizational structure is what sets the alliance apart from the generality of defense pacts.

The essence of that structure is a carefully limited, but nonetheless significant, degree of military integration which welds the NATO armed forces into a coordinated, powerful fighting unit for use in the event of attack on NATO territory. For this purpose an international command system has been created. SHAPE [Supreme Headquarters Allied Powers Europe], near Paris, and SACLANT [Supreme Allied Command Atlantic] headquarters, in Norfolk, both under commanders of American nationality, consist of integrated international staffs.

The officers assigned to these commands are there as NATO officers, not as national officers. They make war plans on behalf of the alliance and set standards on behalf of the alliance. Through the system of commitment of national forces to NATO, they can within broad limits count on the use of known forces to repel attack. The force goals projected by NATO are models influencing the composition and development of the forces of the NATO nations.

The complex of NATO forces is supported by an internationally financed and controlled system of infrastructure facilities, such as airfields, depots, pipelines, and military communications, constructed and maintained through ongoing NATO programs. NATO encourages the standardization of equipment in the forces of the alliance, as well as the joint production of many military items, and forces committed to NATO engage periodically in NATO maneuvers. To sum up, the military success of NATO is in no small part due to the assurance that common action by known forces under integrated command will be forthcoming in the event of attack on NATO territory.

* * *

The Nuclear Problem

The issue of military integration is posed most sharply in the nuclear area. And here I come to my third point of contrast in French and American views. It is as follows: The French regard a national nuclear force as a requirement for great-power status; they have every intention of building it into a significant national force; and they are in principle unsympathetic to proposals for integrated nuclear forces in NATO. For our part, we recognize that the French have attained a military nuclear capability; we continue to hope that it may be possible to head off the creation of additional national nuclear forces; and we sense and sympathize with the desire of many of our NATO allies for a greater share in the alliance organization for nuclear defense.

It is worth noting that the decision to build a French nuclear force goes back to the Fourth Republic, prior to President de Gaulle's return to the French political scene. Thus, successive French administrations have accepted the heavy costs of developing a national nuclear establishment—costs in money and resources—which might otherwise be devoted to other military or social purposes. As the French plans move ahead in the years to come, the French envisage the creation of a *force de frappe* which, though small by American standards, will nonetheless have considerable striking power.

Our concern with the creation of new national nuclear forces lies in the fact that their very existence tends to encourage other nations to acquire their own nuclear weapons, for power and status purposes. One hesitates to contemplate the kind of tensions that would exist if all the nations capable of manufacturing such weapons were to do so. Quite apart from the costs involved, the danger of triggering off a destructive nuclear conflict through miscalculation, accident, or irresponsible decision would increase in geometric proportion as the number of separate forces mounted. And the danger that such a conflict would almost immediately draw in others, raising the destruction to unimaginable proportions, would grow as well.

These are the reasons for our desire to avoid the proliferation of such weapons. They explain our efforts, at the United Nations and elsewhere, to obtain satisfactory assurances against putting nuclear weapons under the national control of still other countries.

* * *

To round out the picture, it must be said that we regret the failure of the French to become a party to the limited nuclear test ban treaty, understandable as that may be in terms of the French nuclear testing program. And we also regret the refusal of the French to occupy their seat at the Eighteen-Nation Disarmament Committee in Geneva—the major forum for the East-West consideration of disarmament problems.

Other Divergencies

I have attempted to outline some of the divergencies between the American and the French approaches to the problems of the Atlantic world. Naturally enough, our policies are also, to some extent, divergent in other areas.

For example, while there are strong tendencies in the West toward bridge building with Eastern Europe, it is the French who are most optimistic as to an eventual association of all of Europe—still unspecific in form—extending from the Atlantic to the Urals. While we too are aware of difficulties standing in the way of German reunification, it was France which first stressed the need to reach agreement on German frontiers. While some NATO nations established diplomatic relations with Communist China at an early stage, France is the only one to have moved to recognition in recent years. The French favor a conference now to end the war in South Viet-Nam and to settle its future. And, like the Communist bloc in the United Nations, the French have refused to pay their share of peacekeeping costs in the Congo and thus risk the loss of their vote in the United Nations General Assembly.

I am not tonight arguing the merits of these positions. The point I would make is that they all have some bearing on the vigor of the Atlantic relationship. For that relationship is political as well as military. No one would argue for strict uniformity in the foreign policies of the NATO allies. The responsibilities of each of them vary so widely that that would be impracticable.

* * *

Bilateral Relations

There remains the problem of bilateral relations between the United States and France. Clearly, in the present atmosphere, there are potential sources of Franco-American friction which will require careful handling if good relations between the two Governments are to be preserved.

A case in point is the recent anxiety in France over large-scale investment by great American corporations in some important sectors of the French economy. This is a sensitive topic, with serious political and economic overtones. It is not, of course, a problem entirely limited to France: American business has been quick to recognize the opportunities provided by production inside the other Common Market countries, as well as elsewhere in Europe. It is anything but a simple problem. Before reaching conclusions about it, one would need to answer a number of important questions. For example, how much of an impact has American investment made on the local economy, and what is the nature of that impact? Has American business observed satisfactory standards of conduct in the local environment? Is American investment a consequence of stringency in European capital markets, and are there alternative sources of needed capital? What is the bearing of American investment on cartel and monopoly policies within the EEC? On the balance of payments problem? Does American entry bring with it advanced technology or stimulate research and development?

Obviously, questions such as these can be answered only on the basis of expert study. The issues involved need dispassionate consideration if they are to be settled in the mutual interest of the parties. Whatever the methods used, they must be designed to produce light rather than heat, agreement rather than irritation.

Indeed, this is the spirit in which we would hope to cope with all of our problems with the French Government. We want no controversy with our oldest ally. We have made it clear that we will support no enterprise directed against France; that we will conclude no agreement in the NATO context that is not open to French adherence; and that there will be a full exchange of views with the French before any such agreements are concluded.

We are convinced that in this friendly spirit solutions can be found for our current perplexities in the Atlantic area. We think the historic forces and the concrete interests impelling Europe toward greater internal cohesion and toward closer transatlantic relations will not in the long run be denied. And we shall continue to bend our efforts toward these ends.

11

Eastern Europe

There are seven nations in the geographical area of Eastern Europe: Bulgaria, Czechoslovakia, Democratic Republic of Germany, Hungary, Poland, Rumania, and the Soviet Union. Two other countries in Southern Europe—Yugoslavia and Albania—have been included in the past, but usually are omitted for ideological and geographical reasons. The U.S. has diplomatic relations with six of the seven; the Democratic Republic of Germany is the only nation that the American government does not recognize. American diplomatic relations have improved with all these countries in recent years; they are best with Yugoslavia and worst with Albania.

Soviet policy after the war

The Iron Curtain fell where the Soviet Army camped. With the exception of Germany, where the Western armies retreated to agreed-on boundaries of occupation zones, the Red army advanced no further than where the fighting stopped. In Yugoslavia and Albania, indigenous Communist forces (led by Tito and Hoxha) defeated the German army; an important fact to keep in mind when analyzing the Yugoslav defection in 1948 and the Soviet-Albanian rift in 1960. Hence, the Russians occupied Eastern Europe by defeating Nazi armies, not the forces of independent states. This point has sometimes been lost in the rhetoric of the Cold War. One leader who foresaw the results of Russian liberation of Eastern Europe was Winston Churchill, who advocated that the allied thrust following the Italian campaign be in Southern, and not Western, Europe. Roosevelt ignored his advice because of intelligence estimates that a southern front would involve more allied casualties than a western front. Also, Stalin twice had been promised a second front in the west, a promise broken twice by the North African and Italian campaigns.

Stalin's attitude after the war was one of "to the victor belongs the spoils." He did not desire an Italian occupation zone even though Italy was a major axis power. The Russian attitude was reinforced by the fact that four of the six East European nations were belligerents against the Soviet Union. Rumania, Bulgaria, Hungary, and of course, East Germany officially declared war on the U.S.S.R. Hence, in 1956, Western concern focused on Poland and Czechoslovakia.

The coup of February 1948 ended the embryonic democratic government that had developed in Czechoslovakia. In Poland, the Western-Soviet debate centered around a memorandum of agreement written during the Yalta Conference in which Stalin pledged to "form interim governmental authorities broadly representative of all democratic elements in the population" in the East European countries, and to hold "free elections" for the "earliest possible establishment . . . of governments responsive to the will of the people." Two problems of semantics were involved in the memorandum: what constituted "democratic elements" and "free elections"? To Stalin, nondemocratic parties were fascist groups, a position that Churchill and Roosevelt agreed to; however, to the Russians most non-Communists were by definition "fascist." "Democratic elections" were interpreted by Stalin as the type of system in force in the Soviet Union rather than that of the Western democracies. The Americans thought that the Polish government-in-exile in London, which had been recognized as the legitimate representative by most Western states, would be part of the "interim government." Stalin refused: he did not want an anti-Communist, pro-Western government in Poland straddling his lines of communication and logistical support to occupied Germany. Nor did he want a strong, independent Poland as a neighbor.

Thus, by February 1948 the Soviet Union solidified its position in Eastern Europe. To maintain its control over the area, the U.S.S.R. developed three instruments of policy. First, in 1947 the Soviet Union established the Communist Information Bureau, or Cominform, to guide the satellite governments in making decisions on domestic and foreign policy issues. Second, the Council for Mutual Economic Assistance, or COMECON, was born in January 1949 in response to the Marshall Plan. The Soviet government did not permit the East European states to accept Marshall Plan aid; therefore, COMECON was intended to compensate for the loss of American capital. Third, a military alliance, the Warsaw Pact, was signed in May 1955. The Warsaw Pact was not in response to the North Atlantic Treaty, which dates from 1949, but to West Germany's rearmament and induction into NATO. In general, these three instruments of political, economic, and military control have not fared well in the post-war period.

If the Czechoslovakian coup of 1948 marked the beginning of the united Soviet bloc, then it was short-lived, for the Yugoslav defection occurred in June 1948. Despite this early crack in the seemingly monolithic structure of the Soviet bloc, U.S. decision-makers tended to underestimate the power of nationalism in East European nations.

Contemporary American policy

As often happens in politics—domestic and foreign—presidential administrations are assigned catch words to describe their policy orientation. U.S. relations with Eastern Europe are no exception. The Truman Administration policy is summarized by the word "containment," which can be defined as the selective use of power to dissuade the U.S.S.R. from acts that threaten the American national interest. Not all Russian diplomatic behavior would be discouraged, only that which tended toward recklessness and instability. This policy of selective use of power meant that the U.S. could refuse to respond to Soviet actions that American decision-makers considered to be non-threatening, or the U.S. could respond with only an increment of its power. President Johnson described the Berlin airlift in 1948-49 as an "act of measured firmness," because it was a less-than-total response to a Russian provocation. Containment was not intended to deny the U.S.S.R. a place in the international system. The Soviet Union should be "taught" or "conditioned" to live in the international system by rewarding constructive behavioral patterns and discouraging acts that were considered inimical by American policy-makers.

The Eisenhower Administration began by talking about "liberation" or "roll back." Containment, the Republicans thought, was too negative. Despite opportunities to "roll back" the Iron Curtain, especially in the 1956 Hungarian revolution, the Eisenhower Administration did nothing, conceding that the East European area was within the Russian sphere of influence. However, the East European states, while forsaken, were not forgotten: in 1959, the third week in July was set aside as "Captive Nations Week" by the Eisenhower Administration.

"Gradualism" was the term ascribed to the Kennedy Administration and "bridge building" to President Johnson. Both connoted the same meaning. Kennedy invited a re-examination of "our attitude toward the Cold War" in his June 1963 address at the American University. Johnson's October 7, 1966, statement illustrated the extent to which this re-examination has progressed. He declared that one goal of U.S. policy was to unite all of Europe, both East and West. This objective could be obtained only with Russian consent; thus, the concept of "roll back" was buried officially. He offered to substitute "peaceful engagement" for "peaceful co-existence" as a basis for East European-American relations.

East-West Trade

Trade with East European states is not prohibited, although goods determined to be strategic by a NATO committee are excluded from economic exchange. U.S. trade with this area is small, but growing as Table 1 shows.

TABLE 1

U.S. Trade With Eastern Europe

Millions of dollars

	1965	1966
Exports	140	198
Imports	138	178
Total	278	376

Source: "East-West Trade," *Department of State Bulletin,* June 12, 1967.

The U.S. possesses a favorable balance of trade with Eastern Europe, a factor which helps the American balance of payments problems. While the increase in trade is impressive, the U.S. share of total economic exchange between East Europe and the West is not. The

Federal Republic of Germany traded more than $2 billion; the United Kingdom about $1 billion; and Japan, France, and Italy between $600 million and $1 billion. Compared with these figures, $375 million for the U.S., the largest exporter in the world, is very small. Mr. Solomon presents the government's case for expanding trade with Eastern Europe.

Conclusion

The two policy statements below capture the contemporary attitudes of U.S. foreign policy toward the U.S.S.R. and her allies—which have been perceived as the primary threat since 1946. While these statements describe a continuing concern for Russian expansion, they also expressed the confidence that the U.S. can live in peace with another superstate, the Soviet Union.

Making Europe Whole: An Unfinished Task

Address by President Johnson[1]

* * *

Today two anniversaries especially remind us of the interdependence of Europe and America.

—On September 30, seventeen years ago, the Berlin airlift ended.

—On October 7, three years ago, the nuclear test ban treaty was ratified.

There is a healthy balance here. It is no accident. It reflects the balance the Atlantic allies have tried to maintain between strength and conciliation, between firmness and flexibility, between resolution and hope.

The Berlin airlift was an act of measured firmness. Without that firmness, the Marshall Plan and the recovery of Western Europe would have been impossible.

That hopeful and progressive achievement, the European Economic Community, could never have been born.

The winds of change which are blowing in Eastern Europe would not be felt today.

All these are the fruits of our determination.

The test ban treaty is the fruit of our hope. With more than 100 other signers we have committed ourselves to advance from deterrence through terror toward a more cooperative international order. We must go forward to banish all nuclear weapons—and war itself.

A just peace remains our goal. But we know that the world is changing. Our policy must reflect the reality of today—not yesterday.

1 Excerpts from an address before the National Conference of Editorial Writers at New York, N.Y., October 7, 1966. Printed in the *Department of State Bulletin*, October 24, 1967, pp. 622-25.

In every part of the world, new forces are at the gates: new countries, new aspirations; new men. In this spirit, let us look ahead to the tasks that confront the Atlantic nations.

Europe has been at peace since 1945. But it is a restless peace—shadowed by the threat of violence.

Europe is partitioned. An unnatural line runs through the heart of a great and proud nation. History warns us that until this harsh division has been resolved, peace in Europe will not be secure.

We must turn to one of the great unfinished tasks of our generation: making Europe whole.

Our purpose is not to overturn other governments, but to help the people of Europe to achieve:

—a continent in which the peoples of Eastern and Western Europe work together for the common good;

—a continent in which alliances do not confront each other in bitter hostility, but provide a framework in which West and East can act together to assure the security of all.

In a restored Europe, Germany can and will be united.

This remains a vital purpose of American policy. It can only be accomplished through a growing reconciliation. There is no shortcut.

We must move ahead on three fronts:

—First, to modernize NATO and strengthen other Atlantic institutions.

—Second, to further the integration of the Western European community.

—Third, to quicken progress in East-West relations.

Let me speak to each in turn.

Vitality of the Atlantic Alliance

I. Our first concern is to keep NATO strong and abreast of the times.

The Atlantic alliance has proved its vitality. Together, we have faced the threats to peace which have confronted us—and we shall meet those which may confront us in the future.

Let no one doubt the American commitment. We shall not unlearn the lesson of the thirties, when isolation and withdrawal were our share in the common disaster.

We are committed, and will remain firm.

But the Atlantic alliance is a living organism. It must adapt to changing conditions.

Much is already being done to modernize its structures:

—We are streamlining NATO command arrangements;

—We are moving to establish a permanent nuclear planning committee;

—We are increasing the speed and certainty of supply across the Atlantic.

However, we must do more.

The alliance must become a forum for increasingly close consultations. These should cover the full range of joint concerns—from East-West relations to crisis management.

The Atlantic alliance is the central instrument of the Atlantic community. But it is not the only one. Through other institutions the nations of the Atlantic are hard at work on constructive enterprise.

In the Kennedy Round, we are negotiating with the other Free World Nations to reduce tariffs everywhere. Our goal is to free the trade of the world from arbitrary and artificial constraints.

We are also engaged on the problem of international monetary reform.

We are exploring how best to develop science and technology as a common resource. Recently the Italian Government has suggested an approach to narrowing the gap in technology between the United States and Western Europe. That proposal deserves careful study. The United States is ready to cooperate with the European nations on all aspects of this problem.

Last, and perhaps most important, we are working together to accelerate the growth of the developing nations. It is our common business to help the millions in these nations improve their standards of life. The rich nations cannot live as an island of plenty in a sea of poverty.

Thus, while the institutions of the Atlantic community are growing, so are the tasks which face us.

Pursuit of Further Unity in the West

II. Second among our tasks is the vigorous pursuit of further unity in the West.

To pursue that unity is neither to postpone nor neglect the search for peace. There are good reasons for this:

—A united Western Europe can be our equal partner in helping to build a peaceful and just world order;

—A united Western Europe can move more confidently in peaceful initiatives toward the East;

—Unity can provide a framework within which a unified Germany could be a full partner without arousing ancient fears.

We look forward to the expansion and further strengthening of the European community. The obstacles are great. But perseverance has already reaped larger rewards than any of us dared hope 20 years ago.

The outlines of the new Europe are clearly discernible. It is a stronger, increasingly united but open Europe—with Great Britain a part of it—and with close ties to America.

Improving the East-West Environment

III. One great goal of a united West is to heal the wound in Europe which now cuts East from West and brother from brother.

That division must be healed peacefully. It must be healed with the consent of Eastern European countries and the Soviet Union. This will happen only as East and West succeed in building a surer foundation of mutual trust.

Nothing is more important for peace. We must improve the East-West environment in order to achieve the unification of Germany in the context of a larger peaceful and prosperous Europe.

Our task is to achieve a reconciliation with the East—a shift from the narrow concept of coexistence to the broader vision of peaceful engagement.

Americans are prepared to do their part. Under the last four Presidents, our policy toward the Soviet Union has been the same. Where necessary, we shall defend freedom; where possible, we shall work with the East to build a lasting peace.

We do not intend to let our differences on Viet-Nam or elsewhere prevent us from exploring all opportunities. We want the Soviet Union and the nations of Eastern Europe to know that we and our allies shall go step by step with them as far as they are willing to advance.

Let us—both Americans and Europeans—intensify our efforts.

We seek healthy economic and cultural relations with the Communist states.

—I am asking for early congressional action on the U.S.–Soviet consular agreement.[2]

—We intend to press for legislative authority to negotiate trade agreements which could extend most-favored-nation tariff treatment to European Communist states.[3]

And I am today announcing these new steps:

—We will reduce export controls on East-West trade with respect to hundreds of non-strategic items.

—I have today signed a determination that will allow the Export-Import Bank to guarantee commercial credits to four additional Eastern European countries—Poland, Hungary, Bulgaria, and Czechoslovakia. This is good business. And it will help us build bridges to Eastern Europe.

—The Secretary of State is reviewing the possibility of easing the burden of Polish debts to the United States through expenditures of our Polish currency holdings which would be mutually beneficial to both countries.

—The Export-Import Bank is prepared to finance American exports for the Soviet-Italian Fiat auto plant.

—We are negotiating a civil air agreement with the Soviet Union. This will facilitate tourism in both directions.

—This summer the American Government took additional steps to liberalize travel to Communist countries in Europe and Asia.[4] We intend to liberalize these rules still further.

—In these past weeks the Soviet Union and the United States have begun to exchange cloud photographs taken from weather satellites.

[2] For background, see *ibid.*, August 30, 1965, p. 375. (The consular treaty was approved in 1967. Editor's note.)

[3] For background and text of the proposed East-West Trade Relations Act of 1966, see *ibid.*, May 30, 1966, p. 838. (This act was not passed by Congress. Editor's note.)

[4] For background, see *ibid.*, August 15, 1966, p. 234.

In these and many other ways, ties with the East will be strengthened—by the United States and by other Atlantic nations.

Agreement on a broad policy to this end should be sought in existing Atlantic organs.

The principles which should govern East-West relations are now being discussed in the North Atlantic Council.

The OECD [Organization for Economic Cooperation and Development] can also play an important part in trade and contacts with the East. The Western nations can there explore ways of inviting the Soviet Union and the Eastern European countries to cooperate in tasks of common interest and common benefit.

Hand in hand with these steps to increase East-West ties must go measures to remove territorial and border disputes as a source of friction in Europe. The Atlantic nations oppose the use of force to change existing frontiers.

Ending the Bitter Legacy of World War II

The maintenance of old enmities is not in anyone's interest. Our aim is a true European reconciliation. We must make this clear to the East.

Further, it is our policy to avoid the spread of national nuclear programs—in Europe and elsewhere. That is why we shall persevere in efforts to reach an agreement banning the proliferation of nuclear weapons.

We seek a stable military situation in Europe—one in which tensions can be lowered.

To this end, the United States will continue to play its part in effective Western deterrence. To weaken that deterrence might create temptations and endanger peace.

The Atlantic allies will continue together to study what strength NATO needs, in light of changing technology and the current threat.

Reduction of Soviet forces in Central Europe would, of course, affect the extent of the threat.

If changing circumstances should lead to a gradual and balanced revision in force levels on both sides, the revision could—together with the other steps that I have mentioned—help gradually to shape a new political environment.

The building of true peace and reconciliation in Europe will be a long process.

The bonds between the United States and its Atlantic partners provide the strength on which the world's security depends. Our interdependence is complete.

Our goal, in Europe and elsewhere, is a just and secure peace. It can most surely be achieved by common action. To this end, I pledge America's best efforts:

—to achieve a new thrust for the alliance;
—to support movement toward Western European unity;
—and to bring about a far-reaching improvement in relations between East and West.

Our object is to end the bitter legacy of World War II.

Success will bring the day closer when we have fully secured the peace in Europe, and in the world.

Why the United States Should Expand Peaceful Trade With Eastern Europe

by Anthony M. Solomon

Assistant Secretary for Economic Affairs[1]

* * *

Today there is no longer a single united Communist world. You know, as well as I, how the once arrogant Moscow-Peking axis has fallen to pieces. The Communist world is split down the middle. On one side is Communist China, paranoid in its hostility to the United States, wedded to the doctrine of inevitable conflict between the Communist and the capitalist worlds, and proclaiming that "power comes out of the barrel of the gun." On the other side is the U.S.S.R., accused of revisionism by the Chinese because it has faced up to the awesome consequences of direct military confrontation in today's nuclear world and is moving slowly and cautiously to increased peaceful intercourse with the West.

The split between the Soviet Union and Communist China and the gradual loosening of Kremlin controls after the death of Stalin have had important repercussions in Eastern Europe. The small countries of Eastern Europe that in Stalin's day were mere satellite appendages of the U.S.S.R. are today increasingly able to adopt internal and external policies appropriate to their interests as they see them. They have expanded trade and cultural relations with Western Europe, Japan, and other industrialized countries from which Stalin had isolated them behind the Iron Curtain. Poland was the first Warsaw Pact country to reduce Soviet domination over its internal affairs. Romania has been pursuing independent initiatives in the area of foreign policy and has actively resisted Moscow's efforts to influence

---

[1] Excerpts from an address made before the Chicago Automobile Trade Show luncheon at Chicago, Ill., on March 2, 1967. Printed in the *Department of State Bulletin,* March 27, 1967, pp. 518-23.

205

the course of her economic development. The ferment of change is at work in other Eastern European countries. Their governments are still Communist, of course, and they are tied to the U.S.S.R. by geography and ideological bonds; but they are neither ruled from Moscow nor excommunicated when they follow divergent lines.

Contrast the situation now with what it was in 1948 when Tito tried to follow an independent course and Moscow mobilized the Communist world to try to whip Tito into line. Moscow did not succeed, as you know. Indeed, Yugoslavia's successful breakaway was the first major crack in the Communist monolith.

The split between Moscow and Peking and the loosening of Moscow's control over the countries of Eastern Europe are not the only important changes we have seen in the Communist world in the past decade. Political and economic changes of some significance are also taking place within the Communist countries of Europe. In most of these countries the hand of the police has become less apparent and less heavy. Compared with the Stalinist period, these peoples live more freely. There is a greater freedom of speech, a freer exchange of ideas, and a growing knowledge of what life is like in the Western World.

We ourselves have official exchange agreements with the Soviet Union and Romania and informal arrangements with the other Eastern European countries. A growing number of persons—well over 1,000 a year—are moving in each direction between the United States and Eastern Europe in these exchanges. The Voice of America no longer is jammed anywhere in Eastern Europe except in Bulgaria. Not only is it listened to for news and information about our country, but it has one of the largest and most enthusiastic American-jazz audiences in the world—stretching more than 5,000 miles from Pilsen to Vladivostok.

Trade and Economic Reform

Changes also are underway in the organization of their economies. The countries of Communist Europe recognize that they have major economic problems, and the U.S.S.R. and some of the smaller countries are experimenting with economic reforms. They are trying, in capitalistic style, to relate production to demand, price to cost, and style and design to consumer taste. "Profit" is no longer a dirty word.

They are moving in varying degrees and by slow stages away from centralized political planning and control over every feature of economic life toward looser forms of organization which give some modest scope to individual initiative down the line.

Eastern Europe's trade with the free world has been an important factor in this movement toward economic reform. These countries have had to submit their goods to the competitive test of the world market when they have wanted to trade, and they have found their products wanting in quality and technical modernity. This has put into question among the peoples and leaders of those countries the economic institutions behind their products and Communist economic dogma itself.

* * *

The winds of change are sweeping all of Eastern Europe, and the direction of change is good. The direction is away from iron discipline and tight central control in completely closed societies toward greater contact with the West, exposure to Western ideas, and internal liberalization.

What is the significance of these changes for United States policy? Should we encourage increased contact and communication with Eastern Europe, the freer movement of people between East and West, a wider exchange of goods and of ideas, or should we stand frozen on the policy we adopted 20 years ago? Can increased contact and increased peaceful trade contribute to the further favorable evolution of Communist society in Europe?

We believe strongly that it can. Our response to the challenge of the Communist world must reflect the changing realities within that world. That is exactly what President Johnson's East-West trade proposals are designed to do. The President has said eloquently that we should try to build bridges to Eastern Europe: bridges of ideas, education, culture, and trade.

To some of our people the very idea of increasing peaceful trade and contact with Communist Europe is anathema. They see it as a snare and a delusion, indeed as fundamentally immoral. Our answer to them is that in this nuclear age it would be both immoral and irresponsible not to try to find areas of agreement, not to try to reduce suspicion, tensions, and hostility that can spill over into violence, not to try to encourage the further opening of the Iron Curtain and the movement toward economic and political liberalization in Communist Europe.

Perspective on Role of Trade

And this is where trade has an important role to play. I think it is fair to say that affirmative action on the President's proposal to increase peaceful trade would be the one most important signal to the Communist world that the United States really wants normal relations and peaceful competition, that we are sincerely interested in increased intercourse, in finding and enlarging areas of agreement. Such action would strengthen the hands of those in the Communist world who favor constructive relations with the West and would undercut those who look to the barrel of the gun. To that extent, it would directly contribute to our objectives in Viet-Nam. On the other hand, rejection of the President's proposal for increased trade and peaceful engagement would chill the atmosphere and strengthen the hands of the Stalinists in the internal Communist struggle who are resisting change.

What are the President's proposals for increasing peaceful trade with Communist Europe? They are in two parts: The first has to do with liberalization of our export controls; the second, with modification of our restrictions on imports. The President has already agreed to modify our export controls. He announced last October that hundreds of nonstrategic items formerly requiring specific license would now be freely exportable to Communist Europe.[2] In addition he authorized the Export-Import Bank to extend its normal guarantees of commercial credits on our exports to Eastern Europe.

Action on our import restrictions, however, is not a matter for executive decision alone. It requires congressional authorization. The President has proposed that he be authorized to extend nondiscriminatory tariff treatment to imports from countries in Communist Europe in return for equivalent benefits to us. At the present time, imports from the Communist countries of Europe, other than Yugoslavia and Poland, are subject to the prohibitively high tariffs that were in force here in 1930. Removal of this discriminatory feature in

---

[2] This is a reference to Mr. Johnson's October 7, 1966, address in New York City, excerpts from which are reprinted in this volume immediately preceding Mr. Solomon's statement. (Editor's note)

our trade relations with Communist Europe would be a significant political gesture. It would also have salutary economic effects because it would enable the countries of Eastern Europe to earn dollars to buy United States products. It would facilitate thereby that two-way flow of trade that is a feature of normal international relations.

To place in perspective the role trade plays—and might play—in our relations with Eastern Europe, we should examine the basic facts. The most outstanding characteristic of our present trade with Eastern Europe is its extremely low level. This is true whether measured in relative or absolute terms.

In 1966 we sold to Eastern Europe goods worth $200 million. Other countries of the free world sold to those same countries goods worth more than $6 billion. Germany's exports to Eastern Europe are six times ours; France and Canada each sell more than twice as much as we do; and even Japan, geographically more distant, sells more than the United States.

Agricultural Sales to Eastern Europe

A second important characteristic of our present trade with Eastern Europe is the large proportion of agricultural products in our total exports. In 1965 five commodities made up more than half of the total: tallow, hides, soybeans, grain sorghum, and other feedstuffs.

We are, of course, not alone in our sales of agricultural commodities to Eastern Europe. Our good neighbor to the north, Canada, sold in 1965 an amount of wheat alone worth almost twice our total exports to these countries.

* * *

While agriculture makes up the bulk of our exports and those of Canada to Eastern Europe, other countries find their principal markets in the East in machinery, in transport equipment, in chemicals, in artificial fibers, and in iron and steel.

The market in Eastern Europe is large and growing. Since 1960 it has roughly doubled. It is a highly diversified market, purchasing everything from foodstuffs and primary products to fairly sophisticated industrial equipment. Our share of this market is very small indeed, barely 3 percent, narrow in product coverage, and declining in relative terms.

209

It is clear from these facts that the United States is not an important factor in trade with Eastern Europe. Even if all our trade were cut off, it would not affect in any significant way the economic position of Eastern Europe. It is also clear that, with few exceptions, the only economic effect of our restrictions is to cede the business to our competitors.

So much for the present. What about the future? What are the possibilities for increased trade with Eastern Europe?

While I doubt our trade with Eastern Europe will ever be vast, I believe a significant increase from present levels is possible. Given active promotional efforts and removal of present barriers, I believe it is quite reasonable to expect a level of United States exports of around $500 million within several years. Exports at this level would still be very small in relation to our total exports, which this year will probably exceed $30 billion. But even in this age of astronomical figures, $500 million is hardly in the category of petty cash.

*   *   *

We believe there is a compelling case both on the broadest political grounds and on the narrower grounds of economic self-interest to expand peaceful trade with Communist Europe.

*   *   *

12

Far East

The East Asian area is comprised of six nations: Peoples Republic of China (P.R.C.), Mongolian Peoples Republic, Republic of China, Peoples Democratic Republic of Korea (North Korea), Republic of Korea, and Japan. Three distinguishing factors characterize U.S. diplomacy in the Far East. First, it is an area that diplomatically is half non-existent in American foreign policy. Three of the six nations are not recognized by the U.S.; diplomatic relations are maintained only with Japan and the republics of Korea and China.

A second characteristic of American policy toward East Asia is the presence of bilateral, rather than multilateral, defense arrangements. The U.S. has employed multilateral treaties of alliance in Western Europe, the Middle East, Latin America, and South and Southeast Asia. In Africa, the U.S. has no alliances at all, either bilateral or multilateral. Thus, the Far East is unique in the single-nation alliance system that the U.S. has built with the three nations it recognizes: (Japan, South Korea, and Nationalist China; a fourth nation in Southeast Asia, the Philippines, has a bilateral arrangement, but also is a member of SEATO.)

Finally, the P.R.C. is found in East Asia, the major concern of contemporary U.S. foreign policy. "Communist China is without doubt the most serious and perplexing problem that confronts our foreign policy today," declares Assistant Secretary of State Bundy in the policy statement reprinted below. P.R.C. has been involved in military conflicts in Korea, Tibet, and India. To the American decision-maker, the problems of containing the U.S.S.R. in 1940's and 1950's have shifted to the P.R.C. in East Asia in the 1960's and 1970's.

Sino-American relations

P.R.C.'s establishment on October 1, 1949, was a traumatic experience for the American public as well as the decision-makers. The event had a profound effect on the bipartisan support of foreign policy, because the Republicans would not share the "blame" for failure in China and wanted to use the event for political purposes. Senator Joseph McCarthy (R., Wisc.) suggested that the fall of China was the result of Communists or "dupes" in the Democratic administration and State Department rather than conditions on the battlefield. On August 5, 1949, the State Department issued a White Paper which officially stated the American position on the Communist conquest of China. It argued that only the massive introduction of American military forces, including land units, could have brought victory.

The Korean war

Eight months after the official founding of the P.R.C., on June 25, 1950, the North Korean armies moved across the 38th parallel. The U.S. immediately supplied assistance to the South Korean forces and then sought support in the U.N. The U.N. forces (largely U.S. units) first retreated and then launched an offensive that carried them across the 38th parallel and on to the Yalu River which separates Korea and P.R.C. Units of Chinese forces were encountered in October and November, and in December a deluge of P.R.C. "volunteers" crossed the Yalu. For the next two-and-a-half years the Korean conflict was stalemated.

After a new administration assumed office in 1953, President Eisenhower ordered the 7th fleet removed from the Formosa Straits in February. Secretary of State Dulles visited India in May and asked Prime Minister Nehru to transmit a message to the P.R.C. government that the consequences would be "grave if the Chinese Communists failed to conclude a truce in Korea." The threat at least included an all-out assault in Korea, and at most, the use of nuclear weapons. The Korean armistice was signed two months later, on July 27, 1953.

U.S.-Chinese hostility

There are numerous roots to the present-day hostility between the United States and P.R.C.: American support for the Nationalist government and ideological differences are but two of them. The Nationalist-Communist civil war and the Korean conflict furnished two major issues that have appeared from time to time in the ebb and flow of Chinese-American relations. These issues were: the release of U.S. airmen captured in the Korean War and American citizens held in mainland China; and the status of Formosa and other offshore islands. On the first issue, the P.R.C. government tried American airmen for treason and espionage rather than treating them as prisoners of war. The airmen were released after visits by U.N. Secretary-General Hammarskjöld in December 1954 and Krishna Mennon, Indian Defense Minister, in May 1955. However, the American citizens remained in prison or under house arrest.

The question of Formosa or Taiwan was a more explosive issue. The Republic of China and U.S. signed a defensive pact in December 1954. In January 1955 a resolution of Congress gave the President advance authorization to use any military action to defend Formosa. Quemoy and Matsu, two islands near the Chinese mainland controlled by the Nationalists, were threatened periodically by the Communists.

Thus, U.S. and P.R.C. relations by 1955 worsened to the point where the two powers were confronting each other with rigid positions over Taiwan. Both nations began to ease off. In March, Eisenhower declared that the U.S. had not undertaken to defend Quemoy and Matsu; in April, Chou En-lai, at the Bandung Conference, requested talks with the U.S. about reducing tensions in the Far East; and in August, the U.S. and P.R.C. began talks at the ambassadorial level in Geneva. Later the talks were shifted to Warsaw and the U.S. ambassador to Poland met occasionally with the P.R.C. ambassador to Poland. The Chinese have from time to time suggested that these talks be raised to the foreign minister-secretary of state level, but the U.S. always has refused.

In 1955, the P.R.C. spokesmen appeared to be conciliatory. The Chinese suggested an agreement between the U.S. and P.R.C. not to use force in settling the Formosa issue. The U.S. government, surprised by the Chinese conciliatory mood or suspicious of it, responded by an outlandish request—that all Americans held by the Chinese be released as a condition to any agreement. Instead of breaking off the discussions, the Chinese partially met the American condition and released two American priests in June 1956. Then came the Navy plane incident of August 22, 1956. The Chinese attacked and destroyed an American Navy plane over what the U.S. considered international waters. The U.S. position stiffened and the American government demanded compensation for damages. The Chinese government flatly refused, arguing that the plane was on an espionage mission and had intruded over P.R.C. territory.

Consequently, American and Chinese policy hardened again to pre-Bandung positions. On June 28, 1957, Secretary of State Dulles made a major address on U.S.-P.R.C. relations. He accused the Chinese of aiding and abetting five foreign or civil wars since 1949 in Korea, Malaya, Indo-China, Tibet, and the Philippines. He concluded that "neither recognition, nor trade, nor cultural relations, nor all three together would favorably influence affairs in China." The only policy he advocated was a policy of patience because "international communism's role is, in China, as elsewhere, a passing and not a perpetual phase." U.S. policy, then, was "wait and see."

In 1958, the P.R.C. began sporatic shelling of Quemoy and Matsu. This time, President Eisenhower declared that the islands were more important than three years ago and that the U.S. would defend them. Again, there was a P.R.C.-U.S. confrontation, and again the response was similar to 1955: the ambassadorial talks resumed.

In 1959 and 1960, conflict shifted away from Taiwan to India, then Laos, and finally Vietnam. A new administration took office in January 1961, and in March, the U.S. initiated its own conciliatory move on the two issues that had proven so thorny: The U.S. was willing to sign a non-use-of-force agreement in the Taiwan straits if (here is the same condition again) the Chinese would release all Americans held on mainland China. Now the Chinese responded in much the same manner that the Americans did in 1955. The next day, March 8, the Chinese declared that their condition for signing the agreement was complete withdrawal by the U.S. from Taiwan. In August, Liu Shao-Chi compared Eisenhower and Kennedy and concluded that the latter was more dangerous than the former. After this exchange, the Kennedy Administration's policy returned to the position of previous administrations: no recognition, no admission to the U.N., and no trade (for the U.S. imposed a *total* embargo rather than strategic goods only as is the case with Eastern Europe.)

President Johnson attempted a more conciliatory move in a July 1966 address when he said, "A peaceful mainland China is central to a peaceful Asia." But the P.R.C. position has remained hardened.

214

Conclusion

The historical record to date of Chinese-American relations reveals several interesting trends. First, the Geneva and Warsaw talks have served as a safety valve and have been used when both countries were on a collision course. Secondly, toward the U.S., China has maintained a prudent foreign policy. In fact, a case can be made for Chinese policy being defensive, rather than revisionist or revolutionary. Finally, American policy is based on the assumption that Chinese foreign policy is motivated by a desire to change its position unilaterally in the international system. Hence, American strategy has been to apply containment to the P.R.C. as it was applied to the U.S.S.R. in the 1940's and 1950's.

But American policy has gone beyond containment to the point of isolating the P.R.C. Assistant Secretary of State Bundy makes a case for the isolation being self-imposed because the P.R.C. has insisted on preconditions unacceptable to the U.S. He also outlines U.S. policy on P.R.C. representation in the United Nations.

The United States and Communist China

by William P. Bundy
Assistant Secretary for Far Eastern Affairs[1]

Communist China is without doubt the most serious and perplexing problem that confronts our foreign policy today. Peking's foreign
policy objectives, and the tactics it employs to achieve these objectives, sharply focus for us the issues of war and peace in Asia and the
freedom and lives of millions of people, not only in Asia but throughout the world.

U.S. Objectives

The key questions we must ask at the outset are: What are our
objectives, in Asia and in the world as a whole? What are Communist
China's objectives? and What kind of policy is best for the United
States in the light of those basic assessments?

And, viewed in this light, the unfortunate fact is that the kind of
world that we seek and the kind of world our Asian friends seek is
totally antithetic to the kind of Asia and the kind of world that
Communist China seeks. What we seek is a situation where small as
well as large nations are able to develop as free and independent
countries, secure from outside aggression or subversion. We look
toward their economic, political, and social development and growth;
we hope their development will be in the direction of increasingly
democratic institutions, but we recognize that these nations must
develop as they themselves see fit, in accordance with their own
traditions and customs. Their rate of progress, we believe, will vary

---

1 Excerpts from an address made before the Associated Students of Pomona College at Pomona, Calif., on February 12, 1966. Printed in the *Department of State
Bulletin,* February 28, 1966, pp. 310-18.

according to individual situations, but progress will inevitably take place and toward goals which are deeply rooted in individual aspirations.

In harsh conflict with these objectives is any situation in which a single nation or combination of nations sets out to control others in the region or to exercise political domination over other nations in the area or any major part of it.

Our objectives are consistent with the spirit of the Charter of the United Nations and, I believe, with the aspirations of the peoples and the governments of the area and of the nations in contiguous and other areas that share with us a concern for what happens in Asia in this and in the next generation. We believe, too, that our objectives accord with the whole tide of history at the present time. They are not abstract principles. They are the bedrock of our policy throughout the world. Governed by what the nations themselves wish to do and by practical factors, what we seek is to assist the nations that are trying to preserve their independence, trying to develop themselves, and, therefore, necessarily trying to resist forces working in the contrary direction.

Chinese Communist Objectives

There is today in Communist China a government whose leadership is dedicated to the promotion of communism by violent revolution.

The present leaders in Peking also seek to restore China to its past position of grandeur and influence. Many of Peking's leaders today, now grown old, are proud and arrogant, convinced that they have been responsible for a resurgence of Chinese power. The China of old exercised a degree of control over Asia that waxed and waned according to the power of the ruling emperor. Under strong rulers this meant a type of overlordship, sometimes benign but frequently otherwise, over the countries around its borders. And the restoration of that image and controlling influence is certainly a part of Communist China's foreign policy today.

In the 1930's Mao Tse-tung called attention to areas controlled by China under the Manchu Empire but since removed from Chinese control: Korea, Taiwan, the Ryukyus, the Pescadores, Burma, Bhutan, Nepal, Annam, and Outer Mongolia. In more recent years,

217

Chinese Communist leaders have added to that list parts of Soviet Central Asia and eastern Siberia. I think we can take this as valid evidence of Peking's Asian ambitions.

* * *

In addition to these historically rooted aspirations, the present leadership is inspired by a Communist ideology still in a highly militant and aggressive phase. This phase is ideologically akin to that in the Soviet Union in the 1920's or early 1930's. It coincides, however, with a situation in which the opportunities for expansion are, or appear to Peking, more akin to those available to the Soviet Union at a much later phase in its ideological development—in 1945 and the immediate postwar years. This Communist element includes the advocacy of change through revolution and violence throughout the world and particularly in China's neighboring areas—not revolution seeking the fruition of the national goals of the people of these areas, but revolution supplied or stimulated from outside and based on a preconceived pattern of historical development.

Their vision of this Communist mission extends to countries far from China—including, as we all clearly have seen, Africa and even Latin America. Peking's plans for carrying out its objectives have been delineated in a series of pronouncements issued by its leaders, one of the latest and most widely publicized having been that issued last September by Marshal Lin Piao, top military leader in Communist China, in which Lin Piao offered Chinese Communist experience in the war against Japan as a lesson to be emulated by the less developed countries in Asia, Africa, and Latin America in their pursuit of "revolution."

As you know, the Lin Piao article draws an elaborate analogy based upon the domestic experience of Mao and his cohorts in taking over China: the organization of the rural areas against the urban ones. It extends that analogy to the thesis that the less developed areas of the world are all in the rural category which will be mobilized in order to destroy "the cities"; that is to say, all the Western, more advanced centers—ourselves, of course, at the head.

I mention this article because it is a clear and comprehensive indication that there has not taken place any moderating, but if anything a solidifying at least at this stage, of this virulent revolutionary policy that is central to our discussion of Communist China. And, of course, we have seen it in action over and over again.

218

The Chinese Threat in Asia

I shall not speak at length of the problems created by Communist Chinese policy in Africa and Latin America. The recent reaction even of Castro suggests that Latin America is reacting adversely to the heavy-handedness of these policies. In Africa, too, there is every sign that the new nations of the area, themselves carrying out nationalist revolutions of their own design, know full well what is meant when Chou En-lai, for example, referred last June to Africa being ripe for a second stage of revolution. The new leaders of Africa have shown no desire to be Kerenskys.

But it is in Asia itself that the major thrust of Communist Chinese policy is felt and must be countered by their neighbors. It is sometimes argued that the ambitions of Communist China in the areas contiguous to it do not mean outright control; and it can certainly be argued that they are tactically cautious in pursuing these ambitions. They have not wished to seek a confrontation of military power with us, and in any situation that would be likely to lead to wider conflict they are tactically cautious. But in looking at the extent of their ambitions one cannot, I think, simply take the historical picture of tributary governments that would be tolerated as long as they did roughly what China wished. That indeed was the historic pattern in many periods when powerful governments ruled in the mainland of China. It is also, perhaps, the pattern one might draw abstractly from the desire any major power might feel not to have hostile military power based in areas adjacent to it. Those two logics, historic Chinese logic and "great power" logic, might appear to point to something less than total political domination as the Chinese Communist objective around their borders.

And yet we must recognize, I think, because of the Communist element in the thinking and practice of the leaders of Peking today, that there is another factor that raises strong doubts whether their ambitions are in fact this modest. We have seen, for example, in the contrast between what the Soviets have done in Eastern Europe and the behavior of predecessor Russian regimes, that there is a Communist logic that does insist on total control, that will not tolerate anything other than the imposition of the full Communist totalitarian system. The experience of Soviet control in Eastern Europe suggests that this same kind of Communist logic does and would apply to the behavior of Communist China.

That it would is further strongly suggested by the way that the Communist Chinese regime has treated Tibet. The fact that Tibet was within the historic limits of Chinese suzerainty does not explain why Communist China has virtually obliterated the culture of Tibet in seizing control of it. One cannot rationalize this on grounds of history or of the need of a great power not to have hostile forces adjacent to it. So I suggest that we must give great weight to the probability that the ambitions of Communist China do extend, not necessarily to the degree of obliteration of the local culture that we have seen in Tibet, but at least to a fairly total form of domination and control in areas contiguous to it.

What, then, would be the consequences if Communist China were to achieve the kind of domination it seeks? Here again one is tempted to look for analogy to Eastern Europe, where there is a growing will to pursue national and independent policies and to adopt domestic policies that differ sharply from the original Communist model. Yet it has taken 20 years of virtual subjugation for the nations of Eastern Europe to move this far, and their nationalism, traditions of independence, and capabilities for independent development were in general far more highly developed than those of the smaller nations on China's borders. To accept Mainland Chinese domination in Asia would be to look forward to conditions of external domination and probably totalitarian control, not merely for 20 years but quite possibly for generations.

Moreover, the spread of Chinese domination would inevitably create its own dynamic and in the end threaten even the most securely based and largest nations within the area of that threat, such as India and Japan. One does not need to subscribe to any pat "domino" formula to know from the history of the last generation, and indeed from all history, that the spread of domination feeds on itself, kindling its own fires within the dominant country and progressively weakening the will and capability of others to resist.

Past Mistakes and Their Relevance to Present

This is what we are dealing with. We can all think, as we look back at the history of China, of errors that we as a nation have made and that other nations of the West have made—errors in justice and conduct in our relationships with China. We should search our souls on these and set our objectives and our principles to avoid repeating them ever again. In Asia, at least, the colonial era is for all significant purposes at an end.

But to say that the West itself bears a measure of historical responsibility for the strength of the feelings of Communist China does not deal with the present problem any more than discussion of the inequities of Versailles dealt with the ambitions of Hitlerite Germany. Whatever the historic blame may be, we have to deal with the present fact of a Chinese Communist government whose attitudes are very deeply rooted in China's national history and ambitions to revive its past greatness, and in an extremely virulent Communist ideology.

* * *

Tactics and Strategy

I would like to emphasize that up to this point I have been speaking of the basic objectives of Peking's policy. To describe these objectives as deeply expansionist is by no means to paint the picture of another Hitler, building a vast military machine with the aim of conquest by conventional warfare on a timetable backed at some point, in the Chinese case, by a nuclear capability.

This has not been the historical Chinese way, and there is every reason to believe that it is not their present preference. Chinese are patient and think in long historical terms. Military force is important and they would like to think that their nuclear capability may at some point be useful in backing the picture of an overwhelmingly strong China whose will must be accepted. But the doctrinal statements of Lin Piao and others speak rather in terms of what they call "people's war," which plainly means the instigation and support of movements that can be represented as local movements, designed to subvert and overthrow existing governments and replace them by regimes responsive to Peking's will.

This is what we are seeing today in Thailand in the form of a so-called "Thai Patriotic Front" established and supported from mainland China. This is the direct form of Communist Chinese tactic that must be met. A variant tactic was reflected in the Communist Chinese role in support of the PKI [Communist Party of Indonesia] in Indonesia.

But equally important to Peking is its encouragement and support of the parallel efforts of the other Communist Asian regimes in North Korea and North Viet-Nam. What is now happening in Viet-Nam is basically the result of Hanoi's own ambitions and efforts. Peking might wish eventually to dominate North Viet-Nam or a unified Viet-Nam under Hanoi's initial control. But if this were resisted by the Vietnamese in the classic historical pattern of relations between the two areas Peking would still gain enormously from the success of Hanoi's effort, which would clear the way for Peking to expand and extend the kind of action it is undertaking on its own in Thailand. It takes no vivid imagination to visualize what Peking would do in Malaysia, Singapore, and Burma if Hanoi were to succeed in Viet-Nam and Peking itself succeed in Thailand.

This, then, is the preferred Communist Chinese tactic and strategy. Ideas are a part of it, although Communist China's image as a successful model of social and political organization is hardly as attractive today as it may have been before the disastrous mistakes of the "great leap forward" and the uneven progress of the years since. Few Asians today think of the Communist Chinese structure as a model, although individual ideas such as land reform and attacks on "feudal" social structures are a part of Peking's tactical efforts.

But essentially we are dealing here not with the power of ideas but with the power of subversive organization—perhaps the one field in which Communist China has shown real innovation and skill. In mainland Southeast Asia, as today in South Viet-Nam, what we could expect to see as the spearhead of the subversive effort would be terrorism, selective assassination, guerrilla action, and finally, if it were required, conventional military forces largely recruited by the tactics of the earlier phases.

These tactics might be varied if Communist China were to decide again to threaten India directly. There the element of conventional forces would play a greater part but would still be backed and reinforced by major political efforts to disrupt the cohesion and strength of India.

Our Basic Policies

I repeat, we must look at things and deal with them as they are, if we are to hope for change. Our basic policy must include, as major elements, two interrelated efforts: to assist the free nations of the area, as they may desire, to preserve their security; and to help them, again in accordance with their own wishes, to improve their political, economic, and social conditions. The latter is an effort that I am sure we would be making even if there were no security threat.

These two fundamental elements of our policy have much in common with the policies that we and our NATO allies pursued so successfully in the areas threatened by the Soviet Union after the war. And surely there is, to a very high degree, a valid parallel between the situation we continue to face vis-a-vis Communist China and that we faced with the Soviet Union after the war. We have dealt with the Soviet Union fundamentally by assisting in the restoration of the power and strength of Europe so that Soviet ambitions were successfully checked. Since 1955, although Soviet ambitions remain, we have seen a trend toward moderation in Soviet policy and a turning inward by the Soviets to their domestic problems.

There are, of course, myriad differences between the situation in Asia and that in Europe in terms of sophistication of economic and political bases, the stability of the societies, and the unity of national cultures. But basic to our policy in respect to Communist China, as in the case of our policy toward the Soviet Union, must be our determination to meet with firmness the external pressure of the Communist Chinese.

* * *

So the effort to assist in preserving security is fundamental to our policy. It is reflected in our treaty commitments—bilateral with Japan, Korea, the Republic of China, and the Philippines, multilateral (but individually binding) through the SEATO [Southeast Asia Treaty Organization] and ANZUS [Australia-New Zealand-U.S. Security Treaty] treaties, and extending to South Viet-Nam through a protocol to the SEATO treaty.

Necessarily, our security effort and commitments have a major military element, for the threat of military action is direct in relation to Korea and the Republic of China and lurks in the background of the Communist Chinese threat to Southeast Asia, as it does for India. The day may come when other nations in the area can join in assuming more of this burden, but the simple fact is that today there cannot be an effective deterrent military force, and thus a balance of power, around China's frontiers without major and direct military contributions by the United States.

But even in the security area the effort is far from merely a military one. Local military forces should wherever possible be adequate, so that an external attack would have to take on large proportions immediately identifiable as aggression. But at least as basic to the preservation of the independence of the nations of Asia is their capacity to insure law and order and to deal with subversion, and this in turn relates to the whole nature of their political structures and to their social and economic progress. So in the end what is done under the heading of "security" merges almost indistinguishably into what is done under the heading of "development."

And so, at one time or another, we have had assistance relationships with all of the non-Communist countries of Asia. Today three of these—Burma, Cambodia, and Indonesia—have chosen to follow paths that involve little or no assistance from us. And there are nations such as Japan, and more recently the Republic of China, which have made such economic progress that they no longer need our direct help. Malaysia and Singapore are other special cases, which look for historical and practical reasons to Britain and the Commonwealth.

So the pattern is varied. In a very few instances we supply major assistance to conventional military forces. In others, such as Thailand, the emphasis is as great or greater on nonmilitary measures to better the lot of the people and thus to strengthen the fabric of the nation. And throughout the area, even where we are no longer giving direct economic assistance, we have joined in supporting the increasing efforts of the World Bank and private lenders to pitch in on the economic side, and more recently the profoundly important regional economic developments represented by the formation of the Asian Development Bank and the growing, though still embryonic, effort to provide an effective framework, through the United Nations, for assistance in the Mekong Basin and on a regional basis to Southeast Asia.

All of these efforts are linked together. They represent the kind of activity which, as I have said, we would be supporting in large part in any case irrespective of the threat of Communist China and the other Communist nations. What they should do, over time, is to help build in Asia nations which are standing on their own feet, responding to the needs of their peoples, and capable of standing up to the kind of tactics and strategy employed by Communist China, backed where necessary and in accordance with our treaty commitments by the assurance that, if external attack in any form should ever take place, the United States and others would come to their help.

This is the essence of what we are trying to do. Containment, yes, but containment carried out by actions that run clear across the board. And containment in the last analysis that depends upon the performance of the Asian nations themselves. As one looks back over the short historical span of the last 15 years, one can surely see throughout the area tremendous progress where security has been maintained. Even though present difficulties are formidable, the nations of Asia have great capacity, and there is much reason for encouragement at the long-term prospect.

U.S.-Chinese Communist Relations

This brings me to the whole question of how we deal specifically with Communist China. Let me briefly review and analyze some of the things we have done or might do.

As far as contacts through diplomatic channels are concerned, we have had 128 meetings at the ambassadorial level with Peking's representatives, first in Geneva and now Warsaw. I think it is fair to say that we have had the longest and most direct dialog of any major Western nation with Communist China.

I am bound to say at the same time, however, that the dialog so far has not been very productive and founders on the fundamental issue of Peking's demand for Taiwan and by its stated conviction that the United States is by historical necessity Peking's prime antagonist on the world scene. But it is fair to say that it is more of a dialog than we could expect to have if we were ever to recognize Communist China, if the experience of Western diplomats in Peking is representative. And it is an opportunity to try directly to make them understand that we have no hostile designs on mainland China or its leaders but that we fully intend to maintain our commitments to defend our friends and allies against Communist aggression and that the United States seeks peace, freedom, and stability for the countries of Asia.

In addition to these direct contacts, we have of course been prepared to deal with Communist China in multilateral forums where its interests are directly involved. This was true of the Geneva conferences of 1954 and 1961-62, and we have made clear our willingness to participate in a Geneva-conference type of format to resolve the present Viet-Nam problem or to have Communist China appear at the United Nations if Hanoi or Peking were ever ready to let the United Nations deal with the Viet-Nam issue.

And there is the possibility that Peking may at some point be prepared to participate usefully in multilateral discussions on disarmament. We have always said that we would envisage such participation if workable arrangements appeared to be in prospect, although I am bound to add that Peking's attitude, particularly since its nuclear tests, has given no ground for supposing that she is prepared to enter disarmament discussions with any constructive position.

Chinese Representation at the U.N.

Some nations at the U.N. hope that Communist China's seating would have a moderating effect on its policies. They advance the thesis that, not being included in the U.N., Peking feels rejected and acts with considerably less restraint than if it were a member with a member's obligations.

We respect those who hold this view, but we cannot agree with it. It seems to us a rationalistic view that ignores the deep-seated historic and ideologic reasons for Peking's current attitudes. Nor does this theory—the "neurosis" theory if you will—explain Peking's behavior toward other Communist nations or its behavior in Afro-Asian groupings to which Communist China has been fully welcomed. (He refers to Professor John K. Fairbank's description of China's "Long background of feeling superior to all outsiders and expecting a supreme position in the world." Editor's note.) Surely this, alongside ideologic differences, lies at the root of the Sino-Soviet split, of Communist China's disruptive behavior in Afro-Asian groupings, and of the heavyhandedness of Communist China's policy from Indonesia to Burundi.

Moreover, we must consider Peking's price for entering the U.N. On September 29, 1965, Chen Yi, the Chinese Communist Premier, made the following demands:

1. The expulsion of the Republic of China from the U.N.
2. The complete reorganization of the U.N.
3. The withdrawal of the General Assembly resolution condemning Peking as an aggressor in the Korean conflict.
4. The branding of the United States as an aggressor in that conflict.

These are obviously unacceptable conditions.

The Republic of China, for example, is one of the original signatories of the United Nations Charter and has lived up to its obligations as a U.N. member in good faith. More than 13 million people live on the Island of Taiwan. This is a larger population than that of 83 members of the United Nations. The United States for many years has had close and friendly relations with the Republic of China, and since 1954 we have been bound by treaty to join with it in the defense of Taiwan. It would be unthinkable and morally wrong to expel the Government of the Republic of China from the U.N. to meet this demand of Peking's.

One must also consider the attitude of Communist China toward conflict, not only where its own interests are directly concerned but even in cases where they are not. Had Communist China been in the United Nations, could there have been a cease-fire resolution on the India-Pakistan conflict in September and could Secretary-General U Thant have received any mandate to bring that conflict to a halt? Peking's critical comment on the Tashkent proceedings is a clear answer. We are dealing with a nation that, at least as far as we can now see, will attempt as a matter of principle to put a monkey wrench into every peacemaking effort which may be made in the world.

Finally, there is the psychological factor: whether the admission to the U.N. of a nation that is dedicated to violent revolution and currently supporting North Viet-Nam's aggression against South Viet-Nam and threatening India in seeking to exacerbate and extend the Indo-Pakistan conflict would, in fact, not encourage Peking to think it is on the right track while deeply discouraging other nations which are resisting Peking's pressures and seeking to maintain their own independence.

It continues, therefore, to be U.S. policy to support the position of the Republic of China in the U.N. For our part, we will also continue to oppose the admission of Communist China.

Bilateral Contacts

Now I should like to talk briefly on the subject of unofficial contacts with Peking, stressing above all one point which has not been sufficiently emphasized.

227

Many people do not realize that it is Communist China which has prevented any movement toward bilateral contacts. The United States over the past several years has tried to promote a variety of contacts, but the Chinese have kept the door tightly barred.

Since 1958, for example, we have validated passports of over 80 representatives of newspapers and other media for travel to Communist China. Only two have been admitted. We have tried unsuccessfully to arrange with the Chinese either a formal or an informal exchange of newsmen, and more recently we have indicated to them our willingness unilaterally and without reciprocity to see Communist Chinese newsmen enter the United States.

In addition, we have a short time ago amended our travel regulations to permit doctors and scientists in the fields of public health and medicine to travel to Communist China.[2] We shall see, but so far the response has been negative.

We have discussed with various scientific and other organizations their interests in arranging people-to-people exchanges with the Chinese. We have encouraged the exchange of publications between various universities and institutions in the United States with Peking. There is a free flow of mail to and from Communist China. All of these efforts have been consistent with our worldwide concern for a freedom of information and for the exchange of knowledge and views in humanitarian fields. Yet they have been consistently rejected by Communist China. If there were a possibility that such contacts might over time develop a broader understanding of the rest of the world in Communist China, it is they, not we, who reject this possibility.

Trade With Communist China

* * *

We have not opposed the trade of other nations with Communist China except insofar as there is a strongly built-up pattern of control in the area of strategic commodities. We have expressed our concerns to other nations from time to time, recognizing that their trade policies were their own decision but raising questions of their vulnerability to possible pressures from Peking in their overinvolvement in trading patterns.

---

[2] For background, see *ibid.*, of January 17, 1966, p. 90.

As for the possibilities of our trade, every time the subject is seriously mentioned in this country, it is shot down immediately in Peking. In 1961, for example, when food supplies in mainland China were very short, President Kennedy made it quite clear that we would take under consideration a Chinese Communist request to purchase grain. The Chinese Communist response was to denounce the President and to reject any possibility of trade, not only in grain but in other commodities with the United States.

Conclusion

These are samples of what we are up against. We are Peking's great enemy because our power is a crucial element in the total balance of power and in the resistance by Asian states to Chinese Communist expansionist designs in Asia. That is the really controlling fact, not sentiment, not whatever wrongs may have been done in the past, but that very simple fact and the very fundamental conflict between their aims and objectives and the kinds of aims that we have—above all, our support for the right of the nations of Asia to be free and independent and govern themselves according to their own wishes.

All of us must hope that this picture will change. Mainland China is, of course, a great power in the world historically. How it will develop economically and in other respects remains to be seen. I myself think that they will have considerable problems that will tend over time to absorb them if their external ambitions and desires are checked. There are those who argue that mainland China's great size and population, its historical and cultural links with the areas around its borders, and its economic potential make inevitable the growth of a Chinese "sphere of influence" in Asia. Those who advance this fatalistic theory discount the aspirations of the peoples in the area, their ability, and the effectiveness of U.S. aid, and they ignore the historical trends of our time.

In sum, I repeat that the problem must be considered basically in the same way we did that of the Soviet Union. We must, on the one hand, seek to curtail Peking's ambitions and build up the free nations of Asia and of contiguous areas; on the other hand, while maintaining firm resistance to their expansionist ambitions, we can, over time, open the possibility of increased contacts with Communist China, weighing very carefully any steps we take in these general areas lest we impair the essential first aim of our policy, including our clear commitments.

It is unlikely that the present leaders, who have become doctrinaire and dogmatic, can be expected to change, but they in due course will be replaced with a new generation of leaders. It is our hope that these men will see with clearer eyes and better vision that China's best interest lies in pursuing a peaceful course.

13

Southeast Asia

Southeast Asia has become the area of primary importance in contemporary American foreign policy. The U.S. government's attention has been focused on Indochina, which in 1954 was partitioned into three nations: Laos, Cambodia, and a divided Vietnam. American relations have varied in friendliness with the nations of this region (Burma, Indonesia, Malaysia, Philippines, Singapore, Thailand, Australia, and New Zealand). But on the subject of the Vietnamese conflict, the United States has received support from most of these countries and strong opposition only from Cambodia. The Vietnamese war is one of the most difficult to analyze, and most controversial subjects in contemporary American foreign policy. The historical background needed to evaluate the State Department's "Fourteen Points" and Ambassador Goldberg's policy statement can be divided into three periods.

The French Period: 1945-1954

On September 2, 1945, Ho Chi Minh declared the Democratic Republic of Vietnam an independent state. The French government attempted to reassert its traditional control over the area. On December 19, 1946, the Indochina war began as Ho's forces (known as the Vietminh) attacked French military installations in Hanoi.

The U.S. entered the picture early. On May 8, 1950, the American government sent aid to the French forces in Indochina. One month later, the first U.S. Military Assistance Advisory Group landed. During the next four years (May 1950–May 1954), the U.S. supplied a majority of the economic aid and military equipment employed by the French in the conflict. When the French effort collapsed, the

Eisenhower Administration seriously considered intervention, but found little or no support among European allies or in Congress. With no one else willing to continue the war, the soldiers gave way to the negotiators at Geneva. The Geneva Conference was held April 26 to July 21, 1954. Its agreements provided for three independent states, Cambodia, Vietnam, and Laos, to be carved out of former French colonial holding. Vietnam, "temporarily" divided, was to be reunited by general elections to be held by July 20, 1956, two years after the Geneva Conference. During that time, neither side would seek outside military assistance and Vietminh troops would be withdrawn from Laos.

The Diem Period: 1954-1963

The United States was not a signatory to the Geneva agreement. Its response was two-fold: to build a regional alliance, and to support the Right-Wing regimes—Ngo Dinh Diem in South Vietnam and Boum Oum in Laos.

The Southeast Asia Treaty Organization (SEATO) was formed in September 1954 with the United States, France, United Kingdom, Australia, New Zealand, Pakistan, Thailand, and the Philippines as members. SEATO began operating on February 19, 1955, and is the only multilateral alliance aimed at the threat of internal subversion as well as overt aggression. Article 2 stated: "If, in the opinion of any of the Parties, the inviolability or integrity of the territory or the sovereignty or political independence of any party ... is threatened in any way other than by armed attack or is affected or threatened by any fact or situation which might endanger the peace of the area, the Parties shall consult immediately in order to agree on the measures which should be taken for the common defense." Protocols attached to the treaty explicated two points: the threat had to be from a Communist source (thus, an Indian attack on Pakistan would not involve SEATO); and the Indochina nations, while not signatories, would be under the protection of the treaty.

On June 17, 1954, Ngo Dinh Diem, who had been in the U.S. since 1950, was appointed Prime Minister by Boa Dai. He received early support from President Eisenhower in an October 23, 1954, letter. Eisenhower expressed the United States' "grave concern regarding the future of the country temporarily divided by an artificial military grouping, weakened by a long and exhausting war and faced with enemies without aid by their subversive collaborators within." These last words began a theme in U.S. policy which has remained until today: that South Vietnamese resistance to Diem was inspired by and directed from Hanoi. President Eisenhower attached two conditions to American aid: the first condition was that the grants would be used wisely; the second was that "needed reforms" would be undertaken so that the government would be "responsive to the nationalist aspirations of its people." American support was further indicated when Secretary of State John Foster Dulles visited Saigon in March 1955.

Throughout 1955, Diem solidified his own position and his government's. In May, he defeated powerful religious sects that had ruled as "states within a state." In October, Boa Dai was deposed as head of state and a republic was proclaimed. Diem became South Vietnam's first president, and on March 4, 1956, a National Assembly was elected. Ho Chi Minh's calls for elections to reunite North and South Vietnam were ignored by Diem and the American government. Diem's growing power was opposed by the Vietnamese Communist Party, or Vietcong, which joined with other dissident political groups in the National Liberation Front (NLF).

The Kennedy Administration continued the Eisenhower policies toward Vietnam, but with three significant increases in commitments in 1961. Kennedy sent Vice President Johnson to Vietnam in May 1961. Johnson offered American assistance to underwrite an increase in the Vietnamese army. Diem replied that his army possessed enough men, but that he needed American help to adequately train them. As a result, in June the Kennedy Administration increased the size of its military advisory group. In October, Maxwell Taylor, Kennedy's special assistant, was sent to Vietnam. As a result of his visit, in November, the U.S. increased its efforts to train the South Vietnamese army, supplied Diem with his first bombers, sent helicopters operated by American pilots, and issued "shoot back if fired upon" orders to U.S. military personnel. Finally, on December 14, 1961, Kennedy wrote Diem that the U.S. was increasing its economic assistance. He echoed the motifs of Eisenhower's October 1954 letter. The attacks on Diem's government, he stated, were "supported and directed from the outside by the authorities at Hanoi."

In 1962, American attention shifted from Vietnam to Laos. While the Kennedy Administration continued the Eisenhower policies of escalating American involvement in Vietnam, it reversed the trend in Laos. The Right Wing group, led by Boun Oum, had been supported by the U.S. against the "neutralist" faction headed by Souvanna

Phouma and the Left Wing, or Pathet Lao. Kennedy shifted American support to Souvanna Phouma. Either to forestall a Pathet Lao invasion of Thailand or to show serious American concern over the possibility of a Pathet Lao victory, Kennery ordered 5,000 marines into Thailand on May 15, 1962. On July 2, the Geneva Conference reconvened and by treaty recognized the neutrality of Laos and Souvanna Phouma as head of state. The American marines withdrew from Thailand on July 30.

When American attention reverted to Vietnam in 1963, it found a gradually worsening political situation. In May, the first of a series of riots in Hue were precipitated by conflict between the government in Saigon, largely operated by Catholic elites, and the Buddhists. On June 11, the first of several immolations by Buddhists monks and other anti-government individuals occurred. U.S.-Diem relations became strained. The American government felt that concessions should be made to the Buddhists because the religious crisis interfered with the war effort against the Vietcong. The situation grew worse throughout the summer and autumn with significant military losses in the field and rioting in Saigon and Hue. On November 1, 1963, Diem was murdered and his administration replaced by a military junta headed by Maj. Gen. Duong Van Minh.

The American Involvement: November 1963 to the present

Within a few weeks, on November 22, 1963, President Kennedy himself was murdered. Thus, two new governments faced the problems posed by the Vietnamese conflict. On November 24, President Lyndon B. Johnson affirmed his administration's commitment to Kennedy's policies. This last period in the Vietnamese conflict was characterized by the Saigon government's political instability and a growing American involvement.

South Vietnamese lack of political stability was evident early in the period. On January 30, 1964, Maj. Gen. Nguyan Khanh deposed Minh. The Khanh junta was subjected to pressures similar to those experienced by Diem: immolations by Buddhists, and demonstrations and riots by both students and Buddhists. On June 19, 1965, Nguyen Cao Ky was appointed prime minister in a military shake-up in which Khanh was replaced. In an attempt to stabilize the political situation, a Constituent Assembly was elected on September 11, 1966. This

Assembly drew up a constitution and on September 3, 1967, general elections were held for President, Vice President, and a Senate. Thieu was elected President and Ky, Vice President. The ability of the Vietcong to penetrate the major cities of South Vietnam during the February 1968 Tet offensive raises the question of whether or not the Thieu-Ky government has attained stability.

The second characteristic of this period is the U.S.'s mounting involvement in the war. The Johnson Administration during its first year in office faced a challenge from the Republican candidate for president, who advocated using tactical nuclear weapons and bombing North Vietnam. In the midst of the campaign, on August 2, three small North Vietnamese naval craft attacked a U.S. destroyer in the Gulf of Tonkin in international waters (30 miles from shore). Two days later, two destroyers were attacked 65 miles from shore. On the same day, August 4, President Johnson ordered a limited, retaliatory, bombing attack on specific targets in North Vietnam. On August 7, both houses of Congress passed a resolution which supported the President in taking "all necessary measures to repel any armed attacks against the forces of the United States and to prevent further aggression," and authorized the President as he "determines to take all necessary steps, including the use of armed force, to assist any protocol or member state" of SEATO which requested "assistance in defense of its freedom." Only two votes, both in the Senate, were cast against the resolution. Two points should be made concerning this incident: (a) the Gulf of Tonkin incident came to be questioned regarding the facts of the case, and (b) the American response was not the beginning of continuous bombing of North Vietnam. The Johnson Administration did not choose to cash in the blank check given it in the Gulf of Tonkin resolution.

An attack on the U.S. airbase at Pleiku on February 7, 1965, triggered the Johnson Administration into making a major response in the Vietnamese conflict. Eight Americans were killed and 107 wounded. On February 28, President Johnson ordered continuous air bombardment of North Vietnam. In March, the U.S. began a massive buildup of forces in South Vietnam.

U.S. policy objectives

What are the policy objectives of the American government in the Vietnamese conflict? Mr. Goldberg's statement reprinted below lists and evaluates the enemy's basis for negotiations, while the famous "Fourteen Points" outline U.S. policy. The Fourteen Points first appeared in Department of State press releases in January 1966, and were repeated by Mr. Rusk with no changes before the Senate Committee on Foreign Relations in February. The Fourteen Points are, in fact, only thirteen in number, since #3 and #4 refer to the same condition, using different words. They may be divided into four major categories: (a) those concerned with conditions prior to negotiations (points 3, 4, and 14) ; (b) those that will serve as a basis for discussion (points 1, 2, 5, 6, and 13) ; (c) those dealing with U.S. intentions in Vietnam (points 7, 8, and 12); and finally, (d) those dealing with the future of Vietnam (points 9, 10, and 11) .

Another attempt to spell out the American position was made by President Johnson during a television interview in December 1967. At that time, Mr. Johnson presented a "five point" program for peace in Vietnam which introduced new considerations as well as amplified selected items from the "Fourteen Points." In his first point, Mr. Johnson declared that the demilitarized zone must be respected, which was not included in the Fourteen Points. Evidently, Mr. Johnson was stipulating that the North Vietnamese government must agree to cease infiltration of men and arms into South Vietnam. This stipulation has come to be known as the "San Antonio formula" because it first appeared in Mr. Johnson's address of September 29, 1967, in San Antonio, Texas. His second item was a restatement of the tenth of the Fourteen Points, *i.e.,* that the unification of Vietnam should be brought about peacefully and through negotiations. However, the third point injected a totally new consideration: Mr. Johnson demanded that North Vietnamese forces be withdrawn from Laos. His strategy of bringing Laos into the Vietnamese conflict is unclear. In fourth place, Mr. Johnson amplified the ninth point of the Fourteen Points by introducing the American principle of one man-one vote as the basis for constructing a South Vietnamese government. In effect, he was denying the National Liberation Front (NLF) coequal status in the new government. Rather, the NLF would occupy a position in proportion to the votes it would garner in a free election. Finally, Mr. Johnson proposed that the South Vietnamese government begin direct negotiations with the NLF. One of the Fourteen Points (13) held open the possibility of NLF participation in a U.S.-Hanoi-Saigon conference, but now Mr. Johnson was proposing bilateral Saigon-NLF negotiations. Mr. Johnson's March 31, 1968, address did not clarify the American position, although he did order a partial bombing halt to encourage negotiations, which began in Paris in April. Johnson ordered a total cessation of all bombardment of North Vietnam in November of that year before the election of Richard M. Nixon as president.

Conclusion

There is no doubt that Southeast Asia has the highest priority in American foreign policy today because of the Vietnamese conflict. The two policy statements below give the U.S. government's position on its own goals, as well as its image of the enemy's stated objectives.

U.S. Offical Position on Vietnam: The "Fourteen Points"[1]

1. The Geneva Agreements of 1954 and 1962 are an adequate basis for peace in Southeast Asia.

2. We would welcome a conference on Southeast Asia or on any part thereof.

3. We would welcome "negotiations without preconditions" as the 17 nations put it.

4. We would welcome unconditional discussions as President Johnson put it.

5. A cessation of hostilities could be the first order of business at a conference or could be the subject of preliminary discussions.

6. Hanoi's four points could be discussed along with other points which others might wish to propose.

7. We want no U.S. bases in Southeast Asia.

8. We do not desire to retain U.S. troops in South Vietnam after peace is assured.

9. We support free elections in South Vietnam to give the South Vietnamese a government of their own choice.

10. The question of reunification of Vietnam should be determined by the Vietnamese through their own free decision.

11. The countries of Southeast Asia can be nonalined or neutral if that be their option.

12. We would much prefer to use our resources for the economic reconstruction of Southeast Asia than in war. If there is peace, North Vietnam could participate in a regional effort to which we would be prepared to contribute at least one billion dollars.

---

[1] The "Fourteen Points" were published first in State Department press releases dated January 3 and 7, 1966. Reprinted in the Senate Committee on Foreign Relations' *Background Information Relating to Southeast Asia and Vietnam* Third Revised Edition. (Washington, D.C.: Government Printing Office, 1967), pp. 184-86.

13. The President has said: "The Vietcong would not have difficulty being represented and having their views represented if for a moment Hanoi decided she wanted to cease aggression. I don't think that would be an insurmountable problem."

14. We have said publicly and privately that we could stop the bombing of North Vietnam as a step toward peace although there has not been the slightest hint or suggestion from the other side as to what they would do if the bombing stopped.

United States Peace Aims in Viet-Nam

by Arthur J. Goldberg

U.S. Representative to the United Nations[1]

* * *

Let me begin . . . by recalling the basic American peace aims in Viet-Nam. These aims have been stated many times by President Johnson and other responsible spokesmen of the United States. They have been stated over a span of 2 years, but the ebb and flow of the military situation during that time has not made them any less valid as guidelines for peace negotiations. We do not subscribe to the false notion that a strong military position obviates the desirability of seeking peace through negotiations. Today therefore, I wish to review the essence of these American aims.

The United States seeks a political solution in Viet-Nam. We do not seek the unconditional surrender of our adversaries. We seek a settlement whose terms will result not from dictation but from genuine negotiations, a settlement whose terms will not sacrifice the vital interest of any party.

* * *

We are not engaged in a "holy war" against communism. We do not seek an American sphere of influence in Asia, nor a permanent American "presence" of any kind—military or otherwise—in Viet-Nam, nor the imposition of a military alliance on South Viet-Nam.

We do not seek to do any injury to mainland China nor to threaten any of its legitimate interests.

---

[1] Excerpts from an address made at a special convocation at Howard University, Washington, D. C., on February 10, 1967. Printed in the *Department of State Bulletin*, February 27, 1967, pp. 310-16.

We seek to assure to the people of South Viet-Nam the affirmative exercise of the right of self-determination, the right to decide their own political destiny free of external interference and force and through democratic processes. In keeping with the announced South Vietnamese Government's policy of national reconciliation, we do not seek to exclude any segment of the South Vietnamese people from peaceful participation in their country's future. We are prepared to accept the results of that decision, whatever it may be. We support the early consummation of a democratic constitutional system in South Viet-Nam and welcome the progress being made to this end.

As regards North Viet-Nam, we have no designs on its territory, and we do not seek to overthrow its government, whatever its ideology. We are prepared fully to respect its sovereignty and territorial integrity and to enter into specific undertakings to that end.

We believe the reunification of Viet-Nam should be decided upon through a free choice by the peoples of both the North and the South without any outside interference; and the results of that choice also will have our full support.

Finally, when peace is restored we are willing to make a major commitment of money, talent, and resources to a multilateral cooperative effort to bring to all of Southeast Asia, including North Viet-Nam, the benefits of economic and social reconstruction and development which that area so sorely needs.

These, then, are the peace aims of the United States. They parallel the objectives stated by the South Vietnamese Government at Manila. Our aims are strictly limited, and we sincerely believe they contain nothing inconsistent with the interests of any party. Our public pronouncements of them—both in Washington and at the United Nations—are solemn commitments by the United States.

Our adversaries have also placed their aims and objectives on the public record over the past 2 years. The major statement of these aims is the well-known four points of Hanoi, which I will summarize without departing too much from their own terminology.

Hanoi's Four Points

The first point calls for recognition of the basic national rights of the Vietnamese people: peace, independence, sovereignty, unity, and territorial integrity. It also calls for the cessation of all acts of war against the North; the ending of United States intervention in the South; the withdrawal of all United States troops, military personnel, and weapons of all kinds; the dismantling of American bases; and the cancellation of what they term the United States "military alliance" with South Viet-Nam.

The United States would not find any essential difficulty with a reasonable interpretation of any of the terms included in this point. Our chief concern is what it does *not* include: namely, that North Viet-Nam also cease its intervention in the South, end all of its acts of war against the South, and withdraw its forces from the South. Such a requirement is obviously essential to the "peace" to which this first point refers.

The second point relates to the military clauses of the Geneva agreements. It provides that, pending the peaceful reunification of Viet-Nam, both the North and the South must refrain from joining any military alliance and that there should be no foreign bases, troops, or military personnel in their respective territories.

Here again, the only real difficulty is the omission of any obligation on the North to withdraw its military forces from the South—although the Geneva accords, which established the demarcation line in Viet-Nam, forbid military interference of any sort by one side in the affairs of the other and even go so far as to forbid civilians to cross the demilitarized zone.

The third point calls for the settlement of the South's internal affairs in accordance with the program of the National Liberation Front for South Viet-Nam. This point, of course, was not a part of the Geneva accords at all. It introduces a new element which I shall discuss later in this analysis.

The fourth point calls for the peaceful reunification of Viet-Nam, to be settled by the people of both zones without any foreign interference. We have no difficulty with this point, as was indicated in my speech to the General Assembly on September 22.[2]

There has apparently been added a fifth point—put forward and repeatedly endorsed by both Hanoi and the National Liberation

---

[2] For text, see *ibid.*, October 10, 1966, p. 518. (Mr. Goldberg's September 22, 1966, statement contained these words: "Our view on this matter was stated some time ago by President Johnson, who made clear that as far as we are concerned, this question would not be 'an insurmountable problem.' We therefore invite the authorities in Hanoi to consider whether this obstacle to negotiations may not be more imaginary than real." Editor's note.)

Front since the enunciation of the four points in April 1965. This fifth point was stated by Ho Chi Minh in January 1966, when he said that if the United States really wants peace, it must recognize the National Liberation Front as the "sole genuine representative" of the people of South Viet-Nam and engage in negotiation with it. This, like the third of the four points, introduces a new element which was not part of the Geneva accords.

Now, from this brief summation of our aims and those declared by Hanoi, it is clear that there are areas of agreement and areas of disagreement. Recent public statements by Hanoi have been helpful in certain aspects, but how great the disagreements are is still uncertain, because the stated aims of Hanoi still contain a number of ambiguities. I would like to discuss some of these ambiguities because they relate to very consequential matters.

Ambiguities in Hanoi's Stated Aims

There is ambiguity, for example, on the role of the National Liberation Front in peace negotiations. I have already noted the statement of Ho Chi Minh and other spokesmen for our adversaries who have said that we must recognize the Front as "the sole genuine representative" of the South Vietnamese people and negotiate with it. If this means that we are asked to cease our recognition of the Government in Saigon and deal only with the Front, insistence on this point would imperil the search for peace. For the Front has not been chosen by any democratic process to represent the people of South Viet-Nam. Nor has the Front been recognized by the world community. It is pertinent to recall that more than 60 nations recognize the Government of the Republic of Viet-Nam in Saigon, whereas none recognizes the National Liberation Front as a government.

On the other hand, some public statements seem to call for the National Liberation Front to be given a place or voice at the negotiating table. If this were the position of our adversaries, the prospects would be brighter; for President Johnson, as long ago as July 1965,[3] said that "The Viet Cong would have no difficulty in being represented and having their views presented if Hanoi for a moment decides she wants to cease aggression." He added that this did not seem to him to be "an insurmountable problem," and that "I think that could be worked out."

---

[3] At a news conference on July 28, 1965.

A further ambiguity relates to the role of the National Liberation Front in the future political life of South Viet-Nam. Hanoi asks that the affairs of South Viet-Nam be settled "in accordance with the program of the National Liberation Front." Our adversaries, in their various comments on this point, take no notice of the internationally recognized Government of South Viet-Nam or of the steps which the South Vietnamese leaders have taken and have currently under way and the institutions they are now creating for the purpose of providing their country with a constitutional and representative government. Nor would their statements seem to leave any place for the South Vietnamese who have participated in and promoted such steps. Such an interpretation would pose serious obstacles to a settlement.

However, some claim that what the National Liberation Front really seeks is no more than the opportunity to advance its program peacefully along with other elements and groupings in the South in a free political environment.

We have already made it clear that we do not wish to exclude any segment of the South Vietnamese people from peaceful participation in their country's future and that we support a policy of national reconciliation endorsed by the South Vietnamese Government in the Manila communique.[4] Indeed, as Secretary Rusk said in an interview last week,[5] if the Viet Cong were to lay down their arms, ways could be found to permit them to take part in the normal political processes in South Viet-Nam.

Further ambiguities arise concerning the question of foreign troops in South Viet-Nam. What does Hanoi mean by "foreign troops"? They clearly include in this term the forces of the United States and other countries aiding the South, but they have never admitted the presence of their own forces in the South. Of course, a one-sided withdrawal by our side would not lead to an acceptable peace. All external forces must withdraw, those of Hanoi as well as ours, if peace is to be achieved.

There is ambiguity also in Hanoi's position on the timing of the withdrawal of external forces. Do our adversaries consider withdrawal of forces as a precondition to negotiations, as some of their statements

---

[4] This is a reference to the communique issued by the October 1966 Manila Conference, the text of which may be found in the *Department of State Bulletin*, November 14, 1966, p. 730. (Editor's note.)

[5] *Ibid.*, February 20, 1967, p. 274.

imply? If so, this again would raise a serious obstacle to progress. But if they look on withdrawal of forces as a provision to be incorporated in a settlement, this clearly could be worked out. The United States and its allies are already on record in the Manila communique that their forces "shall be withdrawn ... as the other side withdraws its forces to the North, ceases infiltration, and the level of violence thus subsides. Those forces will be withdrawn as soon as possible and not later than six months after the above conditions have been fulfilled." Further, we have indicated our willingness to join in a phased and supervised withdrawal of forces by both sides.

Next, there is ambiguity in Hanoi's position on the cessation of bombing of North Viet-Nam. At times their public statements have demanded that the bombing be ended unconditionally, without any reference to a possible response from their side. On the other hand, quite recently a spokesman of Hanoi said that "if, after the definitive and unconditional cessation of the bombardments, the American Government proposes to enter into contact with the [North Vietnamese] Government, ... this proposal will be examined and studied." And just this week we have seen a further statement, in an interview by the North Vietnamese Foreign Minister, that cessation of the bombings "could lead to talks between North Viet Nam and the U.S." Many of their statements insisting that the bombing cease have also contained other expressions, such as that the American military presence in South Viet-Nam be completely withdrawn and that the four points of Hanoi must be recognized and accepted as "the" basis—or possibly as "a" basis—for settlement of the conflict. This creates an additional ambiguity as to whether Hanoi means to add still other prenegotiating conditions.

The position of the United States on this bombing question has been stated by a number of administration spokesmen, including me at the United Nations. The United States remains prepared to take the first step and order a cessation of all bombing of North Viet-Nam the moment we are assured, privately or otherwise, that this step will be answered promptly by a tangible response toward peace from North Viet-Nam.

* * *

We shall continue our efforts for a peaceful and honorable settlement until they are crowned with success.

U.S. Ready To Negotiate in Good Faith

Some analysts contend that our terms of settlement should be more precisely defined. But it is very difficult to be more precise in advance of negotiation and particularly in light of the substantive ambiguities on the other side. But whatever questions may be raised, they should and can best be resolved in discussions between parties who have the power to resolve them. For our part, we stand ready to negotiate in good faith unconditionally to resolve all outstanding questions.

The United States approach to negotiations is flexible. We and our allies do not ask our adversaries to accept, as a precondition to discussions or negotiations, any point of ours to which they may have objections. Nor do we rule out the discussion of any points of theirs, however difficult they might appear to us. We are willing to discuss and negotiate not only our own points but Hanoi's four points, and points emanating from any other source, including the Secretary-General of the United Nations.

It remains to be seen whether our adversaries share this concept of negotiations. As I have already pointed out, their various public declarations of peace aims have often been coupled with statements that the goals they put forward must, for example, be "accepted" or "recognized" as the "sole basis" or "the most correct basis" or "the only sound basis" or "the basis for the most correct political solution."

Such statements contain still further ambiguity—in one sense the most fundamental of all, since it relates to the concept of negotiation itself. Do these statements mean that Hanoi is willing to enter negotiations only if there is an assurance in advance that the outcome will be on their terms and will, in effect, simply ratify the goals they have already stated? Such an attitude would not be conducive to peace and would make the outlook for a settlement bleak indeed.

If, on the other hand, North Viet-Nam were to say that their points are not preconditions to discussions or negotiations, then the prospects should be more promising.

Our negotiating approach would permit each side to seek clarification of the other side's position. It does not require the acceptance in advance of any points, least of all those whose meaning may be in need of clarification. We do not ask that of Hanoi—and progress toward a settlement will be facilitated if Hanoi does not ask it of us.

In this situation, how can we best move toward a settlement?

One essential early step is to analyze the positions of all parties in order to ascertain whether there is some element or some kernel common to all. Many students of the subject have pointed to one fact which may prove to be such a kernel, namely, the fact that both sides have pointed to the Geneva agreements of 1954 and 1962 as an acceptable basis for a peaceful settlement.

But I must add quickly that this does not necessarily indicate a real meeting of the minds, because of doubts that all sides interpret the Geneva agreements in the same light. Hanoi has said that the essence of the Geneva agreements is contained in its four points. But the four points would not put Hanoi under any restraint or obligations in its hostile activities against the South, which the Geneva accords explicitly prohibit. Besides, as I already pointed out, these points insist that the South's future be regulated in accordance with the program of a group which was not referred to in the Geneva accords and did not even exist when they were written. And in any case, if the Geneva accords were to serve as a basis for settlement, it would obviously be necessary to revitalize the international machinery which they provided for supervision, which is presently operating under severe limitations; to incorporate effective international guarantees; and to update other provisions of the accords which on their face are clearly out of date.

Despite these problems of interpretation, it can be said that if the meaning of the Geneva agreements were accepted as a matter for genuine negotiation, then the constant reference to these agreements by both sides would be more than a verbal similarity; it would be a significant and hopeful sign of the prospects for settlement.

Methods for Seeking a Political Settlement

From all this analysis, there emerges one basic and practical question, and it is this: How are all these apparent obstacles to a settlement to be overcome?

The first and essential prerequisite is the will to resolve them, not by unconditional surrender or by the dictation of terms but through a process of mutual accommodation whereby nobody's vital interests are injured, which would be a political solution. Speaking for the United States Government, I affirm without reservation the willingness of the United States to seek and find a political solution.

The next question, then, is by what procedure such a political settlement can be reached. One well-tested and time-proven way is the conference table. President Johnson has repeatedly stated our readiness to join in a conference in Geneva, in Asia, or in any other suitable place. We remain prepared today to go to the conference table as soon as, and wherever, our adversaries are prepared to join us.

There is also a second procedure by which to pursue a political settlement: namely, private negotiations—either by direct contact or through an intermediary. There is much to be said for this private method, for in a situation as grave as this, with its complex historical background and its present political crosscurrents, it would be exceedingly difficult to negotiate in a goldfish bowl.

I therefore affirm that the United States Government stands ready to take this route also toward a political settlement. And we give our assurance that the secrecy and security of such private explorations would be safeguarded on our side. Of course, we do not and should not ask that freedom of expression be curtailed in the slightest degree.

* * *

Let me quickly add that at this juncture I do not want to raise any false hopes by this remark. I am simply stating a principle which is inherent in the concept of the secrecy and security of private explorations.

Such then is my analysis of the problems involved and the methods to be employed in seeking a negotiated solution of the Vietnamese conflict. Nor should we overlook the possibility that negotiations, private or public, might be preceded or facilitated by the process of mutual deescalation or a scaling down of the conflict without a formally negotiated cease-fire. This, of course, would be welcome on our part.

It is altogether possible, too, that there will be no negotiations culminating in a formal agreement, that our adversaries will sooner or later find the burden of the war too exhausting and that the conflict will gradually come to an end.

Perhaps this will, indeed, prove to be the outcome. But our most respected military authorities have cautioned us not to expect that this will happen quickly and that we must face the possibility of a long struggle. Surely, if there is any contribution that diplomacy can make to hastening a just and honorable end of this struggle, we cannot in all conscience spare any effort or any labor, day or night, to make that contribution—no matter how difficult and frustrating the effort may be or how many false starts and failures and new beginnings it may entail.

As students of history know, one obstacle to a negotiated end of any war can be psychological. The frame of mind appropriate to fighting and the frame of mind appropriate to peacemaking are by nature very different. And yet a stage inevitably comes when both these seemingly contradictory efforts must go on side by side.

Many citizens, viewing this complex dual process, are likely to be confused and distressed by what seems like an inconsistency in their leaders' policies. Some complain that the talk of peace suggests a weakening of our resolve and of our will to win. Simultaneously others complain that the continued military effort suggests an attempt to bring the adversary to his knees, to break his will, and thus casts doubt on the sincerity of our will to peace.

The great difficulty of achieving peace should serve to remind us that there are substantial conflicting interests at stake which stubbornly resist solution; that peace cannot be bought at any price, nor can real conflicts of purpose be waved away with a magic wand. By the same token, the ferocity of war should not be an incitement to hatred but rather a stern discipline, a reminder of the imperative duty to define responsibly the limited interests for which our soldiers fight and which a peace settlement must protect.

The effort to make such a responsible definition and to carry it through the process of peace negotiations is piled high with difficulty. A genuine meeting of the minds may never be wholly achieved. It is unlikely that terms of settlement for this stubborn conflict can be found which would be wholly pleasing to either side. But it is in our highest national interest that an acceptable, livable solution should be found.

Let no one suppose that patriotism, which is so inspiringly displayed on the battlefield, is not also present at the negotiating table. All our recent Presidents have testified to our country's dedication to negotiation as a means of peacefully bridging differences.

* * *

14

The Middle East

After the Ottoman Empire disintegrated in defeat with the Axis powers in 1919, independent Arab nations began to emerge in the Middle East. American prestige in the area was at its highest point at the end of World War I for several reasons. Woodrow Wilson advocated that all colonies be placed under the League of Nations' supervision as "mandates" and be programmed for eventual independence. This stand appealed to the Arab nations, many of whom exchanged Ottoman hegemony for British or French rule. Also, the U.S. refused to accept, under League of Nations auspices, supervisory functions over any colony. Furthermore, the U.S. possessed a legacy of goodwill in the Middle East built up by missionaries who brought educational and medical benefits with them. Until the end of World War II, the United States government refused to become involved politically in the Middle East.

Strategic importance of the Middle East

After World War II, the Middle East became a region of primary importance for four reasons. First, the British, whom the American government recognized as the Western power with primary ascendancy in the area, began to experience financial problems which led them to abdicate their position. Second, U.S. decision-makers read into Soviet behavior toward Iran and Turkey an indication of aggressive designs on the area. Third, the war had shown the need to preserve American oil reserves by developing alternative sources of petroleum. Oil shipments to Europe under the Marshall Plan reinforced this need. The Middle East boasted three-fourths of the oil reserves of the world. Finally, the Suez Canal and the Turkish Straits were two strategic waterways which made the Middle East an extremely valuable piece of real estate. The Suez Canal was vital to European economic existence, and Turkish control over the Straits denied to the Russians access to the Mediterranean Sea.

These four strategic factors molded American foreign policy toward the Middle East. In general, the policy response has been uneven, running the gamut from disinterest to unilateral intervention.

1946-1947: the Russian "threat"

Whether or not a Russian threat existed to conquer the Middle East by subversion or aggression in 1946 is an open question. American policy-makers in 1946, however, perceived a threat in four Soviet lines of policy. One was a Russian request for a part in controlling Libya, a former Italian colony. Another was alleged Russian support of guerrillas who opposed the Greek monarchy. A third was the Russian demand presented on several occasions to the Turkish government for a joint Turko-Soviet defense of the Straits (thus infringing on Turkish sovereignty). And the last "threat," and perhaps the most serious, was Russian attempts to establish a satellite government in northern Iran.

The irony of the Cold War was that it began in the Middle East, not Europe. The effect of these four situations was to arouse the Truman Administration's suspicions of Soviet designs in an area of strategic importance. In addition, the British government in March 1947 informed the Truman Administration that it must reduce its commitments in the Middle East. The result was the Truman Doctrine.

Assuming that the four Soviet threats existed, then American policy was successful during this first period of its Middle East policy—a success, unfortunately, that has been rarely duplicated in the following periods. The Libyan question was solved by a U.N. trusteeship arrangement: the Greek Loyalist forces defeated the guerrillas; the Turks, bouyed by American support, refused the Soviet demands for a joint defense arrangement; Russian troops were withdrawn from northern Iran and the Iranian government established control over the area.

1948-1952: a period of pro-Israeli policy and attempted alliances

The United States approached the Middle East in the immediate post-war years with partial, rather than comprehensive, policies. Two indications of partial policies were concern for Soviet threats, which led to attempts to form a regional alliance, and concern for Jewish refugees left homeless by World War II.

President Truman advocated large-scale migration into Palestine as an answer to Europe's refugee problem. Palestine was governed by the United Kingdom as a non-independent territory (or "mandate"). The British, with a more comprehensive view of the Middle East, opposed Jewish immigration for fear of alienating the Arabs. With or without British approval, Jewish immigration continued, the first trickle eventually becoming a tide while the British and American governments looked for a solution acceptable to both Jewish and Arab sides. No solution was forthcoming and in frustration the British terminated its mandate on May 14, 1948. The Jewish community in Palestine declared itself an independent state and received the recognition of both the United States and the Soviet Union. Fighting erupted between the Jewish and Arab settlers. The Arab states, primarily Egypt, Iraq, Syria, and Transjordan, sent troops. In 1949, a ceasefire was negotiated and Israel signed armistice agreements under U.N. auspices with Egypt (February 4), Lebanon (March 23), Transjordan (April 3) and Syria (July 20). No armistice was signed with Iraq although Iraqi troops were withdrawn from Palestine.

Israel owed its existence as an independent state to its military victories in the field and not to American foreign policy. In fact, American policy during this period was divided between a pro-Israeli President, on one hand, and pro-Arab State and Defense departments, on the other. The presidential directives won out, and American foreign policy throughout this period was partial to the new state of Israel.

The second theme of this period—that of building an alliance against Soviet aggression—conflicted with the pro-Israeli policy. To the Arab leaders, especially the Egyptians, the only danger of aggression came from the Jews and not the Russians. The U.S. and United Kingdom first attempted to build the Middle East Command, and then, the Middle East Defense Organization; both efforts failed.

253

1953-1956: Eisenhower impartiality

The Eisenhower Administration formulated the first comprehensive policy toward the Middle East. Secretary of State John Foster Dulles showed more interest in the region than did his predecessors or any of his successors. The U.S. government abandoned the idea of a regional alliance. When the Baghdad pact was negotiated in September 1955 between Iraq and Turkey, and later joined by Great Britain, Iran, and Pakistan, the United States refused to join for fear of alienating Egypt's Nasser.

An impartial policy also meant that the U.S. refused to arm both Arab and Israeli armies. In February 1955, Israeli army units invaded the Gaza area in a raid that showed Egyptian military weakness. Nasser turned to the Soviet Union to purchase arms that the U.S. refused to sell. American-Egyptian relations grew worse. On July 19, 1956, Secretary Dulles withdrew American economic assistance to build the Aswan Dam. On July 26, Nasser nationalized the Suez Canal Company to obtain funds to raise money for the Aswan project. This action precipitated the British-French-Israeli invasion of October 1956.

1957-1960: The Eisenhower Doctrine

The policy response of the Eisenhower Administration following the October 1956 Suez invasion was to apply unilaterally American power in Middle East. The British had been discredited among the Arab governments by the invasion attempt. In January 1957, Eisenhower asked Congress to approve by joint resolution a "doctrine," which became attached to his name. Among its provisions was authorization given to the President to employ the "armed forces of the United States to secure and protect the territorial integrity and political independence of nations" that requested aid and "against overt armed aggression from any nation controlled by International Communism." No new sum of money was appropriated, but the President asked that $200 million be set aside from regular foreign aid funds especially for Middle Eastern countries.

The $200 million were dispensed within a year, but the authority to intervene contained in the Eisenhower Doctrine was not invoked until July 1958. The Iraqi monarchy fell because of a military coup.

The Lebanese and Jordanian heads of state believed themselves threatened and called on the Western powers to save their government from "Communism." British paratroopers moved into Jordan and American marines landed in Lebanon. The U.S. increased its support of the Central Treaty Organization or the Baghdad Pact. In 1959, the American government negotiated bilateral treaties of defense with Turkey, Pakistan, and Iran.

1960-present: Region of low priority

Kennedy continued the Eisenhower policy of impartiality, but he dropped the policy of unilateral intervention contained in his predecessor's "Doctrine." Also, there were indications that Kennedy attempted to come to terms with the nationalism that Nasser represented. The U.S. recognized the republican regime of Yemen which had been opposed by the monarchs of Jordan and Saudi Arabia. As Kennedy (and later Johnson) became more concerned about other areas of the world, primarily Southeast Asia, the U.S. government assigned a low-priority rating to the Middle East. When conflict occurred in June 1967, the U.S. was willing to let the U.N. handle the problem.

Conclusion

American policy in the Middle East, as spelled out in Eugene V. Rostow's statement, has been to walk the taut line of impartiality between Arabs and Israelis and to forestall Soviet penetration into the area.

The Middle East Crisis and Beyond

by Eugene V. Rostow

Under Secretary for Political Affairs[1]

* * *

The Middle Eastern crisis should be viewed ... as one among many problems we have inherited as the consequence of the withdrawal of Europe, the weakness of many parts of the third world, and the fervent ambitions of many schools and sects of revolutionaries.

The Root of the Trouble in the Middle East

The root of trouble in the southern part of the Mediterranean basin is endemic political and social instability. It is typical of similar problems in many other parts of the third world. But in the Middle East and North Africa it is complicated—and made more dangerous as a burden to world peace—by special factors of history, geography, and proximity to Europe.

For centuries the region has not had a stable and independent political life sustained by its own inherent strength. The proud peoples of the area, who have made great contributions to our common civilization, have been governed by a succession of imperial regimes. The rise and fall of alien governments—Turkish, British, or French— have complicated the effort of the peoples of the Middle East and North Africa to establish communities which could actively participate in the common educational, economic, and political life of the modern world. The struggle of the people of the area to achieve

---

[1] Excerpts from an address made before the Lamar Society of the University of Mississippi Law School at Oxford, Miss., on December 8, 1967. Printed in the *Department of State Bulletin,* January 8, 1968, pp. 41-8.

independence has strengthened the spirit of their nationalism. But their nationalism has sometimes taken extreme forms and resulted in political fragmentation, tempting outside intervention. The temptation to intervene has been reinforced by the fundamental human, economic, and strategic importance of the region.

The United States and nations of Europe have had close and friendly relations with the peoples and governments of the Middle East for generations. The Middle East links three continents. Its airspace and waterways are vital to communication between Asia, Europe, and Africa. And they have fundamental strategic significance. The oil resources of the region are a major factor in world commerce. The power to deny access to the Middle East and its resources would be a matter of grave concern to the United States and its allies in Europe and elsewhere.

The reciprocal relationship between inherent weakness and the force of real interests led to the European presence in the region. Until the end of the Second World War, Britain and France sought to protect their many interests in the area through a system of protectorates and other devices of control.

The split between America and her allies in 1956 marked our unwillingness to support an imperialist policy for today's world. In our view, imperialism is inadmissible in an era which accepts the principle of national self-determination and independence. In the 20th century, imperialism would lead not to stability but to endless, brutalizing civil war. It would defeat the goal of order it seeks to fulfill.

U.S. Goal: To Promote a System of Peace

Our policy, on the contrary, has been to protect our national interest in stability by other means. We have used our influence in the Middle East, as we do in other regions of the world, to promote a system of peace, achieved in collaboration with other nations and sustained with their consent and support—a system of diversity, in the spirit of the United Nations Charter, "based on respect for the principle of equal rights and self-determination of peoples"—above all, a system of peace. We believe in reaching that goal through political means and on the indispensable basis of the responsible decisions of the people of the region themselves.

257

Therefore we have sought to foster an environment in which the countries of the region would come to terms with each other and turn their attention toward cooperative efforts necessary for developing their own immense resources. Only such a stable order, rooted in the region itself and at the same time an integral part of the world's economy and society, could deter intervention from without. To assist that process, we have repeatedly announced our purpose to support the territorial integrity and political independence of all the states of the Middle East, with sympathy and understanding for all and special favor for none.

Obstacles to Stability and Progress

In recent years there have been three main obstacles to achieving such conditions of stability and progress. First, there are bitter divisions among the Muslim peoples of the Middle East; secondly, some Arab states have refused to accept the creation of Israel and have insisted on their right to attack its existence; and finally, since 1955 there has been an increasing Soviet presence in the area, as a military, political, and economic influence and, above all, as a source of arms.

I should like to discuss each of these three factors briefly.

1. Some of the divisions among the peoples of the Middle East derive from their history. During the long, slow decline of the Ottoman Empire, many of the peoples of the area lived under conditions of stagnation, isolated from the modern world. The drama of Arab liberation during World War I left a legacy of fervent misunderstandings, haphazard boundaries, and disappointed expectations. After the First World War, Ottoman rule was replaced in many areas by the British and the French, both long active in the region.

The era of European control came to an end after the Second World War. The French lost Syria and the Lebanon and gave up Morocco, Tunisia, and Algeria as well. Britain's postwar withdrawal from empire ended her presence in Cyprus, Aden, Egypt, Jordan, Palestine, and Iraq.

But the political and military departure of the Western Powers did little to resolve the divisions among the peoples and governments of the Middle East and North Africa. They had had differing experiences under foreign tutelage: different levels of education and different patterns of participation in the work of modern societies. The

258

movements against foreign control gave rise to strong nationalist movements throughout the area. But those movements took many forms. It soon became clear that the peoples and governments of the region had different views about how to organize their political, social, and economic life.

In Egypt a revolutionary government led by President Nasser looked to a new pan-Arab state uniting the whole region. For a time at least, revolutions in Syria and Iraq and strong popular support in other countries made this prospect seem likely to succeed.

At present, the states of the area represent a wide spectrum of political forms: There is an extremist revolutionary government in Syria and a traditionalist monarchy in Saudi Arabia. Meanwhile, Iran and Turkey, to the north, are becoming vigorous modern communities with close ties to the West. Thus the Middle East has remained divided, and some parts of the area are in turmoil.

This state of affairs is hardly surprising. In a world where the most advanced technological facilities exist side by side with medieval social customs and appalling poverty, it is no wonder that there is widespread social and spiritual dislocation. Moreover, there is a notable lack of balance between population and resources among the various Arab countries. The principal country of the region, Egypt, has a population of 30 million but has up to now developed almost none of the great oil wealth characteristic of sparsely settled Saudi Arabia or the tiny Shiekhdom of Kuwait. Indeed, Egypt, for all its efforts at economic development, today has a national income of $150 per capita and difficult prospects for the future. Even the benefits of so massive a project as the Aswan Dam are expected to be absorbed by the rapid growth of population.

In short, it is not difficult to explain a high degree of friction and frustration among the peoples of the region as they struggle to adapt themselves and their rich traditions to a new world.

But the inherent difficulties of the task of modernization are only one dimension of the troubles of the region; another is the history of Israel.

2. The modern State of Israel stands as a tribute to the power of an ideal, the ancient Zionist dream of a return of the Jews from their dispersal, revived in modern times by Theodor Herzl.

Herzl's movement appealed to many Western European and American Jews and to many other Europeans and Americans as well. Starting in the late 19th century, support and sympathy rallied steadily to the Zionist cause. Waves of East European Jewish refugees, fleeing the Russian pogroms of the late 19th and early 20th century, swelled the Zionist movement and became the backbone of the early Jewish settlements in Palestine.

In 1917 Great Britain issued the Balfour declaration. That famous document promised the Jews a "national home" in Palestine at the end of the war. The development of this community, according to the declaration, should not prejudice the rights of "existing communities in Palestine." With the British mandate over Palestine at the end of World War I, Jewish immigration expanded. While some Arab leaders welcomed the Jews to Palestine, tension developed between the two communities. A new wave of immigration followed the Second World War, as the survivors of Hitlerism fled from Central Europe. The British authorities struggled to control the flood of immigrants in the interests of peace between the Arab and Jewish communities. In 1947, however, the British Government found the task impossible and yielded its mandate to the United Nations. The U.N. tried to mediate; but in 1947 the Arabs rejected its partition plan. The result was a war between the Arabs and the newly created State of Israel.

Armistice agreements finally concluded the fighting in 1949, but few people expected these interim arrangements to become the basis for stable relations between Israel and its Arab neighbors. Many questions remained unsettled, including a final definition of some borders. A peace settlement was expected to follow soon after the armistice. In the early 1950's the U.N.'s Palestine Conciliation Commission brought the Arabs and Israelis together for negotiations, but the positions of the two sides gradually became irreconcilable.

Many Arab spokesmen profess the view that the establishment of Israel was an injustice that can never be accepted. They insist that the Arab states are at war with Israel and that they have the right, at an appropriate moment, to join in a holy war to destroy it. The Arab states do not recognize Israel, exchange ambassadors, or allow normal trade with it.

On the other hand, many other nations, including the United States, have taken a sympathetic interest in the remarkable development of Israel as a progressive and democratic society. They have steadily insisted that, while they agree with the Arabs on some important aspects of the Middle Eastern conflict, Israel has a right to live, and no member of the United Nations can claim the right to destroy another.

3. The Russian interest in the Middle East has many antecedents. After the Second World War the Soviet Union attempted to gain control of Greece and Iran and sought the Italian mandate in Tripolitania. It began to give active support to Egypt as early as 1955, both in arms and in economic assistance, notably in connection with the Aswan Dam project. Through its arms sales and through its association with revolutionary parties, it became deeply involved in the internal politics of Syria, Algeria, and the other states of the area.

Increasingly massive arms shipments to Arab states complemented another aspect of Soviet policy in the Middle East: a growing hostility toward Israel. While the Soviet Union had supported the establishment of Israel in 1948, it changed its course during the early 1950's when it undertook its ambitious campaign to gain influence throughout the area. As a matter of political doctrine at least, hostility to Israel is a policy in which most Arab states concur. By siding with the Arabs against Israel, the Soviet Union allied itself with these passionate feelings. At the same time and as a result, the Western Powers could be identified with Israel, depicted as a tool of "Western imperialism." Such a posture could strengthen the radical leaders, parties, and revolutionary groups of the region, who hoped to displace moderate regimes oriented to the West.

Events Leading to the 1967 Crisis

Given these trends, it is hardly surprising that peace is not the natural state of affairs in the Middle East. The process of decolonization led to the British and French intervention in Suez, the protracted war in Algeria, and to the wars still in progress in the Arabian Peninsula. Among the Arabs, there has been a long history of a continuing covert struggle, resulting from time to time in attempted coups and revolutions, as in Syria and Iraq, or in open civil war and invasion, as in the Yemen. Meanwhile,.since the armistice agreements of 1949, there has been a smoldering guerrilla war with Israel, a conflict that in 1956 and now in 1967 erupted into full-scale hostilities.

By the middle of 1966 it was becoming clear that the situation around Israel was heading for another explosion. Organized bands of terrorists, trained in Syria, were penetrating Israel at an increasing pace, directly and through Jordan. Their raids caused damage, anxiety, and major Israeli retaliation. The issue came before the Security

Council twice in the fall of 1966.[2] There was no argument about the facts on either occasion. In the first episode, the Government of Syria boasted of its responsibility. But even a mild and ambiguous condemnation of Syria was defeated by a Soviet veto. In the second case, that of the Israeli retaliatory raid against Sam'u in Jordan, Israel was rightly censured.

In the spring of 1967 terrorist penetration of Israel from Syria increased. Rumors spread that Israel was mobilizing against Syria. Arab spokesmen began to taunt President Nasser for his inactivity in the face of the supposed threat to Syria. President Nasser responded by moving troops into the Sinai Peninsula and asked the United Nations to remove the forces that had patrolled the border between Israel and Egypt since 1957. The Secretary-General responded at once, without going through the type of consultations his predecessor had indicated he would undertake before withdrawing the troops. The United Nations Emergency Force was suddenly removed, not only from the border but from the Gaza Strip and Sharm-al-Sheikh as well. Egyptian troops promptly replaced them, and President Nasser announced that the Strait of Tiran would be closed to Israeli shipping.

At that moment the situation became one of full crisis. Sharm-al-Sheikh controls access through the Strait of Tiran to the Israeli port of Eilat on the Gulf of Aqaba. Since Egypt has kept the Suez Canal closed to Israeli shipping in the teeth of two Security Council resolutions, the Strait of Tiran was Israel's only direct opening to Africa and Asia and its most important source of oil. Closing the strait was in effect an act of blockade.

Egypt's announcement that it would use force to close the strait had another set of consequences. In 1957 the United States had taken the lead in negotiating the withdrawal of Israeli troops from Sharm-al-Sheikh and the Sinai as a whole. At that time Israel made it clear that if force were used to close the strait, it would regard itself justified in responding with force as an act of self-defense authorized under article 51 of the United Nations Charter. This carefully considered formal statement was noted at the time as part of the process of settlement. The international understanding was that the Strait of Tiran would be kept open as an international waterway. The United Arab Republic, it is true, never took formal responsibility for this

---

[2] For background, see *ibid.*, December 26, 1966, p. 969 and p. 974.

understanding, as it refused to recognize Israel or to deal directly with her. But in every other sense Egypt was a party to and beneficiary of this arrangement, through which Israeli withdrawals had been secured.

As President Johnson remarked later:[3] "If a single act of folly was more responsible for this explosion than any other, I think it was the arbitrary and dangerous announced decision that the Strait of Tiran would be closed."

Throughout this period, President Johnson directed an active diplomatic effort, which had started as a matter of urgency many months before the events of May and June. The goal of our policy was to prevent the outbreak of hostilities and to help deal with the underlying cause of tension in the Middle East.

U.S. Diplomatic Efforts

The President's strategy had several essential elements.

First, all the parties were urged to refrain from using force in any way. We attempted to mobilize world opinion in behalf of peace. Our views on the nature of the crisis and the dangers of the use of force were communicated to other governments and made public in a Presidential statement on May 23.[4] We invited Great Britain, France, and other interested nations to join with us in a concerted diplomatic effort to prevent war and then to make peace.

Second, we urgently sought a Security Council resolution calling on the parties to heed the Secretary-General's appeal to exercise restraint, forgo belligerence, and avoid all actions which could increase tension.[5] But several key nations refused to take responsibility for a resolution which might have helped to prevent war.

Third, we tried to initiate a series of talks with the United Arab Republic in the interest of finding a basis for a fair and peaceful settlement. The Vice President of that Government, Mr. Zachariah Moheiddin, was scheduled to come to Washington on June 7th, 2 days after hostilities broke out.

---

[3] For an address made by President Johnson on June 19, 1967, see *ibid.*, July 10, 1967, p. 31.

[4] For text, see *ibid.*, June 12, 1967, p. 870.

[5] For U.S. statements in the U.N. Security Council on May 29, 30, and 31, 1967, see *ibid.*, June 19, 1967, p. 920.

Meanwhile, as a fourth element in President Johnson's strategy, we and the British proposed to the leading maritime nations a draft declaration reaffirming the view that the Strait of Tiran and the Gulf of Aqaba were international waters, through which innocent passage could not be denied. The maritime nations had taken this position in 1947, and it had been upheld in 1958 in the International Convention on the Law of the Sea. The declaration was to be issued publicly during what turned out to be the week of hostilities.

While these efforts and others were being urgently pursued, the situation in the area changed radically. Mobilization and counter-mobilization had replaced the closing of the strait as a threat to the peace. A menacing array of force was approaching the borders of Israel from every side. Jordan put her forces under Egyptian command, and troops from Iraq, Algeria, and Kuwait joined the Egyptians and Syrians. President Nasser openly proclaimed the day of the holy war.

The air grew dry with menace.

The explosion occurred on the morning of June 5th.[6]

Principles for Peace in Middle East

President Johnson immediately announced the policy we have pursued ever since: to end hostilities as soon as possible and at the same time to begin the process of seeking to establish true peace in the area—a condition of peace that could replace the precarious armistice agreements whose inadequacy has been proved so often since 1949.

Our policy of peace to replace the armistice regime—a true peace based on the responsible assent of the nations directly concerned—has far-reaching implications for all the issues between Israel and her neighbors: for the achievement of stable and agreed borders, for security arrangements, and, above all, for the tragic plight of the Arab refugees, who have been hostages to politics for nearly 20 years.

The United States sought an immediate cease-fire resolution in the Security Council on the first day of hostilities. But the Soviets and Arabs did not favor such a proposal. Therefore the Security Council was unable to agree on terms. On Tuesday, June 6th, it was at least possible to obtain cease-fire resolutions from the Security Council.

---

6 For background, see *ibid.*, June 26, 1967, p. 949.

Further resolutions, demanding compliance with the earlier call for an end to hostilities, were adopted on June 7th and 9th.[7]

The final acceptance of these resolutions, at least by Israel, Egypt, Syria, and Jordan, opened a period of intense discussions, which have yet to reach a conclusion. The Soviet Union transferred the problem to the General Assembly, a maneuver which delayed the quest for peace for several months.[8] Despite the unceasing efforts of the United States and other governments to get peace negotiations started, it took more than 5 months to achieve a Security Council resolution under which negotiations might begin. According to the British resolution, which was finally passed, a representative of the Secretary-General is to start talks with the parties on the basis of certain agreed principles stated in the resolution itself.[9]

These principles follow rather closely those stated by President Johnson in his speech of June 19th. That address has been generally recognized as a fair and even-handed statement of the issues and a proper guide to a just and permanent solution of the Arab-Israeli conflict.

The essential idea of the President's statement is that the continuation of claims of a right to wage war against Israel has become a burden to world peace. It is therefore a world responsibility and a responsibility of the parties to achieve an end to such claims—a condition of peace in the area. It should be a fair and dignified peace reached by the parties, not one imposed by conquest or by the great powers. It should recognize each nation's right to live and to live in security. And it should rest on the principle of the territorial integrity and political independence of all the nations of the area.

On the basis of such a peace, the other principal features of the Arab-Israeli controversy should be resolved by the parties through any procedure on which they can agree. Israeli forces should of course withdraw to agreed and secure boundaries, which should replace the fragile armistice lines of 1948 and 1949. Those armistice agreements expressly contemplated agreed boundary adjustments when they were superseded by arrangements of peace. The tragic problem of the

---

[7] For U.S. statements and texts of the resolutions, see *ibid.*, p. 934.

[8] For U.S. statements in the Security Council and in the fifth emergency special session of the U.N. General Assembly, together with texts of resolutions adopted in the two bodies, see *ibid.*, July 3, 1967, p. 3; July 10, 1967, p. 47; July 24, 1967, p. 108; July 31, 1967, p. 148; and August 14, 1967, p. 216.

[9] For U.S. statements and text of the resolution adopted in the Security Council on November 22, see *ibid.*, December 18, 1967, p. 834.

Palestinian refugees should at least be solved and solved justly. Guarantees should be provided for the use of international waterways by all nations on equal terms. The special interest of three great world religions in the holy places of Jerusalem should be recognized and protected. No unilateral solution of the problem of Jerusalem can be accepted. The international interests in this sacred city are too important to be set aside. Failure to resolve this crucial problem to the general satisfaction could well prevent a lasting settlement in the region. And a start should be made on agreements of arms limitation for the area, which could protect the world and the peoples of the region from the risk of another war. An arms race is a tragic waste of resources for any country but above all for countries with urgent economic problems. Moreover, the constant need for armaments causes nations to compromise the very independence they have fought so fiercely to gain and hold. It makes the whole region a cockpit for the external rivalries of the great powers, runs the risk of involving its people in alien quarrels, and postpones indefinitely the achievement of internal stability in the region based on the determination and strength of its own societies.

The United States has made it unmistakably clear that it is unalterably opposed to any resumption of hostilities and that its full support will be given to any procedure which gives promise of fulfilling the principles of the President's statement of June 19th.

The effort to translate those principles into a program of negotiation took many months in the Security Council, the General Assembly, and the foreign offices of the entire world. Some of the Arab states and other governments fought tenaciously in the United Nations for a resolution that would seek to restore the situation as it was on June 4th before any negotiations could begin. As the President remarked on June 19th, such a policy "is not a prescription for peace but for renewed hostilities."

On the other hand, the movement from armistice to peace could not condone expansionism. As President Johnson said on June 19:

> . . . no nation would be true to the United Nations Charter or to its own true interests if it should permit military success to blind it to the fact that its neighbors have rights and its neighbors have interests of their own. Each nation, therefore, must accept the right of others to live.

The Security Council resolution of November 22, 1967, should permit discussions among the parties for a settlement of the Arab-

Israeli war at long last to begin. It is 5 months late, but it is nonetheless a welcome and constructive step. The United States will of course actively support the negotiating process under that resolution.

But peace between Israel and its neighbors is only a beginning, though an indispensable beginning, to the task of achieving a stable and progressive order in the area—an order resting on internal stability not external force. The bitter heritage of the past will not vanish overnight. The risk of war cannot be exercised until the environment is transformed by fundamental changes in the relations of the states and peoples of the region. Such transformations are occurring in Europe, under the powerful influence of the ideas and arrangements of the European Community. Similar efforts have been launched in other areas of the world—in Central America and in Southeast Asia, for example.

Like efforts are needed to help the peoples of the Middle East adapt their societies and economies to the level of their aspirations. The Arabs of the area must themselves find the means to restore the fertile gardens of their past. In such an area effort they could have no better partners than the Israelis, their ancient cousins, who have struggled for centuries to preserve their culture and adapt it to the tasks of modern life. What a tragedy it would be if the opportunity for so fruitful a partnership should be lost in fratricide.

Our Government will persevere in the search for peace. As President Johnson has said:[10]

> If the nations of the Middle East will turn toward the works of peace, they can count with confidence upon the friendship and the help of all the people of the United States of America.
>
> In a climate of peace we here will do our full share to help with a solution for the refugees. We here will do our full share in support of regional cooperation. We here will do our share—and do more—to see that the peaceful promise of nuclear energy is applied to the critical problem of desalting water....

But success in such efforts to achieve regional cooperation—and cooperation between the region and the rest of the world—can hardly be taken for granted. It will not be easy for the Middle East to become a stable and progressive region, open to the world but free from outside interference.

---

[10] *Ibid.*, July 10, 1967, p. 31.

Success in that effort cannot be imposed from without, either by the United States or by anyone else. We and other friendly nations can discourage the coercive designs of others. We can and will encourage progressive forces and initiatives originating within the region. We can hope to see a gradual transformation of the environment that will turn people away from the quarrels of the past to the promise of the future.

The Paradox of Interdependence

In these respects, the Middle East is like much of the rest of what is called the "third world." It is a region of promise and yet of instability. There are many divisive forces native to the region which promote unrest and intermittent turbulence. But these internal divisions are frequently fueled from without and thus prolonged. Turmoil of this kind prevents the economic and social progress that might in the end remake the whole environment. If we turn away from these developments in the third world, the result could be serious: harm to our friends and to our vital interests.

What the world faces, not only in the Middle East but in the Far East, Latin America, and Africa as well, is a race between the forces of order and rational progress and the forces of discord and retrogression. The problems of building a stable world order will not go away. For reasons of security—and reasons of humanity—we must help these troubled peoples to solve their problems of order and development. If we and they fail, we could ourselves be embroiled in the resulting turmoil.

We cannot solve these problems alone. We do not have the wealth, the power, the wisdom, or the imperial will to build a world after the manner of the Romans. Ours is a better vision. But it requires, above all, that other people take the principal responsibility for solving their own problems. We cannot ourselves build a new order throughout the third world, but we shall suffer along with the rest of mankind if that order is not achieved. That is the paradox of interdependence in our nuclear world. If we cannot command an end to the world's problems, neither can we refuse to do our part in solving them.

* * *

15

Africa

Africa is the world region which ranks lowest in American foreign policy when foreign aid received and trade exchanged are employed as indicators. Despite the fact that Africa contains more nations than any other area, the U.S. government has paid less official attention to it. American interests, furthermore, were late in forming. It was not until 1958 that African affairs were elevated to bureau status in the Department of State and assigned an Assistant Secretary.

This state of affairs is the result of two factors. First, the U.S. recognized the primary European interests in the area, as it did in the early post-war years in the Middle East. Throughout the Truman and Eisenhower Administrations, the U.S. government was content to support the European colonial or former colonial powers. Second, Africa has remained the "peace model" for other areas of the world, for it largely has been devoid of crises which result in a major commitment of American resources. Except for the Congolese imbroglio in the early 1960's, Africa has not become an area for East-West competition. Consequently, American policy in general has been to encourage the United Nations to assume leadership in solving African political problems. In no other region, with the possible exception of the Middle East, has the U.N. played a leading role.

The Soviet ranking of Africa evidently mirrors the American low priority given to the region. The Russians have not shown a great interest in Africa either in Tsarist or Soviet days. The strategic importance, or lack of it, of Africa contributes to the American and Soviet evaluation. Its armies, except for the Republic of South Africa, are almost nonexistent as efficient fighting machines. It lacks strategic geographical value, except for the southern cape area when the Suez

Canal is inoperable. Africa does produce raw materials of importance, but alternative sources are available.

Despite Africa's lack of emphasis in American diplomacy, the U.S. does have a cluster of policies which can be discussed under three headings: subregional differences, major changes inaugurated by the Kennedy Administration, and the problems posed by white supremacy rule in the Republic of South Africa and Rhodesia.

Subregional differences

In large regions, such as Africa and Latin America, subarea differences in policy emphasis can be distinguished. Africa can be conveniently divided into White South, Arab North, Black West, and Black East; and emphasis in American policy has followed the same ordering. Overall, the U.S. has enjoyed a favorable balance of trade, exporting over $1.2 billion and importing almost $900 million in 1964. An analysis of subregional trade in Table 1 reveals significant differences.

TABLE 1

U.S. Trade With African Regions

1964 in Millions of Dollars

	Exports	Imports
West Africa	288	412
East Africa	50	166
Union of South Africa	392	249
North Africa	495	63
Totals	1,225	890

The U.S. ran a favorable balance of trade with Arab North Africa particularly and the Republic of South Africa. But with Black Africa, the imbalance was impressive, with $2 (for West Africa) and $3 (for East Africa) imported for every dollar of American goods exported. The surplus of American exports over imports to Arab North Africa and White South Africa is responsible for the overall favorable balance of trade, and in a sense, these two regions "support" Black Africa in the total economic picture. Furthermore most of American foreign aid goes to Black Africa.

Kennedy's major changes

Occasionally, a new administration brings about a change in foreign policy, and this state of affairs certainly applies to President Kennedy and Africa. Major policy changes also were attempted, and some were successful, in other areas. In Eastern Europe, he inaugurated the policy of "gradualism" or "bridge-building"; in the Far East, his administration attempted a conciliatory policy toward the Peoples Republic of China, and was rebuffed; in Latin America, the Alliance for Progress heralded a new American policy approach; and in Laos, there was a policy shift from the right to the neutralist wing.

Prior to 1961, the U.S. abstained or voted against Afro-Asian resolutions on colonialism in deference to NATO allies. This attitude changed with the Kennedy Administration. Emphasis was placed on the U.N. as an instrument of policy to keep the Cold War out of Africa. In the Congo, the U.N. was asked to perform a new function: not only to keep the peace but to unite a nation. Peace-keeping operations were not new to the U.N., but nation-building was. In the end, the Congolese operation almost bankrupted the United Nations. When the U.N. troops withdrew in June 1964, the U.S. began unilateral support.

White supremacy in South Africa

In the policy statement below, Assistant Secretary of State Williams states that "South Africa poses one of the most difficult policy problems faced by the United States government." Along with the Soviet Union, Communist China, France, and the United Arab Republic, the Republic of South Africa must rank as one of the most difficult single-nation problems in contemporary American foreign policy. In general, the U.S. has tried to show its disapproval of South Africa's racial policies without showing hostility. The problem confronting American policy has been the demand made by the Black African states for a show of hostility as well as disapproval. The U.S. has not been willing to go beyond a policy of disapproving of South Africa's actions. Toward Rhodesia, on the other hand, the American government has gone further by a policy of limited sanctions. The U.S. has not recognized Rhodesia as an independent state.

Conclusion

In the first statement below, Assistant Secretary Williams looks at the whole of Africa and its political and economic problems. The second statement focuses on the explosive problems in the southern region of Africa.

United States Policy in Africa

by G. Mennen Williams

Assistant Secretary for African Affairs[1]

The most significant reason Africa is of concern to the United States is, properly, that neither we nor our children can live in peace, freedom, and prosperity in the long run unless the peoples of Africa can develop in peace and freedom and fulfill their fundamental aspiration for a better life. Without such development, the continent's troubles will be a continuing threat to world peace and security.

That conclusion is hardheaded, honest, patriotic pragmatism. That is why we are interested now in helping to build stable and independent countries in Africa and in maintaining cordial and lasting relations with them. And that is why we support African self-determination.

Happily, in favoring this course, our traditional beliefs and our national self-interest coincide completely.

There are many other reasons for our interest in Africa.

For more than a century and a half, American missionaries have been active in many parts of the continent.

Long before our missionaries, however, Africa and America were linked together by the slave trade. Although long dormant, that link has in recent years led Negro Americans to become increasingly proud of, and interested in, Africa—an interest that goes hand in hand with their interest in civil rights.

The United States has long had commercial interests in Africa, going back to the days of clipper ships. Although the volume of our

---

1 Excerpts from an address made at Williams College, Williamstown, Mass., on March 18, 1965. Printed in the *Department of State Bulletin,* April 12, 1965, pp. 539-48.

commerce and investment in Africa is still relatively modest in comparison with our volume in other continents, it is not inconsiderable and is of increasing importance.

Some of Africa's mineral resources are of critical importance to American science and technology. For example, our machine-tool industry relies heavily upon Africa's industrial diamonds, and certain comparatively rare African metals are essential to our industrial and scientific community for use at extremes of heat and cold.

In addition, we have important space-age ties with Africa. Our first manned space flight was reported on by two African tracking stations, and African tracking and control stations are essential to our current space experiments and operations.

The United States also relies on various facilities in Africa to maintain our essential worldwide communications net. This rightly suggests that Africa's physical location has important strategic implications. This was demonstrated not only in the past by the use of North Africa as a jumpoff point for the Allied return to Europe in World War II but more recently when Soviet aircraft could not use West African landing facilities during the Cuban missile crisis.

Africa also figures in our concern with Communist subversion, which has turned in the direction of the statement attributed to Stalin: "The backs of the British will be broken not on the River Thames, but on the Yangtze, the Ganges, and the Nile." Communist Party Congresses as early as 1957 resolved to penetrate Africa. Since then, the Communist nations have stepped up their investment of men, money, and subversion in Africa. The entry of Red China into the African Continent, and its competition with Moscow, have increased and made more complex, rather than diminished, the total impact of Communist imperialism in Africa. While it is true that no African country has become a Communist satellite, that danger to African freedom must be of continuing concern to us and to them.

The United States also has an interest in the peoples of Africa because of their tremendous dynamism and their increasingly significant role in world affairs. In the United Nations, where they comprise almost one-third of the voting strength, their vigor and leadership contribute much to the growing importance of the underdeveloped areas of the world.

Furthermore, while American and European interests in Africa are similar to a considerable extent, the United States does have interests and concerns different and apart from those of the European countries that once ruled in that area—such as, for example, Chinese Communist recognition in the U.N.

In brief, then, our interests in Africa must be considered increasingly in the development of our worldwide foreign policy of peace, freedom, and prosperity.

Economic and Social Realities in Africa

Because of our significant interests in Africa, therefore, it is necessary for us to have a clear understanding of that continent's present stage of development and of the realities of African life.

Africa is an enormous continent—more than three times the size of the 50 United States—and, although potentially very rich, for the most part is presently burdened with severe poverty, disease, and illiteracy. Unlike Asia, Africa's 265 million people do not present a problem of overpopulation.

These people speak nearly 1,000 different languages. Although culturally fragmented, the peoples of Africa have many basic similarities in the everyday realities of African life.

For one thing, most of the people of Africa are poor in terms of developed material wealth. The average per capita income for the continent as a whole is about $120 a year and as low as $40 a year in some parts of the continent. This is the lowest per capita income of any geographic region in the world—almost twice as low as the next lowest region—and there is little local capital for economic development. Fortunately there is a pattern of economic growth in most parts of Africa.

Although Africa is primarily an agricultural continent and 75 percent of the people make their living from the land, the average African farmer is only about 4 percent as productive as his counterpart in North America.

Education presents much the same picture. While there is a cultural and sophisticated elite, about 85 percent of Africa's people are illiterate. There is a crucial lack of trained people to perform the many vital middle-level functions so necessary to African development. I might point out, however, that educational facilities and opportunities are expanding. Today some 40 percent of Africa's children are in primary school—a vast increase over a decade ago. In addition, secondary school enrollment has risen from 800,000 to 1.8

million in the last 4 years, and the number of universities has gone up from 24 to 35.

Communications and transportation are extremely poor throughout much of Africa. In many parts of the continent a telephone call from a French-speaking country to an English-speaking nation must be routed through Paris and London. Total improved highway mileage in the whole continent of Africa is only 551,530 miles, compared to 2.7 million miles of improved roads in the United States alone.

Health is another major problem. Every known tropical disease exists in the continent, taking the lives of one of every five African children. There is a severe shortage of doctors, nurses, and other health personnel. Where we have one doctor for every 740 people, the ratio for Africa (excluding South Africa) is one for every 22,500 people.

Another important reality of African life is the instability created when traditional African tribal values meet the modern political, economic, and social concepts of new national governments. In much of Africa—but by no means all—the function of decisionmaking is moving from traditional chiefs and elders in the villages into the hands of younger people in the cities.

Political Realities

Alongside Africa's economic and social realities is an imposing list of political realities we must include in our foreign policy formulation.

The first, and most important, of these realities is Africa's drive for freedom and independence. In less than a decade and a half, 33 new nations have come to independence in Africa, and others are on the way. Although we sometimes lose sight of the fact, these new nations made the transition to national sovereignty in cooperation with the former metropoles in peace and good order—except for Algeria and the Congo.

The major territories without self-government lie in southern Africa, where white minority governments control large black majorities and significant numbers of Asians and coloreds, who are people of mixed blood. In most of these areas little, if any, progress is being made toward self-determination in acceptable terms for the people, and because of this, the future for peace in southern Africa is not promising. The lack of progress there is a major concern to independent Africa and an issue which passionately unites and motivates Africans throughout the continent. Until this problem is solved, there will be trouble in Africa, with worldwide impact.

The desire of Africa's new and developing nations to obtain recognition of their dignity as equal, sovereign states in the world community is another African reality. For this reason they place great faith in the U.N. as a forum where African countries have voices equal to those of other areas of the world.

Later I'll say a word about the African desire for nonalinement and the compulsion toward African unity. These are real and intensely felt African aspirations.

A final African political reality—and one of considerable importance to the United States—is the growing size of Communist activities in Africa. Communist overtures to Africa cover a broad range of activities, from diplomatic on down. To date, the Soviets have 24 diplomatic missions and the Communist Chinese have 16 in Africa. Together, they have extended more than $1 billion in credits and loans to African nations, although much of that amount has not been drawn upon by Africans. Approximately 7,000 African students go to Communist universities in Europe and Asia on scholarships each year. That is about 1,000 more than the number of African students who come to the United States annually, but far fewer than the 30,000—40,000 in the United Kingdom, France, and other parts of Western Europe. In addition to scholarships, the Communists also have increased their use of publications, radio broadcasting, films, and cultural exchanges as propaganda weapons in Africa. Finally, of course, the Communists widely employ undercover forms of subversion.

Although the growing size of the Communist presence in Africa contributes to the recognition of Africa's importance and dignity and promotes an increasing, although overall small, number of African militants, it is also leading to an increasing African awareness of the true objectives of communism. African leaders have seen or heard about Communist interference in the internal affairs of African governments, efforts to win African support for Communist cold-war objectives, and the treatment of African students in Communist universities. As a result, many Africans are seriously concerned with the way Communist deeds and actions conflict with African national interests and their desires to develop themselves in a peaceful climate in which they are truly independent.

277

Five Pillars of U.S. Policy

In the light of these realities in modern Africa, what, then, should be a realistic American policy toward Africa?

The primary purpose of all U.S. foreign policy is, of course, the security of the United States, and this concern is reflected in our African policy. This does not mean, however, that the protection of America's interests in Africa is inimical to the best interests of the African people. Indeed, the situation is quite the contrary. The objectives we seek in protecting American interests in Africa are objectives which also promote the real interests of the African people.

As we have no territorial or other special ambitions anywhere, American policy is directed toward the building of a world of peace and freedom. In today's interdependent world, that is the only way we can guarantee our own peace and freedom in the long run. In seeking peace and freedom for ourselves, therefore, we do it best by seeking it for others. For that reason our basic policy toward Africa is designed to advance African interests as much as our own.

American foreign policy toward Africa is based upon fundamental American principles that are an integral part of our national life and express our national ethos. At the same time, however, our policy is as practical in the protection of our national interests and security as the motto "honesty is the best policy" is essential to the successful conduct of a profitable business.

* * *

Moroccans still have a warm memory of Franklin Delano Roosevelt because of their belief that he advanced the cause of independence for that country. Likewise, President John F. Kennedy is remembered by Algerians for his 1957 speech in the Senate in which he pointed out that there was only one solution—independence—to the vexing Algerian problem. As President, his friendship for Africa has made his name indelible on that continent. Senegalese, too, remember the warm rapport established by President Lyndon B. Johnson during his visit to that country's first independence celebration in 1961.

Throughout Africa the United States is either praised or damned—depending upon the point of view—because of our support for independence. It is interesting, too, that at the first Afro-Asian conference at Bandung in 1955 the meeting's heroes were not Marx, Lenin, and

Mao Tse-tung, as the Communist Chinese hoped, but the fathers of the American Revolution and their Declaration of Independence. Fundamentally, therefore, I believe I can say realistically that Africans have a basic friendship for Americans.

Of the five pillars of U.S. policy toward Africa, self-determination, then, with the several corollaries that flow from it—such as our acceptance of the African desire for nonalinement—is the first and most important.

The second main pillar of that policy is encouragement of the solution of African problems by Africans themselves and support of their institutions through which solutions can be reached, such as the Organization of African Unity and the Economic Commission for Africa.

The third is support of improved standards of living through trade and aid.

The fourth is the discouragement of arms buildups beyond the needs of internal security or legitimate self-defense.

The fifth is encouragement of other countries of the world, particularly the former European metropoles, to recognize their continuing responsibilities toward Africa.

In this statement of our African policy fundamentals, I have not mentioned opposition to, or containment of, communism. However, there is no question that the support of freedom over communism is basic to and a product of, the aforementioned tenets that guide United States policy in Africa. From time to time special measures may be needed to meet crisis situations—and they will be taken vigorously when necessary—but conditions in Africa are such that the support of true African independence and development is, in the long run, the surest guarantee that Africa will remain in the world of free choice and keep communism at arm's length.

Support of Self-Determination

Turning to the first pillar, U.S. support of self-determination includes several facets:

First, our support of the right of African countries to choose whether or not they wish to be independent;

Second, the right of Africans to govern themselves;

Third, the right of Africans to choose the kind of institutions under which they want to live;

Fourth, the right of African countries to a foreign policy of alliance or nonalinement; and,

Fifth, our willingness to support a movement of African unity if that is what the Africans themselves want.

On the first facet—independence—the American policy of self-determination has insisted that the African people be given the right to choose independence if that is what they want. This policy is a practical one, showing preference for a peaceful transition and a recognition that the long-term interests of all concerned may best be served by a progressive approach, over a reasonable period of time, within a framework of agreement by all parties.

* * *

The United States agrees with Great Britain that a unilateral declaration of independence by Southern Rhodesia, in its present state of limited franchise and representation, does not satisfy self-determination. It seems quite evident that a large proportion of that country's people are dissatisfied with the present amount of self-government. Under present arrangements, they see little hope of acquiring satisfactory internal self-government in a reasonable period of time.

Special mention must be made of the lack of self-determination in the Portuguese territories in Africa. Our policy there is to use every persuasive force we have to get the Portuguese Government into a dialog with the Africans concerned. We would like to see such a dialog, looking toward a mutually agreed program of development for self-government with the ultimate right to opt for outright independence, some form of community with Portugal, or even union with Portugal. A resolution reaffirming the rights of the people of the territories to self-determination was approved in the United Nations in December 1963, with the support of the United States, after a series of talks between the Portuguese Foreign Minister and a number of African diplomats at the United Nations. It will be noted that our policy does not demand "one man, one vote" tomorrow, but it does contemplate an immediate recognition of the people's timely right to choose independence or other form of association or disassociation. In addition, it recognizes the right to government by the consent of the governed, with steps being taken to prepare the people for such self-government as rapidly as possible.

On the second facet—self-government—independence and government by the consent of the governed are not necessarily the same thing, I should point out. The Republic of South Africa has independence from foreign domination, but it does not have government by the consent of all the governed nor does its system of *apartheid* portend that there will be a government with the consent of the governed. American policy in this situation has been made abundantly clear in word and action at the United Nations and elsewhere. The United States is in complete and unalterable opposition to *apartheid*. We have unilaterally, and with the United Nations, declared an embargo on American arms for the Republic of South Africa. We have sought by every diplomatic means to convince the South African Government that *apartheid* contains the seeds for destruction for South Africa, as well as trouble for the rest of Africa and the world. As in the case of the Portuguese territories, we seek to impose no special formula upon South Africa. Rather, we seek to induce a dialog between the Government and its citizens with no present voice in that Government, looking toward a mutually agreeable and peaceful transition to government by consent of all the governed.

On the third facet—free choice of institutions—our policy of self-determination also contemplates our acceptance of free choice by African governments of their own form of government and society, so long as they provide government by the consent of the governed and do not injure others. Our policy does not anticipate that every African government will be a faithful copy of the Governments of the United States, Britain, France, or any free-world country, even though we believe in their merit.

In this connection, while we ourselves prefer a two-party system, we can, nevertheless, understand the reasons why many Africans want a one-party system at this time. This is a concept that our policy can live with, especially if it provides a reasonable right to government representative of and responsive to the needs of the people. But this is not to say that we feel the one-party system is an ultimately desirable system.

In judging African one-party systems, however, Americans must be mindful that it wasn't until after a decade of government under our own Constitution that we had national parties ourselves. (The majority of African governments are only 5 years old.) Until recently in some of our States, one-party systems continued to exist. However, within these State one-party systems, there were opposing factions and the people had a choice between them. This also is true in Africa, where the one-party systems have a degree of internal dialog and discussion that distinguishes them from the monolithic one-party systems of Europe, with which we are more familiar.

The question of African "socialism" also falls within the framework of self-determination. Here we must recognize that, in the African context, technical terms do not necessarily have the same meaning as in ours. African socialism is at least as alien to Karl Marx's socialism as today's American capitalism is different from that described by Adam Smith. There is no African state that does not welcome foreign private investment and capitalist enterprise. Indigenous private enterprise flourishes to some extent in every country, although large-scale private enterprise is not in evidence in many states because their economies are not yet rich enough to permit the accumulation of sufficient private capital.

On the fourth facet—nonalinement—U.S. acceptance of the African desire for a policy of nonalinement is a logical extension of our philosophy of self-determination. There was a time when the United States fretted about "true neutralism." But for 4 years our Government has felt it unnecessary for any country which seeks its own independence to have to be alined with us to be seeking the same kind of the world we seek. Any country that seeks independence *ipso facto* denies the subservience that communism demands.

* * *

On the fifth facet—African unity—the United States recognizes the right of Africans to create any form of association among themselves they choose, so long as the purposes of such association are not destructive to the welfare of others. As a practical matter, the United States understands the African desire—I might almost say compulsion —for unity, on the one hand, and, on the other, that unity is so obviously in the best interests of developing economic and political viability for the fragmented and underdeveloped African states. While the United States approves the move for African unity in principle, it is our policy not to take specific action toward this goal

282

unless requested to do so. Thus we have supported the idea of the almost-continent-wide Organization of African Unity and the Economic Commission for Africa, as well as a number of more limited regional groups.

Self-determination inevitably raises practical questions in its application. For example, just who has the privilege of decision? Can a single city, for instance, determine it wishes to be independent from the countryside with which it has been traditionally associated? Specifically, should Katanga, or Orientale, or Kasai Provinces in the Congo have the right to opt for independence?

The United States has felt that, like the question of what constitutes a bargaining unit in labor relations, the right for self-determination has to be based on a practical historical unit in order to permit fast and sensible results. In the Congo, for example, the whole country was defined by a century's experience. In any event, the Africans themselves expressed their respect for the recognition of historical frontiers in the first meeting of the OAU in 1963, and we feel this is a useful and important base and adjunct for our policy of self-determination.

African Solution of African Problems

The second major pillar of U.S. policy toward Africa is our support for African solutions of African problems.

Aid and Trade

The third main pillar of our African policy is our support of African economic development and independence through aid and trade. Aid to Africa is still a relatively new concept, and is only one-tenth of our global aid program. But, in the short time of its existence, our assistance program is beginning to show positive results. For example, as a result of a chicken-hatching program in Nigeria, much-needed protein was provided for the people and the cost of eggs was reduced from $1.25 to 75 cents a dozen. Likewise, in Tunisia, the ability to produce vegetables for home consumption rose to the point that horticultural imports were cut from $14.4 million annually in 1959 to about $1.2 million today.

U.S. aid to Africa is a realistic response to our support of American interest in that continent.

* * *

In addition, there are both long-range and short-term practical reasons for our assistance. The most important long-range basis for aid is that it helps build a world in which we and our children can live in security and peace.

* * *

Thus, unless the rest of the world lives satisfied, it will be constantly in turmoil. Under any circumstance such turmoil would breed trouble. But in this age of cold war there is no doubt there would be serious trouble resulting from Communist activity in areas of continued unrest.

In addition to that long-range consideration, the United States also has a number of specific short-term reasons for desiring to maintain good relations with its African friends through an aid program. It can be argued, with good reason, that aid does not buy friends. One can agree with that. But there are realities we must accept in this world. As an affluent major power, we could turn friends against us if we did not give them a helping hand when it is needed. And aid is an important, even essential, element in creating the mutual understanding and cooperation among African countries that help our friends comprehend the many world problems we all face—the threat of Chinese communism, for example, or the need for international scientific cooperation.

Obviously, in a continent where many of the preconditions for rapid economic development are lacking, the tasks of nation building are difficult. Much of our help, therefore, is directed toward encouraging the African nations to do all they can to spur their progress and to help them develop the tools necessary to do the job. We are putting our assistance into projects that not only reach large numbers of people and improve their lives but those which help countries develop their own resources and increase their ability to help themselves.

Aid is also a necessary ingredient of the economic development needed to build political stability. In every African country—certainly in all those I myself have visited—the people are hungry for economic and social improvement. Any government—however progressive and constructive, however cloaked with the glory of winning independence—that fails to reckon with this hunger will find itself in jeopardy and the order and stability of its people gravely disturbed. This not only adversely affects the country involved but, because of its international repercussions, the United States as well.

African governments are not yet of themselves able to generate the full thrust required for the economic and social improvement needed to satisfy their people. They must seek aid or risk deepening troubles. The key question is from whom aid will be sought, and when it can be delivered and put to work. It is worth noting that in almost every instance the newly independent nations of Africa turned first to the West for aid and looked elsewhere only if they were disappointed by the Western response.

Our overall aid program for Africa embraces a variety of tools—development grants, supporting assistance, development loans, development research, support for international organizations, Food for Peace, and the Peace Corps. We do not conceive the development of Africa as a challenge to the United States alone but a challenge to the whole free world. And this development is a challenge not only to governments but to private enterprise.

As a consequence, the State Department, other departments and agencies of the United States Government, and other organizations—public and private—are initiating and supporting (1) programs to promote aid and assistance to African countries by nations of the free world and (2) all programs to encourage and help private investment and enterprise in Africa.

Africa is magnificently endowed by nature, and with the effective combination of investment, trade, and local initiative, its potential can be realized. For example, the intelligent development of its many important minerals provides scope for private financial and commercial enterprise, as well as an ever-increasing source of livelihood for the African people.

It is no surprise, therefore, that American private companies have shown increasing participation in Africa's development. The need for investment in Africa is great, and the potential of resource development holds much promise for all concerned—Africa, Europe, the United States, and the rest of the free world.

Between World War II and 1957, it is estimated that total investment in Africa amounted to some $10 billion, of which the bulk came from Europe. U.S. investment in Africa reached the $1 billion mark only in 1961. Europe's trade with Africa is about five times that of the United States, which in 1962 totaled approximately $1.7 billion. We have no desire to disrupt or supplant existing commercial ties between Africa and Europe, but we believe there are many commercial opportunities that have not yet been investigated and we have an increasing interest in exploring those opportunities.

American investment in Africa has increased considerably in recent years, rising from $248 million in 1950 to nearly $1.5 billion in 1963. Of that amount, about 40 percent is in South Africa and 60 percent in other African countries. We like to believe that this growth is due to the cooperation between hospitable African countries and the initiative of American enterprise, plus possibly the stress put on the importance of private investment in Africa by U.S. Government agencies. We look forward to further increases as a result of the investment climate and conditions engendered by investment-minded African governments with American government cooperation.

Internal Security and Arms Limitation

The fourth pillar of our policy toward Africa is our desire to discourage arms buildups beyond the needs of internal security or legitimate self-defense.

Our policy is designed to encourage arms limitation in Africa. Generally the military requirements of most African countries have been worked out with the former metropoles, and there has been little need for supplementary arms assistance from the United States. In some cases, however, there is a strong desire to rely on more than one source in this field, and, on request, we have provided limited military assistance.

We feel that the prospects for peaceful settlements of disputes are bettered by avoiding arms races. And, given the very limited economic resources of the newly independent countries, it is imperative for them to devote their resources to economic and social development rather than arms.

Obviously the Communists would benefit from an arms race in Africa, while the free world would not. For that reason our military assistance is designed primarily to meet the minimum legitimate internal security or self-defense requirements of the recipients, and to contribute to economic and social development wherever feasible.

286

This program, which is small compared with those in other regions of the world—only some 2½ percent of our worldwide military assistance—is principally confined to providing military and telecommunications equipment and technical assistance. Such assistance, we believe, can help African nations develop the conditions of law and order which are necessary for steady progress. We do not anticipate significant growth in the military assistance program for Africa, and most of all we do not wish to help generate any form of arms race. Even in countries where we are providing major items, we feel that our sincere efforts to be helpful in assisting in legitimate self-defense and the responsible limitations under which we provide such assistance dissuade those countries from turning to others who might be less concerned with the total arms race in Africa. We would prefer a race in overcoming the economic and social problems that now beset the continent.

While we attempt to stress internal security and civic action programs when called upon for legitimate military assistance, wherever possible we seek to build police programs to limit the need for military programs.

Encouragement of European Concern

The fifth, and final, pillar of our African policy that I would like to discuss is our desire to encourage other countries, particularly the former European metropoles, to recognize their responsibilities toward Africa.

To a large extent this already is being done. We recognize Europe's vital and longstanding interests in Africa, and we have cooperated with them to encourage continuing and expanding mutually beneficial African-European relations. Such relations are well established in many parts of the continent, for which much credit is due both to the former metropolitan powers and to the African countries involved.

With few exceptions colonial ties are being laid aside for new types of cooperative arrangements between Africa and Europe. And, where African aspirations for independence and dignity have been satisfied, it has been the African nations themselves who have sought fruitful and continuing relations with the former metropoles. We consider this sound policy, and we are pleased that the new cultural, economic, and political relationships between the former metropoles and the newly independent African countries are, in most instances, both

287

close and cordial, and politically and economically beneficial. There is no reason why they should not be.

At the same time the young nations of Africa not only want to be independent but they feel compelled to manifest this independence. For that reason they wish to emphasize their individual personalities and characteristics and minimize their dependence upon others in political, economic, or cultural fields. Generally, then, they feel they must avoid exclusive relations with the former metropoles in order not to compromise their feeling or image of independence.

It is our feeling that the United States can give African countries a second "great power" association which will increase their sense of independence. At the same time their connections with the United States will give the African countries a greater political capacity to maintain associations with the former metropoles. We believe that the availability of such an American presence meets the genuine needs of African states without their having to turn to the Communist nations. We believe the United States in this way can enhance the contributions of the free-world community to Africa and contribute to the preservation of the traditional cultural and other friendly relationships. In brief, then, our desire is to supplement and strengthen existing relationships in Africa, not to supplant them, but always recognizing that we have important interests of our own in Africa. In this way we believe the United States can best serve world peace and African and our own best interests.

In brief conclusion, then, U.S. policy toward Africa is based on our support for the African people to chart their own future, to work out their own problems by themselves if they can, to improve their living standards, to maintain internal security without encouraging an African arms race, and to benefit from continued good relations with other free-world nations, particularly the former European metropoles, without jeopardizing their independence.

* * *

In carrying out that policy, the United States hopes:

1. To assist African nations to develop effective governments to assure peaceful progress for their people and to contribute to world peace and stability essential to the security of the United States.

2. To help these nations build solid economic conditions to become

self-sustaining members of the world community and not susceptible to Communist overtures.

3. To encourage peaceful application of self-determination to still-dependent Africa.

4. To develop a true community of interests between Africa and the United States.

If we can accomplish those goals in the face of Africa's rapidly changing situation, the United States believes Africa will—in African terms—contribute importantly to world peace, prosperity, and stability in years ahead.

United States Policy Toward South Africa

Statement by G. Mennen Williams

Assistant Secretary for African Affairs[1]

* * *

South Africa poses one of the most difficult policy problems faced by the United States Government. Essentially this is because of the nature of the problem itself. It is a problem involving one of the most sensitive aspects of human relations, the problem of getting people of different races to live together in harmony, mutual respect, and cooperation.

We know from our own experience, from our own unfinished business in this field, that fundamental changes in longstanding patterns of human behavior are often difficult to achieve. Although the process of change in this country has accelerated in recent years, it is still neither as easy nor as rapid as we would like. This is true despite the fact that we Americans have a common culture, speak the same language, and as a nation are able to enlist an impressive array of constitutional, judicial, economic, political, and moral forces on behalf of change.

In South Africa on the other hand there is no common unifying national culture, no universally spoken national language, and most of the instruments of national power are arrayed against the change desired by the majority rather than in its support. Moreover, in our case deep-seated and irrational fears play a less important role than in South Africa since our problem involves a deprived minority, theirs an oppressed majority.

---

1 Excerpts from a statement made before the Subcommittee on Africa of the House Committee on Foreign Affairs on March 1, 1966. Printed in the *Department of State Bulletin*, March 21, 1966, pp. 431-40.

There are other difficulties. There are deep and honest differences of opinion as to how constructive change can be induced in South Africa. It is frequently said that in the last analysis the peoples of South Africa themselves must work out their own destiny. But how is this to take place with the internal forces for change so effectively repressed? It is also pointed out that in South Africa economic forces are breaking down segregationist practices and isolationist patterns of thought. But how are such changes to be translated into the political and social fields? How long will it take? And what can outside forces properly do to accelerate it? There is no agreement on these important questions.

Contradictory U.S. Interests

Another range of difficulties is the fact that our relations with South Africa involve mutually contradictory American national interests. In formulating our policy one must examine not only the balance sheet of our bilateral relations with South Africa but also the effect of these relations on our national goals elsewhere in the world. Bilaterally we enjoy mutually beneficial relations with South Africa in several fields. On the other hand, the racial policies of the Republic impose severe restraints on these relations. Some forms of cooperation have become impossible because we cannot accept for Americans visiting or working in South Africa the racial conditions imposed by South Africa upon her nationals. Internationally, the racial policies of South Africa have been almost universally condemned, and the U.N. General Assembly has called on all U.N. members to bring pressure on South Africa to change its policies.

Thus in formulating our policy we must take into account the liabilities as well as the benefits from our relations. There is no doubt, for example, that the Communists have had some success in Africa by seeking to identify themselves with African aspirations in South Africa and by identifying the United States with the controlling white minority. A peaceful accommodation among people of all races in South Africa based on respect for the right of the individual would thus be in our interest and that of the free world and a major blow to the Communists. A shift of South African policy away from racialism would improve relations between Africans and Europeans throughout Africa and aid the work of numerous international organizations. Such developments, naturally, would be in the U.S. national interest.

South Africa, with its abundant human and material resources and strong modern economy, could play a leading role in the progress of Africa. Instead, by its racial policies it is isolating itself from the rest of Africa and from most of the international community. It is diverting its own resources to the machinery of security and repression, which might better be used to assist its own people and others in Africa. Instead of mutually beneficial relationships in trade and other fields, all forms of contact with the rest of Africa are minimal. Elsewhere in Africa, too, resentment and fear of South Africa have been among the factors diverting new African nations from full concentration on the tasks of nation-building and provoking them into unconventional actions against South Africa in international organizations. The accelerating cycle of mutual suspicion and hostility is thus not only dangerous but also ill serves Africa's development. It would be in our interests to see this cycle reversed.

Broad Aims of U.S. Policy

* * *

Of U.S. policy in southern Africa Secretary Rusk has said, "In our dealings with those areas our position is based firmly on the belief that governments derive their just powers from the consent of the governed."[2] The late Ambassador Stevenson, speaking on *apartheid* in the Security Council on December 4, 1963, declared his Government's belief "that no longer can any society long endure in peace, really live with itself, really prosper economically, if in that society one race denies to another human and political rights."[3]

These authoritative statements embody our main aim in southern Africa as elsewhere—the evolution of stable, progressive societies based on nondiscrimination and government by consent of the governed. While the form these societies take will and properly should be up to the peoples themselves, it is in our interest to see peace in that area and the development of societies with which we can enjoy relations of mutual benefit and mutual respect.

---

[2] *Ibid.*, October 12, 1964, p. 498.
[3] *Ibid.*, January 20, 1964, p. 92.

The African Context

In most of Africa there has during the past 10 years been a great surge of independence. We have welcomed the emergence of the new African states and are doing what we can in cooperation with others to help them develop firmer foundations for their independence. We recognize that with independence there have come new problems and that there have been setbacks, but on balance we believe that independence has brought new life and hope to Africa. In Africa as elsewhere we see human freedom not as an immediate panacea for all human problems but as a great creative force. Moreover, in Africa, freedom has another dimension. It has brought to an end for millions of Africans the humiliation of domination by members of another race. Thus, as the area of political independence has advanced to the frontiers of southern Africa, so has the area of human dignity.

The remaining problems in the whole region of southern Africa are, of course, the most difficult of all. Each country has its unique and distinctive features but all contain the seeds of trouble, serious trouble, as long as they deny the enjoyment of self-determination, freedom, and human dignity to the majority of their populations. We believe that the forces for change in southern Africa are increasing their tempo. While on the one hand this is encouraging, it also increases the threat of violence. As intensified pressures for change meet intensified resistance, as peaceful avenues to change are blocked off one by one, fewer and fewer alternatives to violence remain open.

I am not here as a prophet of doom. I do not mean that violence cannot be avoided. What I do mean is that the search for peaceful accommodation of the forces for change in southern Africa, both inside and outside the area, must be intensified before it is too late.

U.S. Approach

The U.S. Government has no prescription for South Africa. But if South Africa's peoples are to devise their own solution, it seems to us that a good way to begin would be to start some form of dialog among the racial groups in South Africa. We are alarmed at the severance one by one of constructive contacts between the whites and nonwhites in South Africa. If we and other like-minded nations could contribute to the creation in South Africa of an atmosphere of free

293

discussion and mutual effort to understand and respect the other person's real interests and aspirations, a great stride would have been made toward stable human relations in the subcontinent. It is clear that a lasting solution in South Africa can only be one devised by the South Africans themselves. But it must be the creation of all groups. Whether imposed paternalistically or by force, a formula imposed by one group upon the others will not endure.

It must be recognized that there are serious obstacles in South Africa to the free discussion and compromise we consider indispensable if the long-range trend toward large-scale violence is to be arrested and reversed. While accommodation of conflicting aspirations and interests is vital, the forces within South Africa making for such accommodation are being repressed. There is growing disillusionment in South Africa with *apartheid* as a solution of its problems. Churchmen criticize its morality; businessmen question its practicality; administrators, educators, and the great nonwhite majority doubt its honesty. But the vast machinery of the state and the highly organized Afrikaner Nationalist community repress discussion effectively by means of punitive laws putting the individual at the mercy of the state without recourse to the courts, by control of the radio and much of the press, by intimidation and ostracism.

* * *

U.S. Aims Essentially Political

The broad aims of U.S. policy toward South Africa are essentially political. We support freedom, equality, and justice for the people of South Africa for the same reasons we support them elsewhere, both at home and abroad. We support them because they are the keystones of our heritage. We support them because we believe that at home they safeguard and enhance our enjoyment of life, liberty, and the pursuit of happiness and that abroad in doing the same thing they strengthen the basis for a just and lasting peace.

These basic freedoms are of course fundamental to our role of leadership as a non-racialist nation in a multiracial world. We support renewed efforts to initiate in South Africa a peaceful, evolutionary process toward these goals. Despite the frustrations we must persist in the search for a peaceful solution. A resort to violence would be enormously costly, not only to the peoples of South Africa but also to the peoples of Africa generally. It would also be costly to us and to the free world and would undoubtedly be exploited by forces hostile to us.

These political aims are paramount. In scientific, economic, and strategic respects our bilateral relationships with South Africa are useful to us—even in some fields important—but they are not essential to our national security.

Specific Interests

Before discussing the specific policies implementing our broad aims, a review of our specific interests may be helpful. Many of these interests, while not decisive in determining our policy, are important. They are and should be taken into account in formulating our policy, though they do not, as is sometimes alleged, dominate it. Our basic policies regarding South Africa stem from broad principles much more than from immediate specific interests largely because in southern Africa the clash of basic principles and values threatens our long-range interests in much of the world.

U.S. Facilities in South Africa

The position of southern Africa athwart the sea route around the Cape of Good Hope makes its ports highly useful logistically to the U.S. Navy, particularly in support of Atlantic Fleet ships en route to and from Viet-Nam waters. If the Mediterranean route were closed, the importance of the Cape route would be enhanced.

Space-tracking facilities in South Africa have been, and continue to be, important, particularly for the lunar and other deep-space programs. Sudden removal of these facilities would adversely affect the progress of these programs. However, these considerations cannot override the greater imperatives of the larger principles to which we are committed.

Economic Interests

Other specific interests are economic.

Direct U.S. investment in South Africa was valued at $467 million at the end of 1964. We have no figures for portfolio investment, but according to our best estimates it would bring total U.S. investment in

South Africa up to about $650 million. American direct investment in South Africa is about 28 percent of our total direct investment in Africa, and the 72 percent outside South Africa is growing more rapidly. Our investment in South Africa is only about 1 percent of our total foreign investment.

U.S. trade with South Africa has a favorable balance amounting in 1965 to about $213 million. Our exports, largely machinery, vehicles, and industrial goods, amounted to $392 million in 1964 and our imports, largely minerals, to $250 million. This was a considerable increase over previous years. In 1963 the trade balance was favorable by $19 million, in 1962 unfavorable by $34 million. Our trade with South Africa is about 1½ percent of our foreign trade.

Minerals

South Africa is an important source of strategic minerals, including industrial diamonds, chemical chrome, several types of asbestos, platinum, and gold. The U.S. has been buying uranium oxide under an agreement of 1950. The contract expires at the end of 1966 and is not expected to be renewed, as U.S. sources are adequate for our needs. South Africa's importance as a source of industrial diamonds has greatly diminished because of the availability of industrial diamonds elsewhere in Africa. Furthermore, the U.S. manufactures synthetic industrials. Other minerals, including chemical chrome, asbestos, and platinum, have been stockpiled or are available from other sources, including substitutes.

Main Policies

These specific interests must be viewed against the broad aims of U.S. policy. We have expressed our policy aims with respect to South Africa repeatedly both in the U.N. and bilaterally. Time and again we have pointed out the dangers we see in the policy of *apartheid* and have urged a change in approach more consistent with U.N. principles and present day realities.

U.S. Policy of Persuasion

The U.S. Government over the years has sought to dissuade South African officials at all levels from discriminatory and repressive laws and from employing various oppressive measures. We have, through diplomatic channels, warned against the extension of *apartheid* practices to the international territory of South-West Africa. The U.S. Government has expressed its critical views to South Africans on the basis of a large accumulation of firsthand evidence. American officials have devoted much time and effort to the study of *apartheid* in its many aspects. Despite the many frustrations we have encountered in our efforts to persuade South African leaders to change their policies, the increasingly manifest contradictions and unrealities of *apartheid* give at least some grounds for hope that the situation in South Africa has not rigidified irreparably.

U.S. Nonracial Policies in South Africa

Along with our policy of persuasion, we have followed a policy of continuing certain forms of cooperation with South Africa and keeping open the lines of communication. Pursuing these policies simultaneously has faced us with some difficult dilemmas. Our representatives in South Africa are exposed to strong pressures from the South African Government and its supporters to conform with *apartheid* practices. Wherever it is legally possible to do so, our representatives resist these pressures.

Our Embassy and consulates hold nonracial receptions and individual officers entertain nonracially. Our diplomatic and consular posts hire local employees on a nondiscriminatory basis. The U. S. Government makes clear that it disapproves of the appearance of Americans, whether as amateurs or professionals, before segregated audiences in South Africa. It will not sponsor visits to South Africa of performers who would appear before such audiences. As a result this aspect of our exchange program is virtually suspended. More importantly, we have canceled operational port calls in South Africa of U.S. naval vessels and aircraft rather than accept the application of racial conditions to our personnel.

U.S. Policy in the U.N.

In the U.N. the United States strongly supports the application to South Africa and to the mandated territory of South-West Africa of the basic principles of the U.N. Charter's affirmation of respect for human rights, the dignity and worth of the individual, and the equal rights of men and women. We support the aim of promoting respect for international law. We have supported a number of resolutions against *apartheid* in the U.N. General Assembly.

The shooting of many unarmed men, women, and children at Sharpeville in March 1960 marked a watershed in U.N. treatment of *apartheid*. For the first time the Security Council considered a South African issue. The United States then supported a resolution deploring *apartheid* and the loss of life at Sharpeville and calling for abandonment of repressive policies. We have supported several similar Council resolutions since then condemning repression and injustice in South Africa.

Arms Ban

As concrete evidence of our abhorrence of *apartheid* and our determination not to contribute to its enforcement, we do not sell to South Africa any arms, ammunition, military equipment, or materials for their manufacture and maintenance. Our first step in this direction was when we placed a ban on arms that could be used in enforcing *apartheid* within South Africa.[4] As international opposition to *apartheid* increased in tempo, along with repression in South Africa, the growth of violence, and the flight of refugees, we took a further step in August 1963. We extended our arms ban against South Africa to all arms, ammunition, and military equipment, except those under existing contracts and those which might be required in the interests of world peace.

Ambassador Stevenson, in announcing the arms ban,[5] said that

> . . . the United States as a nation with many responsibilities in many parts of the world naturally reserves the right in the future to interpret this policy in the light of requirements for assuring the maintenance of international peace and security. If the interests of the world community require the provision of equipment for use in the common defense effort, we would naturally feel able to do so without violating the spirit and intent of this resolve.

We adopted this comprehensive ban prior to the adoption of a U.N. Security Council resolution calling on all U.N. members to apply such a ban. We supported the resolution and have strictly observed the ban. In the Security Council the late Ambassador Stevenson explained this policy as intended to contribute to a peaceful

---

4 For background, see *ibid.*, November 19, 1962, p. 791.
5 *Ibid.*, August 26, 1963, p. 333.

solution and to avoid actions adding directly to international friction in the area. In December 1963, in support of another resolution of the Security Council, our ban was extended to equipment and materials for the manufacture and maintenance of arms and ammunition in South Africa.[6]

Economic Relations

Aside from the arms embargo, the U.S. Government does not interfere with trade and investment in South Africa. This is in keeping with our traditional policy of keeping world trade and other economic relations as free as possible from Government interference. An exception is where the national security is directly affected, as in the cases of Communist China and Cuba.

The U.S. Government neither encourages nor discourages investment in South Africa. Potential investors who seek our advice are briefed on the political and racial situation, the outlook, and American policy and interests. The decision about whether to invest remains with the individual or company.

The U.S. Government of course encourages both new and old companies to maintain high standards in the treatment of personnel employed in South Africa. We believe American companies abroad should lead in such respects as fair wages, nondiscrimination, pension systems, and the like. While American companies operating in South Africa are, of course, obligated to abide by South African laws, we are encouraged by their generally progressive record.

Opposition to Economic Sanctions

Despite strong pressures in the U.N. and from various American organizations concerned about civil and human rights in South Africa, we have not been prepared to support U.N. economic sanctions against South Africa. Several problems are involved. These are:

1. the problem of a legal basis for such actions;
2. the problem of economic effectiveness; and
3. the problem of psychological effectiveness.

With regard to the legal problem, the U.S. Government believes that the conditions envisaged in chapter VII of the U.N. Charter for

6 *Ibid.*, January 20, 1964, p. 92.

the imposition of compulsory sanctions, *i.e.,* the existence of a threat to international peace or an act of aggression, do not apply to South Africa at this time.

Much thought has been given in this Government and in the U.N. to the problem of the economic effectiveness of sanctions. In the summer of 1964 the U.N. Security Council established a committee of experts to study the feasibility, effectiveness, and implications of sanctions, or as it described them, measures which might be taken against South Africa within the framework of the U.N. Charter.[7] The committee was requested to make a technical and practical study of sanctions without reference to the circumstances in which their application might be considered. The United States participated actively in the work of the committee. Its report[8] was submitted to the Security Council in February 1965. It emphasized the view that, although South Africa would not be readily susceptible to economic measures, South Africa is not immune to impact from such measures. It concluded that the degree of effectiveness of economic measures would directly depend on the universality of their application and on the manner and the duration of their enforcement. Should a situation arise in which the U.N. appropriately might consider resort to sanctions, the United States believes the availability of this detailed, practical study will be helpful.

Cessation of investment is most often urged as a first step in applying graduated economic pressures. Could the United States exert effective pressure on South Africa by withholding investment? A generation ago the South African economy depended to a very large extent on foreign investment. Now foreign investment plays a much smaller role in the economy. The United States provides only a small proportion either of total investment in South Africa or of foreign investment there. Our investment in South Africa is only 14 percent of all foreign investment there. From 1950 to 1963 U.S. direct investment in South Africa by companies amounted to only 2.3 percent of the total net domestic capital formation there. If one includes portfolio investment, the percentage is still only 3.5.

South Africa is one of the countries which is subject to all aspects of the United States program to improve its balance of payments. This means that all types of U.S. private capital flows to South Africa are subject either to the interest equalization tax or to the President's

---

[7] For background and text of a resolution adopted in June 18, 1964, see *ibid.,* July 6, 1964, p. 29.

[8] U.N. doc. S/6210 and Add. 1.

program of voluntary restraints on private corporate investment and bank lending abroad. It is probable that new U.S. investment in South Africa will be reduced as a result. Even before this program was begun American companies had been financing their investments largely by profits made in South Africa, advances from South African banks, and the issuance of stock both in South Africa and Europe. From 1955 to 1963 the net outflow to South Africa of new American capital amounted to only $9 million. American investment in South Africa is minor—compared with that of the United Kingdom, about one-fourth. The United States, alone, would have little leverage. Since U.S. investment is not essential to South Africa, the argument for such action is largely psychological, *i.e.*, that it would jar South African whites into a better appreciation of the worldwide opposition to their policies.

Discouraging or prohibiting U.S. investment in South Africa would, of course, improve our relations with much of the world. It is also undoubtedly true that the stopping of American investment would have a considerable impact on South Africans. Even though the economy were not shaken, the confidence of those relying on *apartheid* as a permanent pattern for South Africa's economy and society would be undermined. The cessation of investment would be seen as one of a long series of developments tending to isolate South Africa. Many who profit from *apartheid* would be induced to reflect on its long-term disadvantages more seriously than they do now.

Whether increased doubt about the advantages of *apartheid* would affect South African policies beneficially is questionable. It might harden South African policies even further and undoubtedly would impel South Africa to turn to other sources of investment and to accelerate its already considerable efforts to achieve economic self-sufficiency.

While cessation of investment might increase our credibility and influence with African countries in our efforts to encourage a nonviolent solution, it could seriously handicap our ability to carry on a dialog with South Africa. It could cause some damage to our own economic, scientific, and strategic interests.

Cultural and Scientific Relations

The United States, at both public and private levels, has a wide variety of cultural and scientific contacts with South Africa. Such contacts are intended to promote mutually beneficial relations in these fields. We hope they may also have the effect of combating the tendency of South Africa to drift off into sterile isolation.

Both public and private U.S. educational and exchange programs, though small, include all cultural groups as well as supporters of the Government and Opposition. A special effort is made, particularly in Government programs, to reach nonwhites, in view of their greater need and the many obstacles encountered. The South African Government's reluctance to give travel documents to nonwhites is one such obstacle, but we do not believe the effort should be abandoned. Particular aims of these programs include familiarizing South Africans with how the United States is dealing with its own problems, including civil rights, and providing leaders and especially young potential leaders with opportunities for training and observation in the United States. Of the approximately 400 South (and South-West) African students in U.S. institutions of higher learning, 137 are supported by U.S. Government funds. Of this number 122 are nonwhite. The U.S. Government has specific programs in Africa and the United States to help refugees from South Africa and South-West Africa obtain training and education. We have also contributed to U.N. programs for the education of South-West Africans and South Africans.

* * *

Conclusion

* * *

Frustrated by the harm that *apartheid* does to human beings and to our policies, many believe we should manifest our disapproval of *apartheid* in more concrete ways. We in the Department, too, keep looking for new and constructive measures that we can take in dealing with this problem. In doing so, however, we constantly ask ourselves whether a particular action would be effective. That is, would it actually improve the situation in South Africa, or might it even worsen it? We must also ask ourselves what effect the action would have on our position in Africa and the rest of the world and thus on our ability to influence the various forces that may be brought to bear on the situation.

302

We cannot neglect either our own values and specific interests in South Africa or those of major allies whose cooperation is of great importance to our worldwide policy goals. It is a frustratingly difficult set of policy considerations to juggle. In view of our position of world leadership and our commitment as Americans to equality here at home, it is impossible for us to have fully satisfactory relations with South Africa as long as it pursues policies so diametrically opposed to our own fundamental beliefs. At the same time it would be shortsighted and unwise to turn our backs on the South African problem. To the extent that we can without compromising our principles, we believe we must keep the channels of communication with South Africa open. Despite all frustrations, we must keep on seeking ways to influence constructively the problem of race relations in South Africa.

In the meanwhile we must do what we can to encourage more progress on the periphery of the main problem by aiding nonracial states in the rest of southern Africa. It may be that such states, while resisting the virus of *apartheid,* can have constructive relations with South Africa and by their example perhaps may gradually undermine the fear and prejudice which so obstruct healthy human relations at the foot of the continent.

* * *

16

Latin America

As is the case with Africa, Latin America is not a monolithic structure, but a group of subregions distinguishable both geographically and in American diplomatic interest. The *UN Demographic Yearbook* divides the area into four parts: Caribbean, Central America, Tropical South America, and Temperate South America (which includes only four states: Argentina, Chile, Paraguay, and Uruguay). A general overview reveals an unevenness in American foreign policy with more emphasis placed on the Caribbean and Central American republics than the South American nations.

Latin America, according to the popular image, is a region that experienced its revolutions for independence in the 19th century. However, this image is in error, for Latin American nations have been blown by some of the same "winds of change" that have buffeted other areas. In 1962, Trinidad and Tobago gained independence, as did Barbados, Jamaica, and Guyana in 1966. Other Caribbean areas no doubt will follow.

The story of the Monroe Doctrine is an old chestnut in the fires of U.S. diplomatic history. It eventually was interred by the Good Neighbor Policy, popularized by Franklin Roosevelt, but with roots found in the Hoover Administration. A parallel situation existed with the Alliance for Progress, so closely identified with President Kennedy, but the beginnings of which are found in the Eisenhower Administration after the humiliating visit of Vice President Nixon to several Latin American states in 1958. The irony of American diplomacy in this region is that Democratic presidents seem to glean the results of policy changes begun under Republicans.

U.S. policy toward Latin America can be summarized under two major headings: economics and security.

Economic policy toward Latin America

⚡ Despite the U.S. government's protests to the contrary, interest in Latin American economic development is related to military security and in particular the rise of Castro's Cuba. Prior to 1957, the Latin American governments received only three percent of the total of American foreign aid.[1] The threat of Communism in Latin America and the reception of Mr. Nixon led to a rethinking of the comparative neglect of the Latin American states.

President Kennedy proposed the Alliance for Progress on March 13, 1961. He called for an economic approach similar to that used in the Marshall Plan for Europe. The Latin American states were asked to coordinate their efforts, to decide first what they could do for themselves and for each other, and then turn to the U.S. for the balance. The projected cost of the ten-year Alliance for Progress was $100 billion. The Latin Americans themselves pledged 80 percent of the financing while the American government promised 20 percent, or $2 billion a year through 1971. Half of the amount, or $1 billion each year, would come from the regular foreign aid funds and half from international agencies (such as the World Bank) and private funds.

The Alliance for Progress involved economic, social, and political aspects. The Latin American states pledged to undertake land reform which was a socio-economic objective. One political goal of the Alliance was to establish representative democracy in each state. The Alliance for Progress was founded on the premise that revolution would come sooner or later to Latin America; consequently, the Alliance was a vehicle for "controlled" revolution.

The Alliance for Progress has now used up over half of its life span. The results are: a mixed record of successes and failures. The land reform program has lagged, the war against illiteracy has not gone well, and the economic growth of some countries has not lived up to expectations.

For example, a goal of 2.5 percent growth rate each year was set by the Alliance. This is a modest figure, considering the fact that a 5 percent yearly growth is usually thought of as necessary for a developing country to achieve economic "takeoff." Nine of the Latin American states experienced an average annual growth rate for 1961

---

[1] Cecil V. Crabb, *American Foreign Policy in the Nuclear Age*, Revised Edition (New York: Harper and Row, 1965) , p. 280.

through 1966 in real gross domestic product per capita:[2] Nicaragua (which grew the most, 5.3 percent), Panama, Bolivia, Peru, Guatemala, El Salvador, Mexico, Chile, and Jamaica. The remainder fell below it: Honduras, Dominican Republic, Columbia, Brazil, Paraguay, Venezuela, Argentina, Costa Rica, Ecuador, and Uruguay. The 1966 figures reveal that four states in the first group appear to be experiencing a marked decrease in growth (Peru, Guatemala, El Salvador, and Jamaica). On the other hand, only Honduras has shown signs of increased economic growth after a slow start. What is of major concern are those states which did not hold their own during the 1961-66 period, but slipped back with negative rates of economic activity: Argentina, which possessed the worst record (a minus 2.7 percent), Paraguay, Venezuela, Ecuador, and Uruguay.

Why has the history of the Alliance for Progress been checkered with notable failures marring successes? Obviously, there are many "causes"—social, political, religious, cultural, and economic. But since the last factor is an important one in view of the statistical data presented above, two points should be made. First, inflation is rampant in some of the Latin American nations. Using data reflecting the average annual percentage changes in the cost of living in individual countries (1961-66), Brazil registered an astounding increase (60 percent), while Uruguay (40 percent), Argentina and Chile (27 percent each), Columbia (15 percent), and Peru (10 percent) also registered somewhat alarming changes. The remaining nations experienced inflation of less than 10 percent per year. Secondly, the Latin American republics tend to live beyond their means in foreign trade, importing much more than they export. As a rule, they traded little among themselves and mostly with the U.S. and other developed countries. Consequently, as much as one-half of the U.S. foreign aid performs a "bailing out" function for the country's balance of payments. Instead of financing economic development, foreign aid is used to shore up local currencies by providing dollars for the Latin American states to pay their high import bills.

In view of the Alliance for Progress performance—or lack of it—the U.S. government in 1967 began to move toward another approach: a

---

[2] "Real gross domestic product per capita" means that three items are not factors in distorting the economic growth picture: (a) increases due to inflation; (b) decreases due to enlarging population; and (c) increases due to imports from other countries. These statistics and other data that follow are taken from a series of studies published in 1967 by the Senate Committee on Foreign Relations entitled "Survey of the Alliance for Progress."

Latin American Common Market (LACM). Mr. Linowitz, U.S. representative to the Organization of American States, summarized the basis of this decision: " . . . the job begun by the Alliance nearly 6 years ago is already much longer than had been planned. But they also realize, even as we, that only catastrophe can result if we and they quit now. The job must be finished, and all of us must have the patience and the continuing will to see it through."[3] The Market is scheduled to begin in 1970 and, hopefully, will be in complete operation by 1980. Hence, LACM will "tie into" the Alliance for Progress, which ends in 1971, and will mean that American economic assistance will continue for another decade, probably at a slightly higher rate than $2 billion a year. LACM will construct a common tariff wall around the participating Latin American states and will encourage trade among them. The United States, of course, will be outside the LACM tariff wall, as it is outside the European Economic Community's common tariff wall.

Two organizations that precede LACM offer an indication of success, although in one case that "success" is tarnished. In 1960, both the Central American Common Market and the Latin American Free Trade Area were established. The former, which includes five nations, has functioned well, and its successes are heartening to LACM advocates. The free trade area has not entirely lived up to expectations, although trade has been increased among its members.

A common market for Latin America is the contemporary goal of U.S. foreign policy. Hopefully, it will solve the problems that the Alliance for Progress attempted with moderate success to eliminate.

Security

The Pan American community is the oldest regional grouping organization in U.S. diplomatic experience. It pre-dates the Communist threat with roots that reach back to the late 1800's. In 1910, the Pan American Union was formed to collect and disseminate information about the Americas. In 1948, when the Organization of American States (OAS) was created, the Pan American Union became its secretariat and was assigned political duties.

---

[3] Sol M. Linowitz, "The Road from Punta del Este," *Department of State Bulletin,* Vol. 56 (May 29, 1967), p. 823.

In 1947, at the Rio Conference, a treaty of reciprocal assistance was signed, which became the first collective security treaty of the post-World War II period. Hence, an attack against one signatory would be an attack against all. But in January 1960 Cuba "fell" without an "attack." The U.S. government's first response was to topple the Castro regime, which was attempted in the abortive Bay of Pigs invasion in April 1961. Then, in October 1962, came the Cuban missile crisis. U.S. policy since then is outlined in Mr. Ball's policy statement below.

Conclusion

The U.S. has applied policy instruments to Latin America which worked well in Western Europe, *i.e.*, the Marshall Plan through the Alliance for Progress, and economic integration through LACM. The former, though not a failure, has not been an overwhelming success. The Marshall Plan reconstructed a limited subarea within a region, while the Alliance for Progress is attempting to build an entire region without much industrial base. Have American leaders, blinded by the successes of the Marshall Plan and Common Market in Europe, attempted to employ policies which do not fit the different problems of Latin America? Mr. Linowitz's statement below is a realistic evaluation of the Alliance for Progress. He also touches on the problem of Cuba, which is the primary focus of Mr. Ball's address. American policy towards Cuba has not changed since 1964, the date of Mr. Ball's policy statement.

Principles of Our Policy Toward Cuba

by George Ball,

Under Secretary of State[1]

Foreign policies are rarely born full-armed like Minerva. More often they evolve in response to events and circumstances.

In such cases there is a danger that the assumptions on which policies are founded may become obscured.

This has, I think, happened to some extent with regard to our policy toward the present government of Cuba. Some of the public discussion that has surrounded that policy has involved misapprehensions on a number of fronts—misapprehensions as to the nature of the danger posed by the present and potential activities of the Castro government, misapprehensions as to the range of policies available to counter that danger, and misapprehensions as to the objectives that we can expect to accomplish by the policies employed.

In my observations to you this evening, I shall try to answer some of the questions that have arisen with regard to our Cuba policy and shall try to clarify some of the confusion that has been apparent in the public debate.

The Nature of the Threat

First, what is the nature of the threat imposed by existence of a Communist regime in Cuba?

It is not, in our judgment, a *military* threat to the United States. We shall never permit it to menace our own strategic power, as our actions in October 1962 demonstrated. We are taking constant and

---

[1] Excerpts from an address made before a convention of the Omicron Delta Kappa Society at Roanoke, Va., on April 23, 1964. Printed in the *Department of State Bulletin*, May 11, 1964, pp. 738-44.

effective measures to insure that such a threat does not occur again—and we shall continue to take those measures.

Nor do we regard Cuba as a direct *military* threat to Latin America. The Cuban armed forces are large and equipped with modern weaponry. They are by all odds the most powerful military establishment in Latin America. But Cuba does not possess air- and sealift sufficient to permit it to take offensive action against its neighbors, and, in any event, we maintain overwhelming military forces in the area to prevent Cuba from attacking other American Republics.

The menace of Castro communism to Latin America is of a different and—perhaps I might say—a more modern kind. It is the menace of *subversion*, the undermining of existing governments, the arming of organized Communist minorities, and the mounting of campaigns of sabotage and terror.

Latin America, Tempting Target for Communism

Some areas of Latin America are peculiarly vulnerable to such tactics. Vulnerability is greatest where social injustice is widely prevalent, where anachronistic societies remain dominated by small elites—tight little oligarchies that control the bulk of the productive wealth. In some places these oligarchies have only recently—and reluctantly—begun to make concessions to the insistent demands of the millions of economically submerged peoples for a measure of social justice and a decent standard of living.

For Latin America, as has been frequently remarked, is in the throes of a great transformation from a continent of backward societies to a continent of new, modern nations. During this period of change and tension, it offers a tempting target for the Communists. They are at least as conscious as we of the importance and weakness of the area. They are at least as determined as we to see that the brew produced by the Latin American ferment is to their liking. They have, therefore, regarded the establishment of a Communist government in Cuba—a Communist Latin American state at the very doorstep of the United States—as a major asset for communism.

Cuba, a Base for Subversion

In their determination to establish a center of subversion for Latin America in Cuba, the Communists have found a natural lieutenant in

311

Fidel Castro. Castro regards himself as the "liberator" of all Latin America. A born revolutionary, driven by a hunger for power and prestige, he looks upon the southern half of the American Continent as a proper field for the fulfillment of his ambitions. He seeks a revolutionary millennium in which the example of Cuba will have swept the continent, and his position of liberator and leader—not of the small island of Cuba, but of all Latin America—will have been assured.

This vision springs from his psychological and political needs. It is necessary to the man and equally to his followers, whose revolutionary enthusiasm must be constantly fed on the prospect of further advance beyond the confines of the island—an island which they look upon as the base from which the continent-wide revolution will be propagated by word and deed.

* * *

Two Principal Lines of U.S. Strategy

The United States, as the strongest nation in the Western Hemisphere, is faced with a difficult but practical problem. With the existence of a Communist center in Latin America, how do we and our Latin American allies prevent that center from being used as an active center for Communist infection?

The most obvious and direct way to eliminate the Castro regime in Cuba would be by direct military action designed to replace the present government by a non-Communist government friendly to the West. Less direct action might take the form of an enforced blockade—which would still be an act of war.

At the other end of the spectrum from military action is a policy of trying to negotiate with Castro. Taking account of the decisions reached within the American system, notably at Punta del Este in January 1962[2] and later in October 1962,[3] we have consistently maintained that two elements in the Cuban situation are not negotiable. First, Castro's political, economic, and military dependence upon the Soviets; and, second, the continuance of Castro's subversive activities in Latin America.

---

[2] For background, see *ibid.*, February 19, 1962, p. 270.
[3] For background, see *ibid.*, November 12, 1962, p. 720.

We see no present evidence that Castro is prepared to eliminate these two conditions—and, in fact, the evidence thus far is all the other way.

The limits in which we must erect a Cuban policy are, therefore, well defined and narrow. If, on the one hand, we do not wish to adopt policies that involve an act of war—and even the most vigorous critics of our Cuban policy have rejected this course of action—and, on the other, there seems little sign of a possibility of serious negotiation with the present regime, we are left with two principal lines of strategy for dealing with the menace of Castro's Cuba to Latin America.

First, we must take all possible measures to strengthen the Latin American nations so that they may, through individual and collective means, resist Communist subversion.

Second, we must employ all available instruments of power less than acts of war to limit or reduce the ability of the Cuban government to advance the Communist cause in Latin America through propaganda, sabotage, and subversion.

Cooperative Actions of American States

To the greatest extent possible, we are pursuing both these lines of strategy within the framework of the inter-American system. We have sought to make clear to our Latin American friends that the problem of protecting the continent against the menace of Castro communism must be tackled by the American states as a collective undertaking. The Organization of American States is the principal instrumentality for this purpose, but we are also employing other multilateral groupings within the inter-American family.

In January 1962, the foreign ministers of the OAS formally found the Castro regime to be incompatible with the inter-American system and excluded it from further participation in that system. The foreign ministers also approved the immediate suspension of trade with Cuba in arms and war material.

In early October 1962, the foreign ministers of the OAS informally met to consider the problems arising from growing Sino-Soviet intervention in Cuba, particularly the attempt to convert the island into an armed base for Communist subversive penetration of the hemisphere. In their conclusions, the foreign ministers pointed out:

313

1. The need for the American Republics and all other independent countries to review their policies on trade with Cuba, including the use of their ships in the Cuban trade;

2. The importance of intensifying measures against Communist subversion;

3. The desirability of keeping a careful check on the delivery of arms to Cuba; and

4. The need for special studies of the transfer of funds for subversive purposes, the flow of subversive propaganda, and the utilization of Cuba as a base for training in subversive techniques.

The Council of the OAS subsequently directed the preparation of a special study on measures for controlling funds, propaganda, and training for subversive purposes. The Council sent the report, incorporating specific and general recommendations in these three fields, to member governments in July 1963 urging that the recommended measures be carried out promptly.

Meanwhile, in April 1963, the five Central American Republics, together with Panama and the United States, undertook a cooperative effort to safeguard the Caribbean area against Cuban subversive activities.[4] At that meeting, and at a subsequent second meeting in January 1964, the cooperating countries agreed on a series of measures to increase the security of the countries of the area. The program includes the control of subversive travel, funds, and propaganda, the strengthening of security organizations, and the improvement of communications between national security agencies.

* * *

These cooperative actions by the American states have shown considerable success. In order to control movement to and from Cuba for subversive purposes, many Latin American governments have instituted procedures for restricting travel by their nationals to Cuba. As a result of these measures only 50 percent as many Latin Americans were able to travel to Cuba during 1963 as during the preceding year.

We continue to work with individual governments to help them improve the ability of their police and armed forces to deal with terrorism and insurgency. The United States and Latin Ameri-

---

4 *Ibid.*, May 6, 1963, p. 719.

can governments are also cooperating with increasing effectiveness in exchanging intelligence on Castroist subversion activities and in improving communications between their security services.

In the long run, however, Latin America will be rendered immune to Communist infection only by an amelioration of the conditions—political, economic, and social—in which subversion flourishes. The United States and the free nations of Latin America have, therefore, through the Alliance for Progress, undertaken a major collective effort. It is directed at the ambitious target of transforming the structure and productive capacity of the Latin American nations so as to bring about not merely an increase but a more equitable distribution of resources. Given the magnitude of this undertaking, it will be years before major results can be achieved. But until such a transformation is accomplished, Latin America will remain a fertile seedbed for Communist subversion.

Program of Economic Denial

By strengthening the Latin American nations through collective political, economic, and military measures we are increasing their ability to resist subversion. But at the same time we must actively pursue measures against Cuba to limit its ability to subvert.

In this effort we are exploiting the propaganda potential to the fullest. But an information program must be regarded primarily as a supplement to substantive policies. Given the present limits of action, we must rely, as our major instrument, on a systematic program of economic denial.

This is the only policy—short of the use of force—that gives promise of having a significant impact on Cuba and its continuance as a Communist base in the Western Hemisphere. Such a program, in our judgment, can and does work effectively to achieve objectives that are in the manifest interest not only of the United States and Latin America but of other free-world nations.

Objectives of Economic Denial Program

In discussing the effectiveness of this program, let me make one point quite clear. We have never contended that a program of economic denial—short of an act of war such as a military blockade that would cut off bloc as well as free-world trade—is likely *by itself* to bring down the present Cuban regime. The objectives which this program can accomplish are more limited. They are four in number:

First, to reduce the will and ability of the present Cuban regime to export subversion and violence to the other American states;

Second, to make plain to the people of Cuba and to elements of the power structure of the regime that the present regime cannot serve their interests;

Third, to demonstrate to the peoples of the American Republics that communism has no future in the Western Hemisphere; and

Fourth, to increase the cost to the Soviet Union of maintaining a Communist outpost in the Western Hemisphere.

Those are the objectives which we seek to achieve by a program of economic denial against Cuba. That program reflects the purpose of the Organization of American States. In our opinion, it is realistically designed to accomplish the limited but nonetheless important objectives toward which it is directed.

Cuba Vulnerable to Economic Pressure

Economic denial is a weapon that must be used with great selectivity. It can never be more effective than the economic circumstances of the target country. A program of general economic denial against the Soviet Union, for example, would in the long run make little sense, since the Soviet Union imports from the free world only about one-half of 1 percent of its gross national product. But Cuba presents a wholly different situation. It is a small island with meager natural resources and a low level of industrial development. Prior to the Castro regime, its imports from the free world—principally the United States—represented more than 30 percent of its gross national product.

Those imports were the vital elements of its economic prosperity. They consisted principally of industrial goods and equipment, fuel, raw materials, and foodstuffs.

Cuba's industrial installations, its power plants, its sugar mills, its transportation equipment are all of Western origin. After 5 years

316

Cuba's industrial plant is obsolete and rapidly deteriorating. With no continuing supply of spare parts, it has resorted to cannibalizing its existing equipment.

In addition, Cuba has become far more exposed and vulnerable to economic pressure because Castro's internal policies have driven into exile several hundred thousand Cubans—the managerial and professional elite. There is now a great shortage of skills, and much of the equipment in the industrial plant is mishandled. The situation has been further aggravated by management decisions taken on ideological, rather than economic, grounds.

Cuba is, therefore, vulnerable to a policy of economic denial. The proof of its vulnerability is well illustrated by what has happened to the Cuban economy since trade with the West was first restricted. Today the Cuban standard of living is some 20 percent below pre-Castro levels. Such statistics, of course, do not tell the complete story because many essential items are rationed and many imported items, such as fresh fruits and canned goods, have almost disappeared. The Cuban people are allowed, for example, two bars of soap per person per month, three pounds of meat per person per month, and six ounces of coffee per person per month—when they can get them.

Industrial output, which accounts for less than 25 percent of the gross national product, has remained stagnant. Quality has frequently been sacrificed to maintain the volume of production. In many industries output is shoddy, centralized operations inefficient, and labor productivity extremely low, in large part because of lack of morale and incentive. Plants and machinery are often idle owing to a lack of spare parts or raw materials, and breakdowns in water, power, and transport exacerbate the general disorganization.

Cuban sugar production—the basis of the entire economy—has fallen drastically. Last year's production of 3.8 million tons was the lowest since the early 1940's, and the crop for this year will probably be near the same figure.

With the curtailment of free-world trade, exports have fallen drastically—from more than $800 million in 1958 to less than $500 million in 1963. The lines of trade have been completely redrawn. In 1958, substantially all imports came from free-world sources; last year, 85 percent came from the bloc. It is perhaps pertinent to point out that Cuban exports to Latin America fell from $24 million in 1953 to an estimated $8 million in 1962, while Latin American exports to Cuba fell from $78 million in 1958 to an estimated $6.7 million in 1962.

Restrictions on Shipping and on Vital Goods

In order to exploit Cuba's economic vulnerability we have developed programs of common action on two levels:

First, to restrict the availability of free-world shipping to Cuba;

Second, to limit the categories of goods that may be available to Cuba.

In order to make these policies effective, we have sought the cooperation of the other major industrialized countries of the free world, and particularly our NATO allies. We have obtained considerable, although not complete, cooperation.

For example, the number of calls by free world vessels at Cuban ports dropped 60 percent in 1963 as compared to 1962, and there are reasonable prospects that, over 1964 as a whole, there will be a further drop.

Realistically, we must recognize that the restriction of free-world shipping, while useful, is of only limited utility. Shipping under the control of the bloc could transport the goods that Cuba requires, although at the cost of a considerable reorganization and disruption of schedules and charters.

Much more important is the denial of those categories of goods that are most vital to the operation of the Cuban economy. This includes industrial goods, transport equipment, and critical materials. Not only is Cuba wholly dependent on a large and continuing import of consumer goods if it is to maintain more than a subsistence economy, but its limited industrial plant, including the sugar industry, is based on Western equipment that is rapidly becoming worn out and obsolete and on Western transport equipment that is rapidly falling apart. It is important, therefore, that the West should not bolster the economy by providing spare parts and replacements.

This was the reason, for example, that the administration took such a strong position against the recent sale of 450 buses to the Castro government—400 of which are to be used in Habana. Those 400 additional buses will almost double available public transport in the city that dominates Cuba's economic life. Without those buses the efficiency of the Cuban economy and the level of Cuban morale would be further impaired.

The sale of Western locomotives to Cuba, for instance, would have an even greater impact. Movement of sugar to Cuban ports is almost entirely by rail, and the motive power of the Cuban railroad system is presently in a critical state of disrepair. In a late 1963 description of the "desperate state" of the railroad system, a Cuban official organ estimated that only one-quarter as many locomotives were then in operating condition as in 1959. To replace even a part of this equipment would be a very big boon to the Cuban economy.

The position of our Government in seeking to prevent the sale of such heavy equipment to the Cuban regime has, unfortunately, not always been fully understood either in the United States or by some of our friends abroad. The question has frequently been confused by the curious contention that the sale of United States wheat to the Soviet Union somehow justifies the sale of critical supplies to Cuba. Such an argument betrays a misunderstanding of the nature and objectives of the program of economic denial which I have attempted to describe this evening.

As I mentioned earlier, the continent-wide economy of the Soviet Union, which in many ways approaches self-sufficiency, is far less vulnerable to economic denial than that of Cuba. There would be no point in trying to influence Soviet strength or Soviet policy by a *general* effort to deny exports to that country. All that has ever been attempted is a *selective* program of denying access primarily to strategic goods.

The United States has long had a modest trade in agricultural products with the Soviet Union. The special aspect of the wheat sale was its unusual size and character. The Soviet Union has been traditionally an exporter of wheat, and before approaching the United States it had already contracted the bulk of its wheat import requirements from Canada and Australia. Purchases from United States were, from the Soviet point of view, marginal. Even the 2½ million tons originally discussed would have totaled only about 3½ percent of normal Soviet bread grain production.

Under these circumstances it is quite clear that the sale of wheat to the Soviet Union involved considerations quite unrelated to those involved in the denial of economic goods and other capital equipment to Cuba. Thus any sale of wheat to the Soviet Union was not of great importance to the Soviet economy and of slight importance to the food stocks of the Soviet people. But our denial of industrial and transport equipment and spare parts to Cuba can mean a serious impairment in the state of the Cuban economy.

Oddly enough, these two quite distinct questions have been confused—sometimes, I fear, deliberately—by people holding quite disparate views—by those in Europe who would like to find an excuse to sell heavy equipment to Cuba and by those in America who would like to find a basis for attacking the wheat sale. An objective comparison of these two situations reveals the emptiness of the argument.

Cuban Economic Failure

In the course of my observations this evening, I have tried to spell out for you the bases for our policy toward Cuba and to explain particularly the reasons why we are seeking—and shall continue to seek—to limit the supply of critical goods to the Cuban economy.

This program is directed at the present Cuban government. It will be continued so long as that government persists in its efforts to subvert and undermine the free societies of Latin America.

Within recent weeks it has become more than ever apparent that our program is succeeding. Cuba under communism is providing a spectacle of economic failure for all to see. Far from offering a better life for the Cuban people, communism is bringing only depression and want.

Today the Cuban economy is in a mess—a mess produced by incompetent management, ideological interference, and the refusal of the United States and many other Western societies to deal with a government that is seeking to undermine its neighbors.

The magnitude of the Cuban economic failure is clearly apparent in the constant complaints of the present Cuban leaders.

But if our program of economic denial is helping to accentuate the failures of the Cuban economy, let me make it quite clear that it is not aimed at the Cuban people. The United States has no quarrel with the people of Cuba. It feels no animosity, only sympathy and sorrow. We have shown our good will by exempting food and medicines from the restrictions imposed on our trade with Cuba. We have never sought in any way to starve the Cuban people.

For we are confident that the people of Cuba will not always be compelled to suffer under Communist tyranny.

Given freedom and democracy, Cuba could develop its high potential for economic and social progress. The Cuban people should not be forced to serve as a vehicle for the intrusion into this hemisphere of an alien way of life that can bring them neither progress nor liberty. Let one final point be clear. We oppose the present Cuban regime not just because its ambitions menace our hemispheric neighbors. We oppose it, above all, because its standards of conduct and its tyrannical practices condemn the people of Cuba to misery and fear.

The people of Cuba deserve better than that.

The Alliance for Progress: Dramatic Start and Hopeful Future

by Sol M. Linowitz

U.S. Representative to the Organization of American States[1]

* * *

The inter-American system, in short, is a pioneer and a pacesetter in the effective and constructive use of a regional instrumentality to buttress and strengthen a universal system of law and order among the nations. And the two systems are not only complementary; they are, in fact, indispensable to each other.

I emphasize this point because it is one of the most important international developments of the century, and because it points up the importance that we in North America attach to the special ties that bind us to the countries of Latin America. Today we are giving our friendship, our material help, our conviction that even as we, the people of the United States, are not prisoners of the status quo, neither are the people of Latin America. We have made clear our belief that all of us must not only adapt to changing times, but together we must lead the way toward the social and economic transformation of the continent.

In the past, we have been far more successful at expressing declarations than in getting down to work and carrying them out. But this procedure is no longer good, if it ever was; and we know that Latin America can no longer be taken for granted. For if we do, the entire hemisphere may be taken on a ride to oblivion.

It is precisely because we have come to understand this fact—it is precisely because we know that a successful inter-American system can

---

1 Excerpts from an address made before the American Chamber of Commerce of Mexico at Mexico City on August 21, 1967. Printed in the *Department of State Bulletin*, September 11, 1967, pp. 321-24.

show the way to the future for other regional systems facing similar problems and difficulties, both economic and social—that I remind you of the past.

We have reached, I believe, a watershed in terms of hemispheric unity and progress; but the past can show us how far we have come. It points up the significance, as nothing else can, of the anniversary we marked a few days ago[2]—on August 17th to be exact—the sixth anniversary of the date when the American Republics launched the Alliance for Progress, the date when a charter of hope came into being in this hemisphere, giving life to the most ambitious program of human betterment ever undertaken, collectively, by any group of nations.

It would be nice to say on this sixth anniversary that the Alliance is fulfilling all the dreams of its founders; that Latin America is well on the road to prosperity; that its people have already succeeded in building new lives for themselves and for their children; that they have overcome such problems as low standards of living, soaring birth rates, lack of opportunities, underdeveloped industrial and agricultural potential, insufficient housing, lack of schools, high infant mortality rates, widespread disease, short life expectancies. It would be nice to say, but it would, of course, be untrue. For today, 6 years after the Alliance for Progress came into being, Latin America is still in the grip of far too many economic problems and social conditions that conspire to arrest progress and frustrate dreams.

The Record of the Alliance

But that is only part of the story. True, the Alliance for Progress has not yet solved the problems of Latin America, but a dramatic start has been made; and by any standard this is one of the major accomplishments of the decade of the sixties, if not of the century itself.

Indeed, the record of the Alliance, even with all that remains undone, is perhaps the best answer that can be given by the Republics of Latin America to the recent meeting of the so-called Latin American Solidarity Organization in Cuba. (I say "so-called" because it obviously reflected neither solidarity nor organization.)

[2] For remarks by President Johnson on Aug. 17, see *ibid.*, of September 4, 1967, p. 287.

It seems to me that the prime effect of the LASO conference is not to be found in any long-range threat to our free institutions, one it desperately sought to foment. Rather, it will be found in the hatred and the distortions it encouraged among those who should know better and among those who, regrettably, are not being given the chance to know better.

We must not, of course, ignore the threat of Castro intervention in Latin America. There is ample evidence of its handiwork. But we must well understand that communism in this hemisphere will feed on poverty, despair, and social inequality and that in the Alliance for Progress we have the most potent weapon of all to counter it. For the Alliance is attacking those very conditions that offer fertile ground for ideologies foreign to our traditions, institutions, and the character of our people. At the same time we look forward to meaningful action by the Meeting of Foreign Ministers in September, where the more immediate problems of Cuban subversion will be considered.

Seen in its true perspective, the LASO conference represented a confused struggle among Communists in Latin America over tactics, rather than any deep difference over basic objectives. There is no doubt that communism in Latin America remains a threat, and we must not make the mistake of minimizing it. But, by the same token, we must not make the equally great mistake of regarding every dissatisfied person, every leftist or activist in Latin America, as a Communist simply because he desires a change for the better.

For many of these changes, while they may be revolutionary in Latin American terms, are hardly revolutionary in terms of our own history and development, or that of Mexico's. They include changes that would give Latin American farmers the right to own their own land; that would give Latin Americans a tax system based on ability to pay; a chance for their children to obtain a decent education; the opportunity to live in a decent home, to share in the benefits of modern medicine—these are the kinds of changes the people of Latin America seek.

* * *

Lessons To Be Learned From Latin America

Just as we cannot escape the responsibility for bettering the lives of our own citizens, neither can we escape the responsibility that is peculiarly ours in this world because of our great power and wealth.

Indeed, our support of the Alliance program points up how far we have advanced since the days of the great depression in our country when our concern was turned only inward. Our support of the Alliance, even as our previous support of the Marshall Plan, extends to the international sphere what was introduced in the United States at the national level in the thirties: the concept that this is not a world in which only the wealthiest should survive, but a world in which those more fortunate have responsibility toward those less fortunate, that prosperity or depression knows no political frontier, that we cannot be an isolated island of wealth in a sea of poverty, that the welfare of this continent is a continental problem in which we all have equal responsibilities. And the Alliance for Progress, far from being a simple "aid program" is the blueprint for collective effort and collective benefit.

There are many problems within this continent whose solution depends upon what we can learn from each other. The United States, for example, has reached a high level of prosperity. But the problems faced by New York, Chicago, Boston, and Los Angeles differ perhaps in degree only from those confronting the large cities of Latin America in housing, public services, health, educational facilities, to mention a few of the more obvious.

In meeting these, we are no longer businessmen, lawyers, engineers, economists, professors, writers, and the like. We are all developers, engaged in what is in essence still a grand improvisation. But we cannot improvise or build development on any mechanistic models or sterile statistics—not even on pure logic. For development is fundamentally a human and cultural experience. If development starts in the minds of people, it must build and be buttressed by its cultural heritage, its local and national institutions, and its traditions.

Taking Stock

In taking stock on its sixth anniversary of how far we have advanced in the Alliance for Progress, then, we must look not only at the enormous task still before us but also backward at the tasks already done. We must look not only at the speed of the journey but also at the acceleration. Only thus can we see how far we have come. And there have been more tax reforms, land reforms, schools built, students trained, roads built, new institutions created in Latin America in the past 6 years than during any previous decade. In land

325

tenure, tax and administrative reform, there has been greater progress during the past 6 years than in the previous 25 years.

What does this mean in precise terms? Just this: that while the statistician may tell us that the "gap" is widening between the rich countries and the poor countries—the haves and the have-nots—the fact remains that the social welfare "gap" in Latin America is narrowing. Already there have been sufficient redistribution of income, school construction, increase in water supply facilities, and advances in public health services to suggest that it is, in fact, a shrinking gap.

These are some of the reasons why I believe we can feel justifiably encouraged at the progress of the Alliance. We have a right to be impatient; but our impatience must feed our determination to get on with the job of what is, in truth, one of history's great social experiments: a peaceful revolution to transform a continent, to telescope years of development and create worthwhile lives for people whose hopes and aspirations merit every assistance we are capable of rendering.

If the Alliance is to succeed, it must hold true to the original philosophy that gave it life: to satisfy the basic needs of the Latin American people for homes, work and land, health and schools— *techo, trabajo y tierra, salud y escuela.* If it is to do this in fact, it must stimulate the profound social changes that are the prerequisites of a life of dignity. Only thus will the gap between the rich and the poor be narrowed in any meaningful way. Only thus will the dams, the highways, the housing projects, the new schools. the integrated continentwide economy, and all the other goals of the Alliance have any lasting value or true meaning.

Because we know that the most efficient factory cannot justify a city's slums; and economic growth is to no avail if it serves only a fraction of the people. It must serve them all. And that, in sum, is the ultimate goal of the Alliance in the years ahead, the goal to which the Presidents of the American Republics pledged themselves at Punta del Este in April.[3]

Role of American Business

I believe that much of the imagination and vision to realize the opportunities before us can be provided by private enterprise. With

---

[3] For background, see *ibid.*, May 8, 1967, p. 706.

an investment of $10 billion in Latin America, American business has a vital stake in the Alliance for Progress. Whether American investments will grow—and in some cases whether they will be allowed to remain—may well depend on the success or failure of the Alliance. Our business firms, therefore, have an immense responsibility and opportunity. They can do much to assist the nations of Latin America attain their exciting goals, goals which they set for themselves at Punta del Este.

I know that American business has already done a great deal in fields ranging from heavy investments to training for community development. But I hope it will undertake to do even more within the context of each country's individual needs and policies. It can do this in part by utilizing local people not merely for unskilled or assembly-line work but by training them to become supervisors and part of management. It can do this by giving special consideration to becoming active in less developed parts of the continent where efforts are under way to bring the 20th century to areas which have for years remained in darkness. It can do this by joining with national private enterprise, as here in Mexico, in joint undertakings to build new economies and create work and opportunity for a rising labor force.

I hope that our American business firms will always recognize that the needs of the people of Latin America must come first and that their investments can be made most secure by building on solid foundations for the future—taking into account the needs of the community.

This involves, of course, much more than economics. If we know all there is to know about all the rich natural resources of Latin America without knowing or understanding the continent's most important resource of all—its people—we fail in our undertaking.

To know the statistics of Latin America's gross national product without knowing, too, its history and its culture is, in fact, to be ill prepared for the challenges ahead.

Meeting the Challenges Ahead

The Alliance is meeting those challenges. It *is* aimed at the right policies. It *is* attacking the right obstacles. It *is* putting its emphasis where the biggest efforts are required. It *is* the hopeful beginning of a really creative development program. But it will be a long journey,

327

and it will need our continued understanding and support of Latin America's own efforts. In our relations with our Latin American neighbors, we will need, above all, a sense of time, a sense of scale, a sense of destiny.

This must be the highroad we will take, the dream of destiny we will fulfill. How much better, how much more fulfilling it will be than the road being taken by those who have lost the dream of destiny, of partnership, of shared hopes and efforts, who have turned their backs on a geography and history that unite us in this hemisphere.

Success of the Alliance, moreover, will be a testimony to the belief held by the free nations of America in the power of peaceful and constructive change. The peaceful revolution it will inspire will offer a better life, a life of dignity for all who seek it. In contrast, the revolution of chaos spawned by those who would intervene in the affairs of the hemisphere offers hatred and violence and no future.

But there is a future in the Alliance, a future surely in keeping with with the hopes of Latin America's growing millions, with the hopes of Juárez and Bolívar, Martí and San Martín, and our own Founding Fathers. In this future, the hemisphere can and will grow and develop, in prosperity and confidence, into a model of how nations, with all their diversity of culture and difference of resources, can work together to improve, enrich, and ennoble their common life.

* * *

Index

Index

Alliance for Progress, 77, 306-307, 322ff
Anti-ballistic missile system, 37-43
Apartheid, 281, 297-298
Arms control, 286-287, 298

Balance of payments, 47-49, 53-54
Balance of Power, 89

Communist China:
  nuclear threat, 40-41;
  U.S. policy toward, 216ff
Conventional warfare, 25-26, 34-36
Communication in world politics, 138-139

Disarmament:
  Baruch Plan, 120-121, 123-124;
  Committee of Principals, 144;
  impact on U.S. economy, 127-128;
  inspection, 126-127;
  Russian plans, 120-121, 124;
  U.S. policy, 36-37

Economic development:
  Africa, 275;
  investment, 63-65;
  Middle East, 258-259;
  relation to U.S. security, 83-84;